TH...
COM...ANION

**a guide for
New Zealanders
in the UK**

Bronwyn Sell is an award-winning New Zealand journalist. She was born in Auckland in 1974 and grew up there and in the Bay of Plenty town of Kawerau. While on her OE in London, she edited the expat newspaper *New Zealand News UK* and was the *New Zealand Herald*'s London correspondent. Bronwyn hasn't yet made it home from her OE — she is on an extended stopover in Sydney with the Australian partner she picked up in a dodgy antipodean pub in London. She is a newspaper subeditor and freelance writer.

THE BIG OE COMPANION

a guide for New Zealanders in the UK

Bronwyn Sell

RANDOM HOUSE
NEW ZEALAND

Note: The author takes no responsibility for any errors or omissions or for the services of companies and organisations mentioned in this guide. The author has accepted no money, discounts or gifts in exchange for listings or endorsements, and all advice is independent. Prices quoted are at 2004 levels and are subject to change.

National Library of New Zealand Cataloguing-in-Publication Data

Sell, Bronwyn.
The Big OE companion: a guide for New Zealanders in the UK / Bronwyn Sell.
ISBN 1-86941-635-X
1. New Zealanders—Travel—Great Britain. 2. Great Britain—Guidebooks. 3. Great Britain—Description and travel. I. Title.
914.1048608923—dc 22

A RANDOM HOUSE BOOK
published by
Random House New Zealand
18 Poland Road, Glenfield, Auckland, New Zealand
www.randomhouse.co.nz

First published 2004

© 2004 Bronwyn Sell

The moral rights of the author have been asserted

ISBN 1 86941 635 X

Text design: Sharon Grace
Cover design: Matthew Trbuhovic, Third Eye Design and Graphics
Cover illustration: Getty Images
Printed in Australia by Griffin Press

Contents

Introduction: The letters O and E   **10**
The first OE   12
Ten great things about the UK   13
Ten things you'll never understand   13
Phone numbers   15

1. The OErs   16
The Myers/Inkson study   16
Who?   16
Where?   17
Why?   17
    To travel   17
    To explore   17
    To escape   18
    Because it's the thing to do   18
For how long?   18

2. Groundwork   19
Timing   19
Research   20
Travel help companies   21
Starter kits   22
The essentials — getting a passport and visa   22
    Passports   22
    Visas and permits   24
Getting there   29
    Flights   29
Sorting out your finances   31
    Saving money   31
    Sorting out your New Zealand bank accounts   32
    Opening a UK bank account   33
    Cash   33
    Tax   34
    Student loans   34
Power of attorney   35
Accommodation   35
Communications   36
    Email and internet   36
    Mobile phone   36
Get prepared for work   37
    Research   37
    Registration   38
    Police checks   38
Other logistics   38
    Leaving work   38
    Moving out   38
    Driver's licence   38
    Car insurance   39
    Poste restante   39
    Health   39
    Discount passes   40
Packing   40
    Audit your belongings   40
    Choosing luggage   40
    What to pack   41
Planning calendar   43

3. Your first week   44
Arrival   44
    Arrival card   45
    Immigration   45
    Customs   45
    Money   45
Transport from the airport   46
    Underground   46
    Other options   46
Going Underground — the Tube for beginners   47
    Figuring out your route   47
    Zones   47
    Buying a ticket   48
    Using the ticket   48
Luggage storage   48
Getting mobile   48
Meeting up   49
Get lost   49
An introduction to London's sights   50
The lingo   52
Orientation parties   53
A note on personal safety   54
Street dwellers   54
    Beggars   54
    Big Issue   55
    Charity sellers   55
Your second week   55
A lesson in London English   56
The Koiwi uccent   58
How to speak New Zealander   58

4. Enjoying the UK — 60

The culture — 60
Best places to marvel at posh UK — 61
Best places to meet the everyday Brit — 61
When the UK is not Great Britain — 62
The pub and the pint — 62
   Chains and independents — 62
   Early closing — 63
   Pub crawls — 64
Notable pub crawls — 64
Food — 64
Best places to soak up culture — 65
   Takeaways — 65
Cost of going out — 66
   Café culture — 66
   Restaurants — 66
Best places to chill — 67
   Taking tea — 67
Royal events — 68
Best places to spot royalty — 68
National Trust Working Holidays — 69
Live and armchair sport — 69
   Football — 69
Football tournaments explained — 69
   Cricket — 70
   Rugby — 71
   Tennis — 71
Music festivals — 71
Going out in London — 72
   Theatre — 72
Best places to party — 72
   Music — 73
   Cinema — 74
   Clubbing — 74
Celebrity spotting — 75
   Sightseeing in London on the cheap — 76
Worth the money — 78
Overrated and overrun — 78
Highlights of the UK calendar — 79

5. Transport and orientation — 83

Around the UK — 83
   Information — 83
   Trains — 83
Tips on catching trains — 84
   Coaches — 85
   Postbus — 86
   Driving — 86
   Buying a vehicle — 88
   Air — 88
In London — 89
   Finding your way around — 89
London postcodes — 90
   Public transport — 92
Public transport survival kit — 92
Famous Tube announcements — 95
Tips for Tube and train travel — 96
   Taxis — 99
   Driving — 100
   Cycling — 101

6. Accommodation — 103

Temporary accommodation — 103
   Dossing — 103
Dossing etiquette — 103
   Hostels — 104
Where to live in London — 105
Areas of London — 105
Flatting — 108
   Costs — 108
   Where to look — 108
   What to look for — 108
   Culture and flatmates — 109
Some peculiarities of flatting in the UK — 111
Taking on a lease — 111
Why live in London when you can live in . . . — 112
   Utilities, etc. — 113
Contents insurance — 114
Moving in and kitting out — 114
Tenancy advice and your rights — 115
The terminology — 115

7. Work — 117

Searching — 117
   Websites — 118
   Recruitment agencies — 118
   Temping work — 118
   Finding an agent — 119
Selling yourself — 119
Filling in time — 120
Tips for staying sane when you're looking for work — 120
Live-in jobs — 120
Playing rugby — 121
Registration and certification — 121

Contents

Advice from a Kiwi human resources manager in London	122
Health and social work	123
Teaching	124
Law and finance	125
Engineering and trades	125
Police checks	126
Unions	126
British working attitudes	127

8. Money matters — 128

Banking in the UK — the basics	128
Opening an account	128
Fees	129
ATM cards	129
Chequebook	129
Credit cards	129
Internet banking	129
Cashback	129
Eftpos	130
Getting a National Insurance number	130
Tips for conserving money (while still having a life)	131
Tax	132
Arrival	132
Tax rebates	132
Personal tax rates	133
Claiming a personal tax return	133
Being self-employed	134
Setting up a limited company	134
National Insurance taxback	135
Getting professional help	135
Individual Savings Account (ISA)	136

9. Health, fitness and sport — 137

Health	137
Emergency number	137
NHS Direct	137
GPs	137
Dentists	138
Walk-in centres	139
Hospitals	139
Prescriptions	139
Contraception, etc.	139
Student clinics	139
Winter survival strategies	140
Fitness and sport	141
Playing sport	141
Avoiding the Heathrow injection	142
Gyms and pools	145

10. Communications and media — 146

Phones	146
Finding numbers	146
Call rates	147
International calls	147
Calling the operator	147
Money savers	147
Time difference	148
Mobile phones	148
Things to check	150
Post	152
Postage costs	152
Cyberspace	153
Accessing the internet	153
Media	154
Newspapers	154
Television	155
Radio	156

11. Shopping — 157

The high street	157
Supermarkets	158
Department stores	158
Markets	159
The London markets	159
Speciality shopping areas	160
London	160
Rest of UK	161
Elite shopping	161
Auction houses	162
Loyalty programmes	162
Cost of basics	163

12. Getting your Kiwi fix — 164

Antipodean media	165
Newspapers and magazines	165
Websites	165
Television	166
New Zealand/UK history	166
New Zealand media	166
New Zealand events	167
Waitangi Day, February 6	167
It's the little things you miss	167
Anzac Day, April 25	168
Toast Life	169
New Zealand art and music	169
Getting tickets to All Blacks games	170
New Zealand shops	170

New Zealand fashion	171
Buying gifts for people at home	171
New Zealand cafés and restaurants in London	171
Gourmet Burger Kitchen	171
Sugar Club	172
Suze of Mayfair and Suze Wine Bar	172
Tapa Room and The Providores	172
Truc Vert	172
Antipodean pubs	173
Walkabout	173
The Redback	173
The Church	173
Others	173
New Zealand clubs and societies	174
Sporting	174
Words to the All Blacks' haka	175
Social	175
Professional	176
Political	178
Maori culture	178
Hinemihi marae	180
Art and culture	180
Homesickness remedies	181
ANZSAC/ANZSAF/SANZA explained	182

13. New Zealand government in the UK and Europe — 183

New Zealand House	183
The New Zealand High Commission	184
Role of the High Commission	184
The New Zealand High Commission — contact details	185
Registering with the High Commission	185
Information office	185
Library	186
Honorary consuls	186
Other New Zealand government agencies in New Zealand House	187
Defence	187
Department of Internal Affairs Identity Services Office	187
New Zealand Immigration Service	187
Tourism New Zealand	187
New Zealand Trade and Enterprise	188
Voting in New Zealand elections	188
Voting in UK elections	188
New Zealand diplomatic posts in Europe	188

14. Tracing your family history — 193

Getting started	193
More information	194

15. Travel on the Continent and beyond — 195

Planning	196
Timing	196
The big festivals of Europe	196
Guidebooks	197
Travel insurance	198
Travel warnings	199
Visas	199
Leave a record	199
Flight/hotel packages	200
Money	200
Euro	200
Credit cards	200
ATMs	201
Tipping	201
Communications	201
Internet	201
Phones	201
Cycle touring	202
Transport tips	204
Trains	204
Buses	204
Driving	204
Budget airlines	205
Navigating London's terrestrial airports	206
Case study — how a £9 flight can break your budget	208
Bus tours	209
Kiwi pilgrimages	210
Van Tour	210
Running of the Bulls in Pamplona	211
Anzac Day in Europe	212
Accommodation tips	213
Camping	213
Hostels	214
Private rooms	214
Bed and breakfast	214

Luggage tips	214
Packing tips	215
In case of emergency	217
A highly subjective list of where to go and how long for	218

16. What next? — 219

Not ready to leave?	219
Immigration and Nationality Directorate	219
Work Permits	219
Getting British citizenship	220
Ancestry Visas	220
Leaving?	220
Sorting out your finances	220
Mobile phones	221
Other logistics	222
Going home?	222
How to know you've been in London too long	223
Shipping your belongings to New Zealand	224
New Zealand Customs Service in Europe	227
Sending money home	228
Booking a flight	228
Delay tactics	229
Taking the long way home	229
Reverse culture shock	229
A 'To do' list on your return	229
Things to expect	230
Dealing with culture shock	230
Moving on?	231
Other Working Holiday Visas	231
Other overseas working options	236
Quiz — what next?	237

Acknowledgements — 240

Introduction:
The letters O and E

There is probably no country in which the letters O and E resonate as strongly as they do in New Zealand. In just a few generations of our country's short history the Overseas Experience, or Big OE, has become a national ritual. The fact that we even have a name for it is evidence of its hold — Australians do a similar thing but have no name for it. It's one youthful impulse that parents and employers understand, even encourage.

Its popularity is something to do with the weakness of the Pacific peso. It's also the fact that you can't hop on a train in Auckland and be in Paris three hours later. OE is a gateway to those magical places we grew up hearing about — Rome, Venice, Berlin, Moscow, London. New Zealand's geographical isolation makes it logical to set up a base camp in Europe.

But another motivation for the OE is far more whimsical. It's about freedom, escape and independence. Reinventing yourself, expanding your horizons. Loosening the bonds of study and career before you are stuck with the commitments of a mortgage and family. It's probably the only time in your life that you will live without immediate demands on your attention from parents, grandparents and children — even pets.

OE veterans love talking about their experiences. Their eyes glaze over as they romanticise about the London winter they probably loathed at the time. Get a few OE veterans in the same room and they'll gravitate towards each other to swap stories of the pubs they haunted and the epic trips they had. Their stories prompt others to go.

When we come home — and most of us do come home, for all the panic over the 'brain drain' — we have a better understanding of who we are as New Zealanders. Of what makes us different from other cultures. Of how we fit into the world.

New Zealand has signed working holiday visa agreements with at

Introduction

least fourteen countries besides the UK, and the number grows every year. But the UK, and London in particular, is still the destination of choice. Why? Aside from its unmistakeable buzz, London provides a comfort zone that other foreign cities don't. No one is sure how many New Zealanders live and work in Britain. The British High Commission in Wellington issues about 19,000 British passports and about 10,000 working visas to New Zealanders in an average year. The New Zealand High Commission in London estimates there are between 100,000 and 200,000 Kiwis in the UK at any time. With those kinds of numbers, there's a good chance you'll have Kiwi friends there, and if not you'll make them easily in the transient New Zealand circles that are constantly expanding for a new friend or contracting when one goes home. You can buy Pineapple Lumps and Burger Rings and go to antipodean pubs if you want to. On the face of it the language and culture are familiar and unchallenging — although you'll find hundreds of subtle differences. And while the strengthening euro is challenging the pound's dominance, it's still easier to earn a crust in a country that speaks your language.

The modern OE began some time around the 1960s, when a few young New Zealanders added a new phase to the Kiwi life cycle, somewhere between leaving school and getting married. Back then it was a long boat trip to the other side of the world, but as aeroplanes opened a bridge between New Zealand and Europe the Overseas Experience became more accessible. Every traveller who returned impressed on another Kiwi the desire to go, and the numbers leaving escalated.

> The OE is more than a positive self-development experience. It is indeed a national icon, a jewel embedded in our folklore and in the messages our young people learn. Long may we promote it. OE is potentially a precious gift not just for the traveller, but for all of us. In its encouragement of initiative, independence, networking, improvisation and intercultural experience, it is surely a telescope focused on our country's future. Every young New Zealander who has not yet had the experience should ask: 'Is there something in this for me?'
> — Barbara Myers and Kerr Inkson, lecturers from Auckland University of Technology and Massey University respectively, in *The Big OE: How it works and what it can do for New Zealand*

The first OE

The OE has always had a profound effect on New Zealand, but it's unlikely that anyone's OE had as much impact as that of the first two travellers. In 1820 missionary Thomas Kendall took Ngapuhi chief Hongi Hika and his kinsman Waikato to England in a whaling ship, so the Maori men could advise on the first Maori language guide.

The two men — 'handsome and manly in bearing' and 'entirely covered by deep lines and high colours of grotesque intricate carving and tattooing' — were a sensation, according to the *Cambridge Chronicle*. They told a reporter, with the help of Kendall's interpretation, that they had come because, 'They wish to see King George, the multitude of his people, what they are doing, and the goodness of the land.' The King treated them royally and presented them with gifts. At the time he was embroiled in a divorce — Hongi Hika is said to have wondered why a king could not handle one wife when he coped easily with five.

In December they caught a lift home on a convict ship bound for Australia. There they exchanged the gifts for guns, and on their return to New Zealand Ngapuhi swept through the North Island, slaughtering thousands. The devastation they wreaked is partly blamed for destroying the traditional Maori way of life.

But the Kiwi OE goes back further than the sixties. Two earlier generations clambered to volunteer for world wars that would expand their horizons even as they shattered their innocence. Their legacy remains throughout Europe. In the small French town of Le Quesnoy, for example, streets are named in honour of the New Zealand troops who liberated them.

Before that the traffic was mostly one-way, as Britons shrugged off the shackles of class for the prospect of a sparkling new egalitarian society half a world away in New Zealand. A few early colonials, including writer Katherine Mansfield, went to the 'Home Country' to find that even in the short time of colonisation New Zealand had become part of their blood — blood they had probably considered British.

Despite the fact that it is so embedded in our culture little research has been done on the OE. No one even knows for sure how many Kiwis are in Europe, let alone what they're doing there. Most of what we know is anecdotal, forming a folklore revolving around travelling, drinking and having a good time.

But the OE is constantly evolving. If there was a heyday in which jobs in the UK were plentiful and life was carefree, it has passed. It's common these days for New Zealanders to stall their OEs until they have

Ten great things about the UK
- Wintry Sundays spent in cosy pubs reading the great UK newspapers
- The long, long days of summer
- Scottish accents
- Strolling London's South Bank on a summer evening
- Free world-class museums and galleries
- Cheap flights to Europe
- Royal fervour
- Daily world-class music offerings
- London's West End and Soho
- The countryside — stone walls, rolling farmland, fields of rapeseed, centuries-old cottages, fallen castles . . .

Ten things you'll never understand
- Mushy peas
- 11 pm pub closing
- Tabloid obsessions
- Washing dishes in a bucket
- Class distinctions
- Topless sunbathing in Hyde Park
- How young women survive winter nights out wearing so few clothes
- How the country can shut down under 1 cm of snow
- The Eurovision song contest (that's not to say you won't watch it)
- Why it takes two years to fix an escalator in a Tube station.

graduated from university and worked for a few years. Consequently, they find themselves in far more serious and time-consuming jobs in the UK than their predecessors might have.

While the traditional van tour of Europe is always popular, long summer excursions are giving way to regular, shorter stints away from work — a weekend here, a fortnight there. While there are still plenty of Kiwis working in bars in the UK, this is becoming more the domain of Eastern Europeans perfecting their English, as New Zealanders move into higher-skilled work. The lifting of work restrictions on the Working Holiday Visa — not that many New Zealanders obeyed the rules when they existed — is a nod to this evolution.

A caveat must be put on the OE. Many Kiwis go on OE to escape their lives. You must realise before you leave that while you can escape a humdrum job or a dead-end relationship you can't escape from yourself. Your insecurities, foibles and anxieties will come with you — and might even multiply when you are left to fend for yourself. For all its well-deserved appeal, the UK can be an overwhelming, lonely place and living there can be an emotional rollercoaster.

You will get homesick, for things you would never have expected — a pohutukawa in bloom, the remembered smell of the sea, the taste of feijoas, the sound of cicadas, Dave Dobbyn's guitar. If you are prepared for this and you know how to deal with it, you'll find the down times — and there *will* be down times — far easier.

Until now, Kiwis have flown into London relatively blind, with random snippets of advice gleaned from friends here and there, and arrived at Heathrow blinking and overwhelmed. We all reinvent the wheel and make the same mistakes.

This book is designed to make things easier. To bring together the body of knowledge gleaned by OE veterans in order to make the path smoother for the next person bitten by the OE bug. You, maybe.

Introduction

Time to leave your street, shed the comfortable colonial skin, have a bit of a wander round, try your luck, get a better perspective on life, don't take Columbus' word for it — find out yourself that the world isn't flat, see what's out there, see where things take you. For some it's still a bull-dodging two-year mobile beerfest, but I think most nowadays leave with slightly broader plans. In base camp — London — every second building is at least 100 years older than our whole country's colonial history. From here we can take on the world because we're Kiwis, everyone loves us and we all know someone in the All Blacks.

— Mike Stead

 Phone numbers

With the exception of the phone numbers listed in *'Groundwork'*, all numbers in this book are in UK national format. To call a UK number from New Zealand dial 0044 at the start and drop the first 0 of the listed number. For example, 020 1111 1111 becomes 0044 20 1111 1111.

As in New Zealand, you drop the STD code in Britain if you are calling within your local area. For example, 020 1111 1111 becomes 1111 1111. (020 is the STD code for London.)

For more information about telecommunications, see 'Communications and media'.

1.
The OErs

You won't be alone in the UK. At any time there are thought to be at least as many Kiwis in the UK as there are in Hamilton, New Zealand. Beyond that, little is known about Kiwis on OE in Britain. Despite its pervasiveness, little research has been done into the OE — who goes and why and what makes them come back. The following is what we do know.

The Myers/Inkson study

The first significant research into the New Zealand OE was released in 2003 — a report by Barbara Myers of Auckland University of Technology and Kerr Inkson of Massey University, called *The Big OE: How it works and what it can do for New Zealand*.

Between 1998 and 2001, the pair interviewed in-depth 50 young New Zealanders who had been on an OE of at least six months. Three-quarters had spent most of their time in the UK, the vast majority in London.

Myers and Inkson concluded that the OE changed young New Zealanders' lives through the learning experience. 'The effect is created by a "king hit" of novel experience allied to the responsibility for self that OE inevitably carries.'

Who?

New Zealanders in the UK tend to be young professionals. We know — from a UK Labour Force Survey presented to the Home Office in 2002 — that in the year 1999 most (60.8 percent) of the New Zealanders and Australians working in the UK were aged 25–39, and almost half (44.3 percent) were working in professional or managerial jobs. In the early 1990s, by comparison, less than one-third were in professional or managerial jobs.

Of the participants in the Myers/Inkson study, 26 had had tertiary education and just two had been manual workers before going overseas. The median age for departure was 24, and 90 percent were in their twenties. The academics concluded that the OE was primarily a middle-class phenomenon undertaken by young, educated people.

> For the UK there are benefits in positively welcoming [working holidaymakers] — the acquisition of a youthful workforce with less demanding requirements for permanent accommodation and support services and the establishment of long-term links with countries of origin . . . While little is known of their characteristics it may reasonably be assumed that they are generally well-educated and adaptable.
> — 'International migration and the United Kingdom',
> UK Home Office paper, 2002

Where?

Like most foreigners living in Britain, for better or worse we stick to London and its surrounds, according to the Labour Force Survey. In 2000 more than half (54.4 percent) of the New Zealanders and Australians in the UK lived in greater London, another 17.7 percent lived elsewhere in the southeast of England, with the remainder scattered through the UK.

Why?

To travel

In a 2002 survey of more than 300 New Zealanders living in London, by UK-based company 1st Contact, 88 percent said their main reason for going to the UK was to travel. Less than six percent said they went for career reasons.

To explore

Half the OE veterans interviewed by Myers and Inkson expanded on their reasons for going. They spoke of a desire for exploration — to see the world, have an adventure or experience other cultures. They did not generally do an OE to improve career opportunities or learn work skills, although work and career objectives tended to develop over time.

To escape
Escape was a secondary motivation for the Myers/Inkson group — from humdrum jobs and lives or personal relationships.

Because it's the thing to do
Virtually all of the Myers/Inkson group said they had been encouraged to go by friends and family. Sixteen mentioned a long-term predisposition ('I had always intended to go').

> The self-directed, improvisational character of the typical OE makes it a good analogue and preparation for the flexible, insecure, entrepreneurial character of work and careers in the 21st century and equips New Zealanders to be self-reliant and to cope well in a rapidly changing economic environment.
> — Barbara Myers and Kerr Inkson

For how long?

Longer than you might plan. Many of those in the Myers/Inkson study had drastically underestimated the amount of time they would spend on OE. On average they had planned to be overseas for less than two years, but had spent four years abroad, according to personal whim and the ebb and flow of opportunity. 'And of course our study considered only those who had returned,' Inkson said. 'It seems that OE is seductive.'

Almost all the UK-based Kiwis in the 1st Contact survey (91 percent) said they intended to go home within five years. Half said they'd be home in two years.

> Travellers were unanimously positive in their evaluation of OE. Typically, they said that the experience had boosted their self-reliance and self-esteem, helped their interpersonal and communications skills, made them more open-minded, more tolerant of other cultures, and more independent and flexible — all big advantages in today's economy.
> — Barbara Myers and Kerr Inkson

2. Groundwork

Unless you are an asylum-seeker and can prove you have spent the last decade being tortured in an underground bunker at the Beehive, you won't want to arrive at Heathrow without a work visa. There are some things you can wing when you make the big move, but this is not one of them.

It is entirely possible to leave New Zealand with just a work visa and a plane ticket. But there are a dozen other things you can arrange far more easily in New Zealand in advance than in a panic in the UK. Do yourself a favour and be as prepared as you can be.

Timing

The stereotype of a Kiwi on OE is someone in his or her early 20s, spending a couple of years working behind a bar in London while boozing it up through Europe on the side. Although that person does exist, New Zealanders go to the UK for a lot of different reasons and at different times of their lives. It's not uncommon to meet empty-nesters in the UK — older couples who use their children's departure from home as an excuse for a long-delayed OE.

If there is a typical OEr, he or she is probably a 20-something professional, holding down a half-decent job and holidaying on the Continent as often as possible.

You can go at any age — as long as you qualify for a visa or British passport.

There is merit in having a growth experience immediately after school, especially if you don't know what you want to do next — in the UK this is an institution called a Gap Year. There is also merit in waiting until you graduate, and starting the career ladder in the UK — although you'll probably be paid poorly. And it is also worthwhile to get a few years of work experience under your belt first.

And hell, if you're 65 and newly retired, why not throw some of your retirement savings into living in Cornwall for a year?

Whatever stage of life you go, you'll probably want to time your arrival so you get to the UK in spring (March to May). That way you'll get cheaper shoulder season airfares, two summers in a row, and arrive when everyone's just starting to perk up after the long winter. In most sectors the job market will also be looking up, and temporary contracts often become available as Brits fly off to Spain en masse for holidays. And if you find yourself unemployed for a while, there are plenty of things you can do for free to keep your spirits up.

Arriving in December can be dispiriting. It's getting dark by 3.30 pm, people are gloomy, the job market can be equally depressed, and you can't go and sun yourself in a park if it all gets to you. That's when the pub culture starts to make sense.

There are exceptions. Teachers might find it easier to come in July or August, before the school year starts in September. People in the financial sector might be more likely to pick up temporary work in the months leading up to the end of the financial year in March. Pilots are more likely to be accepted for training in winter when the airline business is quieter. And retail workers will be in most demand in the lead-up to Christmas.

There are advantages to going in the UK winter: low airfares and cheaper accommodation, for a start. And there's a romantic thrill in strolling across the cobblestones of Covent Garden at Christmas time, wearing a coat so thick it could stand up on its own, with every surface of your body covered in a hat, scarf, gloves and boots, while a string quartet plays carols and people hurry past with big packages.

Research

The best research is talking to New Zealanders who are already in the UK or have recently returned. But remember that everyone has a different experience, so two people can give conflicting advice. Don't be put off by horror stories.

The British High Commission in Wellington periodically runs free

Groundwork

OE evenings in the main centres in New Zealand, at which you can get advice on applying for a visa, and talk to travel agents, recruitment agents and other companies with an interest in New Zealand travellers. For information, email the High Commission at oemail@fco.gov.uk or call 04 924 2849.

The British High Commission has a website, www.britain.org.nz, with stacks of information on working holidays and visas. The UK tourist authority, Visit Britain, has a website dedicated to New Zealanders, www.visitbritain.com/nz. Its UK websites are also worth a look: www.visitbritain.com, www.visitlondon.com and www.uktheguide.com. The Foreign and Commonwealth Office has also developed a website for visitors to the UK: www.i-uk.com. And the New Zealand High Commission in London has an informative website for New Zealanders living in the UK and Ireland: www.nzembassy.com/uk.

There are several antipodean publications in London, all with websites, and there is a burgeoning trade in websites with advice and links to recruitment, travel agents and accommodation. *For lists, see 'Getting your Kiwi fix'.*

Travel help companies

There are a few savvy companies that offer a range of services for antipodean travellers, from their departure from New Zealand to their return home.

The ubiquitous 1st Contact — with a Kiwi at the helm — provides a wide range of services from starter packs, information packs and help with opening bank accounts to recruitment, tax and finances, vaccinations and shipping. To contact them: in New Zealand, phone 0800 224 322, email nzoffice@1stcontact.co.uk, website www.1stcontact.co.uk/nz; in the UK, phone 0870 1STCONTACT (0870 17826 68228), website www.1stcontact.co.uk.

ANZSAC is also aimed at the traveller and expat market, directing its customers to businesses that service the Australian, New Zealand, South African and Canadian communities in the UK. Phone +44 20 7562 7900, email info@anzsac.com, website www.anzsac.com, address 1st floor, 43 London Wall, London EC2M 5TF.

The Big OE Companion

Starter kits

1st Contact and several web companies offer OE starter kits for around $75. These can help you open bank accounts and international phone accounts, give you discounts, provide guidance, and get you into social events. *Antipodean web companies are listed in 'Getting your Kiwi fix'.*

International Exchange Programmes, website www.iepnz.co.nz/britain, goes a step further, offering an all-inclusive package for around $2100. For that, they book you a one-way ticket including stopover, apply for a visa on your behalf, help you open a bank account, offer a mail-holding service, give you a travel guide, book you into a hostel in London, organise transport from the airport, etc.

You can do all these sorts of things by yourself, but if your time's worth more than your money or you're hopeless at organising yourself, they could be worth investigating.

The essentials — getting a passport and visa

Passports

GETTING A NEW PASSPORT

If you don't already have a New Zealand passport you can apply for one from the Passports Office. Download an application form from www.passports.govt.nz, phone 0800 22 50 50, email passports@dia.govt.nz to have one sent to you, or pick one up in person from a travel agent or any of the following:

New Zealand Passports Office
Level 3
Boulcott House
47 Boulcott Street
Wellington

Department of Internal Affairs
Level 6
AA Building
99 Albert Street
Auckland

Department of Internal Affairs
Hodgetts Building
Cnr Amersham and Osterley Ways
Manukau

Department of Internal Affairs
48 Peterborough Street
Christchurch

The standard turnaround time is up to ten working days, and the cost is around $70. Urgent service (three working days) costs around $150 and a call-out service costs around $400, so best you think about this one in advance.

The process is straightforward if you were born in New Zealand. You'll just need to get a witness to verify your identity, and send in the completed application form with two passport photos.

RENEWING YOUR PASSPORT

If your passport is due to expire within a few years, renew it before you leave. It's also a good idea to get a new passport if yours isn't machine-readable. The letters X, L, N, F, AA or AB at the beginning of your passport number denote a machine-readable passport. Without one you'll need to apply for a visa in advance to go to the United States. To renew your passport, you'll need the same forms as for a new application (see above).

GETTING A BRITISH PASSPORT

If you were born in the UK before 1 January 1983; or you were born in the UK after that date and one of your parents was then British or settled in the UK; or if your father was born in the UK and you are his legitimate child; or you were born to a UK-born woman after 1 January 1983, then lucky you. You can apply for a British passport and thereafter waltz through immigration in the UK. It will cost you $164.20 to apply — based on 2004 costs — and will be worth every cent. For information, contact the British High Commission in Wellington on 04 924 2889, email passportmail@wellington.fco.gov.uk or go to the website www.britain.org.nz, from which you can download application forms.

The Big OE Companion

GETTING A EUROPEAN PASSPORT

If you or your parents were born in Europe you may be eligible to hold a European Union passport. It's just as valuable as a British passport, as it gives you the right to work anywhere in the EU (which includes Britain). Contact the embassy or consulate of the appropriate country in New Zealand.

Visas and permits

If you don't have a British or European passport, you'll need a work visa of some sort to live and work in the UK. The most common are the Working Holiday Visa and the Ancestry Visa, but there are more than a dozen others. If you are applying for a visa in New Zealand, you'll deal with the British High Commission in Wellington.

You can download application forms from the High Commission website www.britain.org.nz, or email visamail.wellington@fco.gov.uk or phone 0900 4VISA (0900 48472) to have them sent to you, or pick them up in person from their offices in Wellington (address below) or the British Consulate General office at 151 Queen Street, Auckland. (The staff at the Auckland office don't deal with visa applications.) The British Foreign and Commonwealth Office has a facility for online applications on its website www.visa4uk.gov.uk. After applying online you forward the documentation to the High Commission in Wellington.

There is a hotline on which you can get advice, which costs a few dollars per minute. Call 0900 4BRIT (0900 42748) to charge your phone account, or 0800 4THEUK (0800 484 385) to pay for the service by credit card.

Listed below are the main requirements for the various visa applications. However, you may be invited to an interview and asked to furnish more documentation and answer more questions.

Have copies of all this documentation in your hand luggage when you fly into the UK, in case an immigration officer asks to see it on arrival. If you are on a Student or Working Holiday Visa, you may also be asked for evidence that you have the means to support yourself initially.

For more information on visas, look on any of these websites: www.britain.org.nz, www.ind.homeoffice.gov.uk and www.ukvisas.gov.uk.

The visas cost between $100 and $310. Working Holiday Visas and Student Visas are the cheapest, the Certificate of Entitlement to Right of

Abode is the most expensive. Turnaround time is four to six weeks — the busy season for the High Commission, when applications take longest, is January to May. You have to send in your passport with your application, so make sure you won't need it in the meantime.

> British High Commission
> 44 Hill Street
> Thorndon
> Wellington
> 04 924 2888 or 04 924 2889
> www.britain.org.nz

ENTRY CLEARANCE

If you don't need a visa (if you are travelling as a tourist, for example) but you plan to stay in the UK for more than six months, you will still need to apply for Entry Clearance — even if you have a work permit. Apply through the British High Commission.

CERTIFICATE OF ENTITLEMENT TO RIGHT OF ABODE

Almost as handy as a British passport. If you and/or your parents were born in the UK you may be eligible for a Certificate of Entitlement to Right of Abode, which means that you'll be able to skip through UK immigration and you have the right to live and work in the UK indefinitely.

You'll need a completed application form, your passport, two identical passport photos, your birth certificate and marriage certificate if you are a married woman, your parents' marriage certificate, and evidence that you or your parent is a British citizen.

ANCESTRY VISA

The next best thing to a British passport is the four-year Ancestry Visa. You can apply if a grandparent was born in the UK, or a grandparent was born in what is now the Republic of Ireland before 31 March 1922. You won't have recourse to public funds (which means you can't get a benefit while in the UK) but you can work freely and can apply for permanent residence when your visa expires — as long as you can prove you have been working continuously for your four years.

To apply, you'll need the completed application form, your passport, two passport photos, your birth certificate, a marriage certificate if you are a married woman and the birth certificates of the parent and grandparent through whom you have UK ancestry. You might also need your parents' marriage certificate, and any adoption certificates.

Note: after you arrive in the UK, keep all your bank statements, payslips, tax documents, etc. if you intend to try for Right of Abode after four years. You will need all the paperwork you can get.

WORKING HOLIDAY VISA

Even if you don't have a parent or grandparent who was born in the UK, if you are aged 17–30 inclusive and have no dependents, you can apply for the Working Holiday Visa, which allows you to work in the UK for two years. You must be able to prove you have means to support yourself in the UK for at least a month, and to pay for a journey home.

The visa used to be frustratingly restrictive, but the British Home Office eased restrictions in 2003. Officially, you are still going to Britain for the main purpose of travel, so you will be expected to take a holiday during your stay. Obviously, this won't be hard. You are allowed to work full-time in any occupation and you can switch to work permit employment (*see below, and 'What next?'*) after a year, if you find an employer willing to sponsor you. You won't have recourse to public funds, which means the dole is out of the question.

The two years starts from the date written on your visa and expires exactly two years later, immaterial of whether you come and go from the UK during that time. You can ask to defer entry for three months from the time of application, which is useful if you want to travel on the way to the UK. You'll need to send in a completed application form, your passport, two identical passport photos and three months' worth of bank statements to show you have the means to support yourself. At peak times — December to May — you should submit your application six to eight weeks before your intended date of departure. If you are pushing the upper age limit, keep in mind that your application must be approved before your 31st birthday.

STUDENT VISA

Getting a Student Visa is more straightforward if you have been accepted into a recognised course in the UK before you leave New Zealand. You can also go over on spec for up to six months — if you can demonstrate that you plan to enrol and agree to leave if you don't start studying within six months. (If you go on spec, you'll still need Entry Clearance from the British High Commission, assuming you are planning to stay longer than six months.)

You'll have to demonstrate your ability to support yourself financially. If your course is longer than six months you are allowed to work in the UK for 20 hours a week or less.

You'll have to pay non-residents' fees in the UK, which can be crippling on a New Zealand dollar. Do some research into scholarships and fellowships. The Link Foundation offers half a dozen fellowships. For information, email link-foundation@clear.net.nz, or look on the website http://britain.org.nz/link.

If you are accepted for a course while still in New Zealand, don't pay the fees until your visa comes through. Useful websites for people intending to study in the UK are the British Council's www.educationuk.org and the Foreign and Commonwealth Office's www.i-uk.com. You can also search for courses on the website www.studyinbritain.com.

WORK PERMIT

The Work Permit is a bit more complicated. You will need a sponsor in the UK who can put up a good argument for employing you over anyone else in the European Union. They can apply to the UK Government agency Work Permits (UK) on your behalf. If you can get in on another working visa, it's probably best to do so. For more information on getting a work permit, go to the website of Work Permits (UK), www.workpermits.gov.uk, call them on 0044 114 259 4074, or email wpcustomers@ind.homeoffice.gsi.gov.uk. If you get a Work Permit and you plan to stay in the UK for more than six months, you'll still need to apply for Entry Clearance from the British High Commission in Wellington. *More information on Work Permits in 'What next?'.*

HIGHLY SKILLED MIGRANT PROGRAMME

This programme is designed to attract people at the top of their professions who want to seek work in the UK with a view to settling there. You will be assessed on a points system, taking into account your education, work experience, earnings and other career achievements. There's a special category for people aged under 28, and one for general practitioners.

TOURISTS
If you are a New Zealand passport holder visiting the UK as a tourist for less than six months you don't need a visa — but you can't switch to another visa while in the UK. When you arrive, you may be asked to show onward or return tickets and prove you have sufficient funds for your trip.

OTHER VISAS
For other visas, including Spouse Entry, look on www.ukvisas.gov.uk or www.britain.org.nz or contact the British High Commission, Wellington.

APPLYING OUTSIDE NEW ZEALAND
You are supposed to apply for UK visas through the British mission in the country in which you are normally and legally resident. You can also apply at other UK overseas missions, but they might not accept your application if you are planning to go to the UK for a long time or permanently, and if they do accept it the process may be lengthy. If you are outside New Zealand, call your nearest mission before travelling for three days on a camel to get there, in case they can't help you. (There is a list of missions on www.fco.gov.uk)

The closest overseas post to the UK is in Paris. You can use this office if you don't normally live in New Zealand or if you plan to travel for

> Don't apply and then leave Paris assuming it's under control. Find a benevolent Parisian friend who will let you stay as long as needed, and keep turning up at the UK embassy just enquiring whether it's come through yet. It took phone calls to the New Zealand end as well to finally sort mine out. Spring would be the recommended season for applying because Paris is beautiful and warm and you therefore can't get too stressed or grumpy about being stuck there waiting for your visa to come through.
> — Anonymous

more than three months on the way to the UK. The Paris office is at 16 Rue d'Anjou, 75008 Paris, phone +33 1 4451 3301. It's open Monday to Friday, 9 am to midday.

Getting there
Flights

You can book a flight while you're waiting for your visa to come through, but try to put off paying for it in full until you have your visa and passport back in your hands.

WHAT TICKET?

You'll probably want a one-way ticket to the UK, with perhaps a stopover in Asia or the United States on the way. If you don't know where you want to base yourself in the UK, start in London. Pick a flight that gets you to your stopover city and the UK early in the day, so you have plenty of time in each city to find your accommodation.

If you are planning to be home within a year, you might want to consider a return or around-the-world ticket. Some travel agencies, including STA Travel, offer return tickets that are valid for 18 months. The best advice is to shop around. Look on travel and airline websites, visit a few travel agents — in person and online — and keep an eye out for advertisements.

Some starting points:
- Flight Centre, phone 0800 243 544, website www.flightcentre.co.nz
- Holiday Shoppe, phone 0800 808 480, website www.holidayshoppe.co.nz
- STA Travel, phone 0508 782 872, website www.statravel.co.nz
- Online travel companies www.travel.co.nz and www.travelonline.co.nz

MILEAGE PROGRAMMES

Consider joining an airline loyalty programme. The main ones are the Star Alliance (www.staralliance.com), which includes Air New Zealand, and the One World alliance (www.oneworld.com), which includes Qantas and British Airways. You'll have to pay about $75 to join, but you will probably reap that back. As you travel you accumulate points that you can swap for flights later on — and because of the distance between New Zealand and the UK the points can add up pretty quickly.

SURVIVING THE FLIGHT
The 23- to 25-hour haul to the UK can be soul-destroying. Consider breaking the flight with a stopover of at least a few days in Asia or the United States.

Ask your travel agent to book a seat for you when you buy your tickets — some airlines allow you to book in advance a window or aisle seat and/or one with extra leg room. (A window seat gives you something to lean on if you want to sleep, an aisle seat gives easier access to the toilets.) You don't want to be shoved into a rear seat that doesn't recline, with people crammed in either side of you. If your travel agent can't book you a seat, call the airline in advance or turn up to check in ridiculously early. You'll also be able to opt for vegetarian or special meals when you book.

The best way to survive a long-haul flight is to be a flight nerd. Consider packing an eye mask and good ear plugs, a travel pillow, a change of clothes, toiletries, a huge bottle of water (you never get enough from the flight attendants), deodorant, a pen (for filling out your UK arrival card), reading material, music and other toys to keep you occupied.

Wear comfortable clothes and dress in layers. Sometimes it can be warm enough on a plane to wear shorts and a singlet, other times you'll want trousers and a fleece. Wear sunscreen if you have a window seat — there may be ice on the outside of the window, but you can still get sunburnt.

Make sure there's nothing sharp in your hand luggage — you can get hauled off and interrogated for something as harmless as a pair of tweezers or a nail file these days.

TRAVEL INSURANCE
Get insurance to cover your journey to the UK, but don't bother taking out a year-long policy to cover you while you're there. The UK travel insurance market is very competitive and you'll probably get a better deal once you get there. (*See 'Travel on the Continent and beyond'*.) Your

travel agent can organise insurance for your flight to London, although it can be cheaper to sort it out yourself. It's unwise to travel without insurance.

Sorting out your finances

Saving money

The New Zealand dollar doesn't go far in the UK. The object of the game is to get a decent job soon after you land, but if it takes a while, you'll need enough money to keep yourself, and enough money to get home if things get really tough (which hardly ever happens). The British High Commission used to recommend you arrive with £2000 to spare, which is good advice, although you can get away with less if you scrimp. That's on top of the cost of the flight, visa, your pack and a hundred other things. How much money will you need? About $8000–10,000 will get you to the UK with a comfortable safety net, after a week in Asia or a few days in the United States. You could probably do it for little more than the cost of the flight and visa, if you're prepared to take the first badly paid live-in pub job you find in the UK.

The more money you have, the easier your transition will be. If you start out in the UK with nothing, it can be a long time before you've recouped enough money for a decent holiday in Europe — which is what it's all about for most Kiwis.

How much?
HERE'S A ROUGH GUIDE:

One-way flight and insurance	$1400
Stopover	$400
Visa	$100–300
Passport	$70
Pack, sleeping bag, and a dozen other things	$700
Money for London	$6000

SORTING OUT DEBT

Try to clear any debts before you go and put your credit card in credit, so you can use it for emergency money. Triple-check you've paid all outstanding bills. The exception is a student loan. Pay off as much as you can in New Zealand, but if you're canny with your money you can get stuck into it while you're earning pounds. More about that later.

Sorting out your New Zealand bank accounts

- Let your bank know you're going overseas — you might be able to negotiate a different fee structure.
- If you have several accounts you might want to consolidate them to minimise fees.
- Make sure you are set up with Internet banking before you leave, so you can manage your funds from overseas. It's also a good idea to give someone you trust authority to deal with the bank on your behalf, in case of problems.
- Get your bank statements mailed to that person's address, or ask the bank to stop sending them at least until you get settled in the UK (and even then you might find that Internet banking is sufficient).
- Check that you can use your ATM card overseas (look for Plus, Visa Interlink, Maestro or Cirrus symbols on the back), get a new one if it's about to expire, and find out what fees you'll be charged for withdrawing money.
- Make sure you have stopped automatic payments you no longer need to make.
- Don't close your bank account, as you'll need it to transfer money to when you leave the UK.

CREDIT CARDS

- If you have a credit card, make sure it's not about to expire.
- If you don't have a credit card, consider getting one — it might take a while until your UK bank trusts you enough to give you one, and there will be times when it is more convenient to use a credit card than a debit card or cash.
- Try to keep your credit cards in credit to avoid being charged interest and penalties while you're overseas, and to save yourself the bother of last-minute panics to make payments.
- You can send sterling cheques home to pay your credit card bills, but the New Zealand bank will charge a fee to convert them.
- Write down the number to call if your credit card is lost or stolen.

It's a good idea to get credit card insurance to cover fraudulent transactions.
- Make sure you have a pin number for your credit card, so you can use it at ATMs if necessary.

Opening a UK bank account

Next to getting a passport and visa and booking a flight, opening a bank account in the UK is the most important thing to do before you leave.

It can be difficult to open an account when you get to the UK. Most banks will demand to see proof of your UK address, in the form of something official like a rental contract, a power bill or a payslip — and you can't usually get any of those things unless you already have a bank account.

If you are an HSBC or ASB Bank customer, you can ask the bank to open an account on your behalf with HSBC in the UK — which has a good reputation among Kiwis in the UK. National Bank has the same arrangement with Lloyds, and BNZ has an agreement with Clydesdale. You have to transfer over a minimum opening balance (usually £500–1000), and it takes about six weeks. Some travel agencies and travel companies, including Travelex, will also be able to open an account for you.

You will need to provide the bank with your UK address. It's best to ask a trustworthy friend in London if you can use their address, otherwise you can use the address of your accommodation. It's easy to change the address once the account is open.

Once in the UK you'll have to go to a branch to pick up your card and chequebook. If you are asked to nominate a branch when you apply for the account in New Zealand, and you don't yet know where you'll end up, choose one in central London.

If you are planning to try your luck once you arrive, get a letter from your bank saying what a good customer you are, pack some bank statements and try to get some official-looking mail sent to the address you're heading to in the UK, so you have proof of your address.

Cash

It's a good idea to take a couple of hundred pounds in cash to tide you over until your bank account is sorted at the other end. Get small bills — £20 notes — if possible.

Tax

Call Inland Revenue and let them know you're leaving the country — they will suggest you become a non-resident for tax purposes if:

- you intend to be away for more than 325 days (in total) in any 12-month period, and
- you don't have a permanent place of abode in New Zealand, and
- you have a continuing source of New Zealand income (other than interest or dividends) while living overseas.

You might wish to nominate someone you trust to deal with Inland Revenue on your behalf while you're away — especially if you have a student loan, continuing New Zealand income or other matters to complicate tax affairs — and ask for all correspondence to be sent to him or her.

Make sure you file a tax return if you won't be earning any more money in New Zealand in the financial year — if you have only worked for part of the year you may be due a handy refund. Order tax return forms by phone, download them from the Inland Revenue website or fill them out online.

You can also register with Inland Revenue's secure email facility through its website, so you can communicate with them by email from the UK.

Inland Revenue New Zealand — contact details

Phoning from New Zealand: 0800 377 774
Phoning from overseas:
— for tax residents, +64 4 801 9973
— for tax non-residents, +64 3 467 7020
Student loan enquiries:
— from New Zealand, 0800 377 778
— from overseas, +64 4 381 9435
Website: www.ird.govt.nz

Student loans

If you have a student loan, you must tell Inland Revenue you are leaving the country. You will still be expected to make payments while overseas but they will change the way your repayment amounts are calculated.

Instead of taking a chunk of your salary, they'll expect quarterly payments, which are calculated on the basis that you will pay off the loan in 15 years. You cannot put your student loan on hold while you're overseas, but if you ask nicely you might be able to put off a payment or two if you are not going to be earning for six months while you travel. There is a repayments calculator on Inland Revenue's website.

From overseas, you can make a student loan repayment by:
- Sending a cheque to Inland Revenue, PO Box 39050, Wellington Mail Centre. Include your IRD number, your name and contact details, and a note that the payment is for your student loan.
- Telegraphic transfer through your UK bank. Download a telegraphic transfer form from the Inland Revenue website, fill it out and give it to your bank.

You can also pay by automatic payment or online through your ANZ, Kiwibank, National Bank or Westpac account in New Zealand. See the Inland Revenue website for details.

Power of attorney

You might want to nominate someone you trust to have power of attorney to deal with all your financial and legal matters while you are away. You can get power of attorney forms from some bookshops. For 'ordinary' (temporary) power of attorney, all you need to do is get the donor (you) and the attorney (the person you nominate) to sign the form in front of a witness. For more information, go to the Consumers' Institute website, www.consumer.org.nz, or the New Zealand Law Society website, www.nz-lawsoc.org.nz.

Accommodation

You'd be crazy not to sort yourself out somewhere to stay before you arrive in the UK. It's a good idea to arrange a minimum of two weeks' accommodation. Whether you're dossing or hostelling, note the address and postcode of the place. Not only will you have to be able to find it when you arrive, but you'll need to write it on an immigration card at the airport and you'll need it to open a bank account. *For information on finding a place to stay see 'Accommodation'.*

The Big OE Companion

Communications

Email and internet

If you don't already have an internet email account, get one. Hotmail (www.hotmail.com) and Yahoo (www.yahoo.com) are the most popular. However, you might find that your employer in the UK blocks these web addresses out of a well-founded fear that you'll waste company time on personal emails. Also, the free accounts don't give you much storage space and can be targeted by spam — internet junk mail.

Good alternatives are Ekno (www.ekno.com), Fastmail (www.fastmail.fm), and Mail (www.mail.com), which offer more generous storage space, attract fewer spammers and are unlikely to come under your boss's radar. If you want a New Zealandish address, check out Kiwismail (www.kiwismail.com). With any of these email accounts, you can choose free membership — which is still usually more generous with storage space than Hotmail. However, it doesn't cost much to become a paying member — about $25 — and in so doing you get extra storage space for those travel photos. Some offer virtual vaults — in which you can store copies of important documents — but usually you can just keep these in a folder.

If you are technically minded, consider getting a website to display a travel diary and photos. Yahoo, for example, offers a free photo gallery on which you can display your photos. You can also host your own web pages free on Geocities, www.geocities.com.

It's a good idea to introduce your parents and even grandparents to the wonder of email if they haven't discovered it already. It'll really help the communication once you're on the other side of the world. If necessary, take them by the hand, walk them down to the nearest internet café and stand over them while they open an internet email account and practise sending emails. But make them promise to write real letters occasionally. Everyone appreciates a real letter from home — and you don't want your mum turning into a spam fiend.

Mobile phone

Cancel your mobile phone connection and settle the bill. You might want to arrange it so your current connection is active for your first week or two in the UK, while you arrange a UK connection. If so, make sure you have international roaming and get a UK/NZ electrical adaptor (and use your phone very sparingly for those few weeks). If you are planning to use your handset in the UK, make sure it's unlocked — some mobile phone companies will have locked it to their network before you bought it. Some will refuse to unlock it until you have been with them for a minimum period — usually six months or a year. Ring the mobile provider to get it unlocked. *See also 'Communications and media'.*

Get prepared for work
Research

Do some research into the kind of work you'll be chasing in the UK. A bit of planning can save you time — and thus money — when you get there. If you are in a high-demand occupation — in health or education, for instance — you might be able to land a job before you leave. If you know anyone who's working in your industry in the UK, get in touch and ask how they got their job. Search for UK websites related to your occupation and UK job sites *(see 'Work')*. Have a look at the antipodean publications and/or their websites *(listings in 'Getting your Kiwi fix')*.

> Having already used my two-year Working Holiday Visa I had to arrange my second stint in the UK by getting a Work Permit to practise as an occupational therapist in the NHS. This required securing a job before I left New Zealand. After telephone interviews, I was accepted for two positions, and chose the one which offered opportunities for professional development within a well-resourced department.
>
> When I arrived I found nine therapists had to hot seat on five desks in an office no bigger than the average bathroom. Resources were piled on the floor and along the windowsills. Formal assessments were carried out in the kitchen. There was a freeze on funding for courses, stress levels were very high and staff morale was very low.
>
> But what can you do? You believed all you were told over the phone interview, you tried to do a bit of background research, you aired all your concerns and were reassured. I had signed a contract so I felt I had no option but to continue working.
>
> — Anonymous

Registration

Now the next bit's crucial, so pay attention. Check if your occupation requires you to be registered in the UK, or if you need to get your qualifications certified. This is most likely if you're working with children or in the caring or health sectors. Some tradespeople are also affected. Registration can be complex and time-consuming so it's best to find out what you need to do — and if necessary start the process — while you're still in New Zealand. In some cases you can enlist the help of a recruitment agency in the UK, which can save a lot of hassle, but it can be costly and can leave you beholden. *For more information about registration, see 'Work'.*

Police checks

If you are going to be working with children or as a social worker or carer you'll need a report on your criminal record from the Department for Courts (if you have no criminal record the letter will say so). Get an application form from your local District Court, or by phoning 04 918 8800, or download it from www.courts.govt.nz/privacy. Post it to the address on the form. Allow at least two weeks.

Other logistics

Leaving work

Give yourself a bit of time between leaving your job and flying out. Take a week if you're fairly well organised, more if you're not.

Moving out

If you're moving out of a rental property, don't forget to:
- get your mail redirected, perhaps to your parents' address;
- advise the world in general of your change of address;
- get the utilities disconnected and quit the lease, or transfer the accounts and lease to your flatmates.

Driver's licence

Make sure your New Zealand driver's licence is up-to-date — you can't renew an expired licence if you are overseas (although you can get a replacement if it is lost or stolen). You can use your New Zealand licence in the UK for a year, after which you must apply for a UK licence (see 'Transport and orientation'). It's not necessary to get an International Driving Permit for the UK, but it can be handy if you plan to do a lot of driving in Europe. It must always be accompanied by your New Zealand licence. You can get one by popping into a New Zealand Automobile Association shop with your licence and a passport-size photo, or you can apply online. It costs $15 plus postage if necessary.

New Zealand Automobile Association: phone 09 966 8979, email internationalmotoring@nzaa.co.nz, website www.nzaa.co.nz.

Car insurance

If you think you might buy a car in the UK (and if you are going to be living in London you can get away without one), get a letter from your New Zealand car insurance company testifying that you've made no claims.

Poste restante

You can get mail sent to you care of a post office in the UK. The service is only for travellers, and is available for a maximum of three months at any one post office. Letters from abroad are kept for one month, letters from within the UK for only two weeks. You can pick them up with ID. A list of post offices is available on www.postoffice.co.uk.

To send something post restante to yourself at the central London Trafalgar Square Post Office, address it to:

```
[Your name]
Poste Restante
Trafalgar Square Post Office
24-28 William IV Street
London WC2N 4DL
```

Health

It's a good idea to get your health sorted before you go, although once you're registered on the National Health Service (NHS) in the UK (see 'Health, fitness and sport') most basic medical needs are free, as are visits to the doctor. Pay a visit to your doctor and dentist, stock up on contact lenses, and pack a copy of any prescriptions, including glasses prescriptions. Condoms are expensive in the UK so you might want to take some with you. If you're on the contraceptive pill, get enough to tide you over for a couple of months until you can get to a doctor in the UK (the pill is free in the UK).

Discount passes

If you are a student, pack your student ID and get an International Student Identity Card — ISIC (www.isiccard.com). It will pay dividends in discounts in Europe. You can pick up forged cards on the streets in some Asian cities, but of course this is illegal and you're running a risk. Don't worry about scrambling to get a youth hostel membership before you leave, unless you're going straight into a YHA or Hostelling International hostel in the UK or you know you will be spending a lot of the year using them. You can get one at any time, and many hostels in Europe are independent and don't accept them anyway.

If you are aged under 26, you can get an International Youth Travel Card from STA Travel. Details at www.iytccard.co.nz. People under 26 are considered youths in Europe, and you'll get discounts to match.

Packing

Audit your belongings

Moving to the other side of the world gives you the perfect opportunity to spring-clean your belongings. Have a ruthless purging session and throw out as much as you can bear. If you end up splitting your remaining belongings among your friends and family, keep a list of where you leave everything. After four years away, you probably won't remember what your microwave oven looks like, let alone who kindly offered to look after it.

Choosing luggage

Sturdy packs with frames and daypacks attached are the preferred luggage of most Kiwis in the UK. Macpac, Kathmandu and Fairydown have good reputations. You might find a 90-litre pack too big — especially if you have a small frame and you have to lug your stuff for miles to your hostel or dossing house. It might be better to take a 60- to

70-litre bag and a smaller roll bag if you need it. Don't take too many items of luggage, and make sure you can carry everything in one go. Having a big suitcase is okay if you're wealthy enough to take taxis, and/or have permanent accommodation to go straight into. Make sure you can lock your luggage — using padlocks if necessary — and do so before you check your luggage in at the airport.

What to pack

Don't bother about shopping for a new wardrobe before you leave, although you might want to get a good-quality New Zealand wool jumper and a possum fur scarf as a bit of a comfort blanket, especially if you are going straight into a UK winter. If you are going to be seeking a professional job in the UK, pack a suit. If you're a tradesperson you might want to take some tools (you might have to declare them at Customs in the UK). Otherwise pack as lightly as possible, because you'll probably be carrying your life on your back until you get set up in a flat. And you'll be limited by the airline's baggage weight restrictions — usually 20 kg for checked-in baggage if you are travelling via Asia and 32 kg through the United States. (Carry-on baggage — around 7 kg maximum — is additional.) Remember that you are packing for a civilised country, not for survival, so you might not need your survival blanket and first-aid kit.

CAMERAS AND VIDEO CAMERAS

Your photos of Europe will probably be your most valued souvenirs, so it's worth splashing out on a good camera. Consider buying an SLR camera with two lenses — a standard one which widens to 28 mm or less (handy for photographing all those historic buildings in Europe) and a 300 mm long lens. Alternatively, consider getting a small digital camera. It's not a silly idea to get both, if you can afford it, so you have a bit of flexibility.

Buy a video camera only if you trust yourself to use it selectively and promise your family and friends to edit the tapes before showing them. It's disturbing how many people walk through Europe with video cameras attached to their faces.

When you're travelling, don't get so obsessed with taking photos or filming your trip that you see the best bits of Europe through a lens. Remember that you can always buy postcards.

The Big OE Companion

BEDDING

A compression pack from a camping store will squash your sleeping bag in half.

If you're staying in a hostel on arrival in the UK, they might ask you to supply a sleeping sheet — two single sheets sewn together to make a sack.

PAPERWORK

Prepare a few sets of photocopies of essential documents — passport, UK visa, travel insurance details, airline ticket, driver's licence, medicine prescriptions if necessary, glasses prescription, academic qualifications, car insurance records, references from employers and landlords, professional registrations, your birth certificate, bank records, etc. Take sets with you, post one on ahead, and scan the documents into a computer and email them to yourself if you can. Leave a set with your parents or someone else responsible in New Zealand. Compile a CV before you go (*for tips on CVs, see 'Work'*). If you have something you can bang into shape quickly, you might save yourself having to spend money on internet cafés in the UK.

If you're going through the United States on the way to London, it's unwise to carry a CV or related documents with you. In the unlikely event that US immigration officials suspect you of intending to work in the country illegally, a CV might be hard to explain.

USEFUL EXTRAS

- A greenstone or bone pendant, or paua necklace. (You'll get sentimental.)
- An All Blacks jersey or scarf. (You'll get patriotic.)
- A small photo album with sentimental pictures in it, and New Zealand music. (You'll get homesick.)
- A travel guide to Europe, the UK and/or London. (*Lonely Planet*, *Rough Guide* and *Time Out* guides are popular.)
- A roll-up toiletries bag.
- A sarong (even if you're a boy). Doubles as a towel, picnic rug, skirt, curtain, scarf, even a rope.
- An outline of your UK family tree as far back as you can go — names, places, dates — if you want to trace your heritage.

Groundwork

Planning calendar ⏱ 🔆

One year to go
Start saving and researching.

Six months to go
Set a date.
Buy your air ticket and travel insurance (but don't pay the full amount until your visa comes through).
Check if you need visas for stopover countries.
Check if you need to be registered in your occupation in the UK. If so, start the ball rolling.

Twelve weeks to go
Send passport application.

Ten weeks to go
Send visa application.

Eight weeks to go
Check if you need vaccinations for stopover countries.
Research the job market.
Renew your driver's licence, if necessary.

Six weeks to go
Open a UK bank account.
Sort out your student loan.

Five weeks to go
Give notice at work and ask for a reference.
Give notice on your flat and ask for a reference.
Start sorting out your belongings.
Start buying anything you need.
Book accommodation.

Four weeks to go
Contact your friends in the UK.

Compile an address book (on paper as well as online).
Set up an international email account and give the address to your friends.
Apply for a copy of your criminal record if necessary.

Three weeks to go
Organise final utility payments (electricity, gas, etc.) and sort out your mobile phone.
Sort out your New Zealand bank accounts and apply for a credit card, if necessary.
Do a trial pack.
Get paperwork in order and photocopy it.

Two weeks to go
Get an international driver's licence.
Cancel memberships, subscriptions, insurance policies, etc.
Send out change of address notifications.
Organise for your mail to be redirected.
Email your CV to a few recruitment agencies in the UK (**see 'Work'**).

One week to go
File a tax return.
Move out of your flat.
Get some pounds.
Have a party.
Savour a last good flat white coffee and have it with a chocolate fish.

One day to go
Do your final pack and triple-check you have your passport and tickets.

Leaving day
Quadruple-check you have your passport and tickets.
Kiss your Mum/Dad/dog/cat goodbye.

3. Your first week

Let's assume that, like most people, you'll spend at least your first week in London. No matter how well you prepare, London can feel daunting, especially if you're jet-lagged. Even when you have lived in the city for years it's hard to fathom its immense, sprawling size and sheer number of inhabitants, of every nationality and ethnicity. Its cultural and ethnic diversity can be a surprise — more than 300 languages are spoken in London's streets.

But daunting be damned — you're more likely to find it downright exciting. All those Monopoly board names — Leicester Square, Piccadilly Circus, Trafalgar Square, Oxford Street, Regent Street — the sense of history at Westminster, the buzz of Soho, the peace of the parks, the dozens of fascinating museums and galleries, the foxes and squirrels, the plethora of West End shows. You'll find it all magical in your first week. Etch into your brain how good it feels to see it all for the first time and you'll never take London for granted.

The Golden Rule for your first week is to open your eyes and stretch your legs. Don't even think about looking for work or a flat yet — the serious stuff can wait.

Arrival

Most international flights land at Heathrow Airport, in the west of London. If you're lucky you'll have a window seat — planes often do a swoop over the central city before they land and you'll get a view of an eternity of neat rows of terraced houses.

Your first week

Arrival card

If you don't have a British passport you'll need to fill in an arrival card — the airline staff usually hand these out on board, or you can get one in the airport. It will ask for your name, birthdate, place of birth, nationality, passport number, occupation and address in the UK.

Immigration

After you land you'll be herded to Immigration, which will be the first of many queues you'll find yourself in during your time in the UK. Best you get used to it now. Hand your passport and arrival card to the immigration officer. The officer might eye you suspiciously and ask random questions, such as 'What's your grandmother's name?' if you're on an Ancestry Visa, or ask for details of your job and employer if you're on a Work Permit. They used to give Working Holidaymakers a particularly hard time under the old restrictive rules. Although the rules have been loosened up, don't be surprised if they make up new questions. They're just trying to catch you out, in case you fold under pressure and admit to a penchant for international terrorism. Assuming you're not a terrorist and you're following the rules, be courteous and forthcoming and do nothing to annoy them.

WHICH QUEUE?

If you have a British or EU passport, you're a lucky bugger because you get to waltz through in a short queue. Usually they don't even look inside your nice red passport. If you have an Ancestry Visa or a Work Permit and you arrive into Terminal 1 or Terminal 3 at Heathrow there is a separate queue. All others have to suffer in the Other Passports queue.

Customs

After you've picked up your bags you'll go through Customs, which is usually devoid of customs officers. Go through the green line unless you have goods to declare.

Money

If you haven't brought sterling with you, there are plenty of currency exchange shops at the airport, where you can exchange cash or traveller's cheques. Ask for low denominations — £50 notes are hardly ever seen in the UK and can create problems at the local store. You can also use an ATM to withdraw money from a Visa card or a New Zealand bank account. Your bank will charge for the service, so don't do it too often.

If you opened a bank account before you left New Zealand, you'll probably have to go to the nominated branch to activate it.

Resist the urge to convert prices to New Zealand dollars, or you'll have a coronary before the week is out. Instead, get used to the local currency and the local prices.

Transport from the airport

There's no need to book transport in advance.

Underground

The best way to get to London from Heathrow is by London Underground, known universally as the Tube. It's easy, relatively quick (about 50 minutes to the centre of London) and cheap, although it shuts down around midnight and restarts between 5 am and 7 am, and if you've got a lot of luggage you might have a hard time hauling it around. London Underground: phone 0845 330 9880, email customerservices@tube.tfl.gov.uk, website www.tfl.gov.uk.

Other options

- The quicker (15–20 minutes) but more expensive Heathrow Express train to Paddington (phone 0845 600 1515, website www.heathrowexpress.com).
- The National Express A2 Airbus, which takes about 1 hour 40 minutes to get to King's Cross and inexplicably costs more than the Tube (phone 08705 808080, website www.nationalexpress.com).
- A black cab, which will cost around £45 to central London — more in heavy traffic.
- Or, if you're really, really lucky, you'll have a generous friend with a car and a lot of time on his/her hands.

If you're flying into a different London airport, see 'Travel on the Continent and beyond' for transport information.

Going Underground — the Tube for beginners

The Tube has its faults, but most first-time visitors to London love it because it makes navigating the city a breeze. It might look daunting at first, but you'll have it sussed within a couple of hours.

> To the average antipodean turning up in London, the Tube seems like a magical fairground ride. Let's face it; trains in New Zealand are for freight, not people. Unless you are a King's College student living in Newmarket and travelling to Papatoetoe, it's likely you've only ever been on a train as a special treat. You'll probably ride around the city all day, popping up like a meerkat to see where you are. You'll feel like Captain Kirk, with Scotty beaming you all over the place.
> — Andrew Knight

Figuring out your route

First, you should buy a *London A–Z* map book if you don't already have one and look up the street you need to get to. A street name can be shared by 40 streets, so check it against the postcode *(for a list of postcodes see 'Transport and orientation')* and suburb of your destination. On the map, find the Underground or overland station nearest your destination.

London A-Z map books have Underground maps on the back cover, or you can pick up a map from a Tube station. The *A–Z* also has overland train maps in the middle. The Underground map is colour-coded, with each of the 12 lines in a different colour. It's designed for simplicity and is not to scale. Heathrow is at the western end of the Piccadilly line (dark blue). Trace a route from there to your destination station — if you need to change lines, look for the stations where the lines intersect. If the station at the intersection is marked with a single circle it'll be a quick change. If there are two or three circles you might be facing a long walk between platforms — best avoided if you have a lot of luggage.

Zones

The Tube is split into six geographical zones, which determine how much you'll pay. The West End and the City are in Zone 1, and the other zones are in concentric circles around it. Heathrow is in the outer circle,

Zone 6. Check which zone you're going to on the big Tube map in the station. (If you have to go through Zone 1 to get to your destination you must have a ticket valid for Zone 1.)

Buying a ticket

The automatic ticket machines are easy to figure out. You'll probably want a single (one-way) ticket. At some machines you can pay with Visa or ATM cards, coins or notes. The older ones take only coins.

Using the ticket

At most stations you have to put the ticket in a slot at the Tube gates (some stations don't have machines). It'll pass through and pop out again for you to remove, and the gate will open. You have to do the same to leave the Tube at your destination, but the machine will keep the ticket if it was a single. If you have bulky luggage, get an attendant to let you through.

If any of this confuses you, ask a London Underground staff member and/or get a ticket from the ticket window. The staff are usually helpful, if not always cheerful. *See 'Transport and orientation' for more information.*

Luggage storage

You can store your luggage for short periods of time while you get yourself sorted, although most London stations and airports have canned left-luggage facilities because of terrorist threats. An exception is Victoria Coach Station.

The private company Excess Baggage offers storage facilities at Heathrow Airport (phone 020 8759 3344), Gatwick Airport (phone 01293 569900), all London mainline rail stations, and for up to four weeks at its offices in Earl's Court and Wembley/Park Royal. Phone 0800 783 1085, email sales@excess-baggage.com, website www.excess-baggage.com.

Getting mobile

The one chore you should tick off in the first week is buying a mobile phone — indispensable for meeting up with friends and for flat and job hunting. *For mobile phone advice, see 'Communications and media'.*

Meeting up

If you're planning to meet up with someone in London, be very specific about where you're meeting, especially if you don't both have mobiles. Be aware that Underground stations — the usual meeting places — can have many different exits, and there are stations of the same name in different places. Even naming a shop in a train station to meet outside can be problematic — there are two Boots chemist stores in Waterloo Station, for example.

Get lost

For your first week, lose yourself in London. Be a tourist. That's where most Kiwis go wrong. There's a temptation to dive straight into the serious stuff without giving yourself time to marvel at the whirr of London, to orientate yourself and to get over jet lag. Resist the temptation. London will swallow you up into its hectic ways soon enough, and unless you take the time to do the tourist thing you could find yourself leaving after three years having never seen Tower Bridge. Use the week to get a feel for your new city and to get accustomed to the transport. Take photos. Don't think, 'I'm here for five years, there's plenty of time for pictures of Big Ben.' You could end up going home with an entire photo album dedicated to one tiny village in Scotland and no pictures of London.

Buy a one-week travel pass, which is valid for all tubes and overland trains within the stated zone and buses throughout London. Go exploring with the wide-eyed wonder of a kid at a theme park. Your week of sightseeing needn't mean you have to spend a lot of money — London can be one of the cheapest places in Western Europe if you watch your pennies.

While you're in no hurry, you should spend as much of the week as possible above ground. Because the Tube pops up at most of London's big attractions, it's tempting to rely on it for navigation, to the detriment of your understanding of London's geography. Once you're in the West End and the City, most of the distances you're covering aren't great. It can be more pleasant and interesting to walk — and in some cases quicker — and you'll impress your friends if you learn the short cuts as well as a geezer.

An introduction to London's sights

- Take a day to wander around the West End.
  Take your *London A-Z*, explore side streets and alleys, and follow whims. The West End is loosely bordered by Mayfair in the west, Oxford Street in the north, Covent Garden in the east and Trafalgar Square in the south. Many of London's most famous streets and attractions — Leicester Square, Trafalgar Square, Piccadilly Circus, Covent Garden, Chinatown — are within a few square kilometres. You can pop into the Britain Visitor Centre at 1 Regent Street (just south of Piccadilly Circus), London SW1. If it's a sunny day, have a picnic lunch and a snooze in St James' Park or Hyde Park.
- From Trafalgar Square do a loop west down The Mall to Buckingham Palace, then along Birdcage Walk to Westminster Abbey, Big Ben and the Houses of Parliament. From there, take Parliament Street, which passes Downing Street before changing into Whitehall and rejoining the square by Nelson's column.
- Spend another day walking the riverside Thames Path from Westminster Bridge (on the opposite side of the river to the Houses of Parliament) to the Tate Modern, passing the London Eye, the South Bank and Shakespeare's Globe Theatre. At the Tate take the Millennium Bridge across the river to St Paul's Cathedral and the City, or continue beside the river to Tower Bridge and the Tower of London.
- Check if there is any Royal pomp and circumstance scheduled, on the Royal website www.royal.org. If not, there's daily pageantry at the changing of the guard: at Buckingham Palace daily at 11.30 am April to July, and every other day at other times of the year; at the Tower of London daily at noon; at the Horse Guards at 11 am daily (10 am Sunday).
  Website www.changing-guard.com.
- Take a bus sightseeing tour. It will cost about £12 but it is a good way to see central London overland and find your way around. Or save yourself money by buying a London bus map and a London travel guide and figuring it out on your own. The

regular Number 11 London Bus route is a good orientation to the city. It runs between Liverpool Street in the East End to Chelsea, via St Paul's Cathedral, Trafalgar Square, Westminster and Big Ben, Harrods of Knightsbridge and Sloane Square. And if you've got a travel pass it's free.

- A London Pass gets you free or discounted entry to most London attractions — although since most museums and art galleries are free and some key attractions don't participate, check what it covers first. Prices start at £23 for a one-day pass — which is worth it if you have the stamina to get your money's worth. Don't underestimate the time it will take to get between the attractions, and keep in mind that many attractions close early in winter. In one day you could see the Tower of London and St Paul's Cathedral in the morning, take a canal boat trip through Regent's Park (summer only) and on to London Zoo in the afternoon, and take an evening Original London Walks tour. On a two-day pass (£36) you could also fit in a trip to Windsor Castle and Eton College. For information and to book, go to www.londonpass.com. You can also buy passes from travel information centres at the main Underground and train stations.

For tips on London sightseeing on the cheap, see 'Enjoying the UK'.

During my first week in London I met a friend near Blackfriars Bridge for a drink. Later that night when we were walking back over the bridge to the Tube station I looked along the river to see St Paul's standing there, illuminated by all the uplights, and realised 'Wow, I'm really here.' Now, nearly four years later, whenever I walk over any of the bridges with a view to St Paul's I still remember what it felt like that first time.

When I started visiting European cities and going around London, I was advised that when looking at buildings, 'Don't forget to look up.' It has been a great piece of advice and has meant that I have seen gargoyles, frescoes, curlicues, hidden balconies and many other interesting details that I might never have seen if I had only focused on the first ten feet of the building.

— Natasha Speight

The Big OE Companion

The lingo

abroad — overseas; Brits don't use the word 'overseas'
antipodeans — in the UK this covers New Zealanders, Pacific Islanders, Australians and sometimes South Africans
blag — lie or steal
bog standard — usual, average; as in, 'It was a bog-standard night at the pub.'
chip butties — chip sandwiches
chippie — fish and chip shop
chips — hot chips, not the potato chips in the packets
cinema — not 'the movies'
crisps — potato chips
dead — very; as in, 'She's dead fit.'
doss — stay with a friend
Essex facelift — a slapper hairstyle — a tight ponytail drawing the hair off the face
fancy — to be attracted to someone
fit — attractive (especially women)
flatshare — rented shared accommodation
flip-flops — jandals
gaff — home
geezer — an English man, often a cockney; diamond geezer — a good man
ginger — a redhead (pronounced with a hard 'g' at the beginning)
greasy spoon — a café not known for its culinary expertise which serves all-day breakfasts, and where the coffee comes in mugs that are hand-me-downs from the proprietor's mother
Heathrow injection — the weight you'll put on in the UK if you're not careful
housemates — flatmates
innit — an abbreviation of 'isn't it?', but used by some at the end of every sentence, the way some New Zealanders use 'ay'
jumper — not 'jersey'
ketchup — tomato sauce
lager top — beer served with a dash of lemonade

Your first week

> lashed — drunk
> liquid paper or White Out — not 'Twink'
> lock-in (sometimes called 'afters') — the period after closing time in a pub, when the doors are locked but the customers keep drinking, as 'friends' of the owner
> minging — drunk or disgusting
> motor — a car
> muppet — an idiot
> offie, off-licence — the local dairy, which also sells alcohol
> pants — underwear, not trousers (can be embarrassing if not used in the correct sense); also means no good, rubbish, and is used as an expression of annoyance
> peaky — unwell
> quid — a pound
> rambling — walking in the countryside
> slapper — a loose woman
> sweets — lollies
> swimsuit — not 'togs'
> Switch card — an ATM card
> trainers — sneakers
> treble — not 'triple'
> trekking — hiking (not 'tramping', which is another thing altogether)
> well — very, as in 'it's well cold, innit?'
> you a' right? — a rhetorical greeting

Orientation parties

Some of the antipodean publications and websites host orientation parties. *TNT Magazine* hosts free Getting Started parties once a month, at a central pub or bar. Check the magazine for details, look on the website www.tntmag.co.uk, phone 0870 7522701 or email gettingstarted@tntmag.co.uk. *Other antipodean media companies offering similar parties are listed in 'Getting your Kiwi fix'.*

A note on personal safety

London is no more dangerous than any other of the world's big cities — in fact it's probably safer than most. You should follow the usual global rules of avoiding dark alleyways at night and staying alert to what's going on around you. Don't carry your wallet in a pocket from which it can be stolen easily, especially in crowded places. People have been shot for their mobile phones, so use yours discreetly. *For tips on mobile phone safety, see 'Communications and media'.*

Bag snatchings are common, especially when you're in a pub, bar or café. The thieves are so quick you'd think they were invisible — your bag can disappear even when it's surrounded by some of your burliest mates.

Take a few precautions:

- Keep your belongings where you can see them — preferably touching you. Many restaurants and bars provide bag hooks under the tables.
- Keep records of all your bankcards, credit cards and the like at home so you can cancel them quickly.
- Carry as few valuables as possible in your bag. If you know you won't need a credit card on a night out, leave it behind. Get into the habit of carrying a bit of cash and/or your ATM card in your pockets, so if your bag is taken you won't lose everything.

Street dwellers

Beggars

Most New Zealanders aren't used to being confronted by beggars, but they are a fact of life in the UK. You'll develop your own policy on whether or not you contribute. The government says there's no need for people to beg because they have access to benefits and social services, but homeless charities argue that many beggars have mental health and/or drug and alcohol problems and that treatment is inadequate. Most of the beggars in London are polite and passive and you'll have no problems. If you are confronted with an aggressive beggar it's best to walk away quietly rather than aggravate the situation. If you're in a transport station, you can ask the staff there for help if necessary.

The most annoying beggars are the hordes of women who trudge through tubes and trains, usually with babies who are always sleeping (the theory is that the kids are drugged). They are known as 'travellers' and they are usually Romany people from Eastern Europe — you've probably heard them called 'gypsies'. The women will hold out a sign claiming they are a refugee from the latest war spot. During the Afghanistan invasion they all claimed to be Afghan. During the Iraq war they claimed to be Iraqi. Sometimes they send small children ahead to do the begging for them. They all meet up on train platforms every now and then and swap the baby around.

Big Issue

A good way to help homeless people is to buy a copy of *Big Issue* magazine. Homeless people sell it on the streets, and earn a portion of the takings. Think of it as helping them to help themselves. The magazine is operated on a shoestring budget so don't expect *Newsweek*. However, they secure interviews from some big-name celebrities keen to support the cause. The sellers wear ID cards so you know you're buying from a legitimate source.

Charity sellers

Charity sellers are a scourge of London. You'll know them by their brightly coloured bibs and clipboards — and because they'll be the only chirpy people on the streets. They'll try to reel you in as you're walking with a question like, 'Excuse me sir/madam, do you care about our children?' Then they'll try to sign you up as a donor to a charity. They can be very persistent. If you're a charitable person, you're best to donate straight to the charity yourself, as these sellers take a sizeable commission.

Your second week

After you've kicked back for a week and acclimatised, you may start thinking about looking into the serious stuff — work, accommodation — but try not to get discouraged if everything doesn't fall into place immediately. A quick task for your second week is to register online with the New Zealand High Commission — it's not compulsory but it could be important in an emergency. *For more information, see 'New Zealand government in the UK and Europe'.*

A lesson in London English

On a lazy Sunday afternoon, John met Mike and Jane for a pint at the pub.

'All right geezer?' Mike said to John.

'Wotcha,' said John to Mike and Jane. 'Who's getting them in?'

'Not me,' Mike said, 'I'm boracic. All the readies I've got is a Godiva in my skyrocket and that's it 'til Monday. At this rate I'll end up on the jam roll. Can I borrow a pony off you to tide me over?'

'Go on then, I've got shedloads,' said John. 'And I'll get 'em in then. What are you having Jane?'

'Lager top thanks,' Jane said.

'So what did you two get up to last night?' John asked.

'Well, we were meant to be having it large,' Mike said, 'but it all went Pete Tong. The doorman threw me out because I was well battered. But I did see Chris there — haven't seen him for ages — he's a diamond geezer. Jane got the hump because she thought I was getting off with some bird. I was only talking to her, but she was well fit though.'

'You must be having a giraffe,' Jane said; 'she was a minger.'

'She wasn't that minging,' Mike replied. 'Anyway, then some bloke at the door tried to cop off with Jane and snog her, so we legged it before it kicked off.'

'And then when we got back to the gaff, the lecky was off,' Jane said. 'Because Mike, the muppet, forgot to pay the meter. So he went down to the newsagent to get some credit.'

'Yeah,' Mike agreed. 'So I couldn't cook any grub when we got home and I was Hank Marvin. Plus the flat was Baltic. By the time I got up this morning I was cream crackered.'

'Sounds like pants, innit?' John said.

'It was an' all,' Jane agreed.

'So what time does the footy start this arvo?' Mike asked.

'I haven't got a Scooby Doo,' John replied; 'ask the gaffer.'

'I will,' Mike said, 'and I'll get 'em in while I'm up there.'

A Kiwi translation

'Hello mate,' Mike said to John.

'Gidday,' said John to Mike and Jane. 'Whose turn is it to buy drinks?'

'Not mine,' said Mike, 'I'm broke. The only cash I've got is a five-pound note in my pocket and that's until Monday. At this rate I'll end up on the dole. Can I borrow £25 off you to tide me over?'

'Of course you can, I've got heaps,' John said. 'And I'll buy this round. What are you having Jane?'

'A pint of lager with a dash of lemonade in the top thanks,' Jane said.

'So what did you two get up to last night?' John asked.

'Well, we were meant to be going out for a big night drinking,' Mike said, 'but it all went horribly wrong. The bouncer threw me out because I was really pissed. But I did see Chris there — haven't seen him in ages — he's a really nice guy. Jane got upset because she thought I was chatting up some girl. I was only talking to her, but she was very attractive though.'

'You must be kidding,' Jane said, 'she was a bush pig.'

'She wasn't that ugly,' Mike replied. 'Anyway, then some bloke at the door tried to chat up Jane and kiss her, so we took off before any further trouble started.'

'And when we got home, the power was off,' Jane said. 'Because Mike, the idiot, forgot to put credit into the prepay-meter. So he went down to the dairy to get a prepay card.'

'Yeah,' Mike agreed. 'So I couldn't have any munchies when we got home and I was starving. Plus the flat was freezing. By the time I got up this morning I was knackered.'

'That's no good, is it?' John said.

'It certainly wasn't,' Jane agreed.

'So what time does the soccer match start this afternoon?' Mike asked.

'I haven't got a clue,' John replied. 'Ask the landlord.'

'I will,' Mike said. 'And it must be my round.'

— Andrew Knight

The Big OE Companion

The Koiwi uccent

If you're a Kiwi abroad you can count on getting hassled over your accent. The main area of confusion is the way we say our 'e'. English people think it sounds like an 'i'. Thus 'seven red pens on a desk' will sound like 'sivin rid pins on a disk'. If you want to make yourself understood, speak slowly and clearly, and repeat ten times a day: 'savan rad pans on a dask'. New Zealanders haven't developed a distinction between the words 'beer', 'bare' and 'bear', or between 'ear' and 'air' — but get an English person to say them and listen for the subtle differences. In the States you'll get hassled for not pronouncing your 'r's — which makes 'beard' and 'bed' sound the same to them.

To get an idea of how New Zealanders sound to people of other nationalities, here's a translation that's been doing the rounds of websites and emails for a while.

How to speak New Zealander

amejen — visualise
beggage chucken — place to leave your suitcase at the airport
brudge — structure spanning a river
bug hut — popular recording
bun button — been bitten by an insect
cuds — children
cuttin — baby cat
dick cheese — deck chairs
ear roebucks — exercise at the gym
ever cardeau — avocado
fitter cheney — type of pasta
fush — marine creatures
guess — vapour
iggs ecktly — precisely
inner me — enemy
jumbo — pet name for someone called Jim
jungle bills — a Christmas carol

Your first week

leather — foam produced from soap
lift — departed
McKennock — a person who fixes cars
mere — mayor
mess kara — eye make-up
munner stroney — soup
nin tin dough — computer game
one doze — well-known computer program
peck — to fill a suitcase
pigs — for hanging out washing
pissed aside — chemical which kills insects
pits — domestic animals
pug — large animal with a curly tail
pump — to act as an agent for a prostitute
sivven sucks sivven — large Boeing aircraft
sucks peck — half a dozen beers
tin — one more than nine

Don't whinge about how cold it is, how crap the Tube is, how polluted it is, how great New Zealand is, or how unfriendly the people are when you get here — the standard response (whether spoken or unspoken) will be, 'Sod off home then' (and rightly so).

— Reuben Woods

4.
Enjoying the UK

There was once a Kiwi guy who was so consumed by his London lifestyle that in his two-year UK stint he never got around to going to Europe — or anywhere outside London for that matter. He once got as far as stopping at his local for a pint on his way out of the country, and got no further. Now that's freakish and not at all recommended, but it's entirely possible because there is so much to do in London.

Conversely, it's common to come across New Zealanders in the UK who have taken off to the Continent at every opportunity and haven't explored the richness of the festivals, cities, villages and landscapes of the UK. We don't tend to give the UK the credit — or time — it deserves. But you could feasibly spend all your holidays for two years within the UK and not get bored — although you might feel a little bereft of warm sun and inviting beaches.

The culture

Before we get to the UK, we tend to think that the culture we will find there will be much like ours — we are, after all, its former colony and many of our towns and cities were created in its image. You might not notice the subtle differences between the two countries until you've been in the UK for a while. The biggest gulf is probably class distinctions. Sure, there are ever-growing distinctions between rich and poor in New Zealand, but in the UK this gap has been growing for more than a millennium. And it's not just a matter of wealth — there is the

Enjoying the UK

complication of lineage. Thus you'll find vastly different cultures in a pub in an industrial town in the north of England and in the tearooms of London's Ritz Hotel.

Even today the upper classes like to be able to pigeonhole people. Every now and then you'll come across an upper-crust person who will disdainfully categorise you as colonial — as if you are the crass offspring of a prodigal son, or a favourite pet that went feral.

> I hadn't long moved into a flat with a very posh English girl when she asked me, 'Are you Town or Country?' Puzzled, I didn't know what to say. 'Well, where did you grow up?' I stammered that I'd been born in Auckland but had moved to a small town as a young child. 'Oh, you're Country then.' That seemed to satisfy her.
>
> I later found out that you're considered a bit common if you're Town. She was only 25 but was clinging desperately to class distinctions — even though we were living in a squalid flat and she was getting paid peanuts. She would get sniffy if some young geezers dared to talk to her in the local. She was embarrassingly rude to them.
>
> — Anonymous

Best places to marvel at posh UK
- Henley Regatta
- Royal Ascot
- The Ritz
- Mayfair
- The Oxford–Cambridge boat race on the Thames
- A polo match
- Wigmore concert hall
- A local cricket match
- Eton College
- Harrow on the Hill

Best places to meet the everyday Brit
- A club football game
- Any pub not frequented by antipodeans
- A car boot sale, anywhere
- Markets in London's East End
- The last tube home
- At a fruit machine (the pokies) in Blackpool
- On the streets of any northern city after closing time
- At the counter of a B&B in any town or village
- A farmer's market in a market town

> **When the UK is not Great Britain**
> **— why you'll get bollocked if you call a Scot English**
> The United Kingdom is England, Scotland, Wales and Northern Ireland. Britain is a more colloquial term for the United Kingdom. Great Britain is a less modest version of the above. The British Isles comprise the UK, the Republic of Ireland, the Channel Islands and the Isle of Man.
>
> Politically, Northern Ireland is part of Britain, but in many practical ways it's considered part of Ireland.
>
> The four countries of the UK compete individually in the Commonwealth Games but as one Great Britain team at the Olympics. In cricket the Scots have their own team but the Welsh play for England. Each has its own rugby team, with the exception of Northern Ireland, which plays with the Republic of Ireland.
>
> There are also regional differences. In Cornwall, for example, there are those who consider themselves Cornish rather than English.
>
> Never call Welsh people or Scots English. You might be assigning them the nationality of those who persecuted their forebears.

The pub and the pint

If you're catching up with a friend in New Zealand, you tend to meet for coffee. In the UK you catch up over a pint. It's something to do with the convivial atmosphere of pubs and the fact that they're everywhere, while good cafés are comparatively hard to find. Good coffee is even more elusive.

If you're going to develop a drinking habit in your lifetime, the UK is where it's likely to happen. To compound the national pint culture, if you're living in London you'll very rarely be driving home from the pub because you probably won't own a car. Thus you don't have concerns about drink-driving to curtail your intake.

The drinking age in the UK is 18.

Chains and independents

It's sad that just about every pub in the UK is part of a chain — the Young's pubs and Wetherspoons pubs, which aren't always evident from the name — the Rat and Parrot, All Bar One, Hogshead, the Pitcher and Piano, the Slug and Lettuce, O'Neill's, etc., etc. It's hard to find an independent pub, but there are still plenty of gems. The words 'freehouse' indicate an independent pub — one that's not affiliated with a particular brewery.

A lobby group called Campaign for Real Ale actively promotes the independent pubs and traditional British beers. They publish the *Good Beer Guide*, and have a website www.camra.org.uk on which you can find information about independent pubs and beer festivals in the UK. Incidentally, the town of Burton-upon-Trent in Derbyshire is renowned as the boutique brewing capital of the UK.

Early closing

Nearly every new Kiwi on the block gets caught out by 11 pm pub closing time. On a Friday night in New Zealand you'll finish work around 5.30 pm, go home and shower, have a few drinks at home and go to the pub around 9.30 pm, ready to stay for the long haul. Do this in the UK and the last drinks bell will ring while you're halfway through your first pint. (Edinburgh is an exception — there, most pubs are open until at least 1 am.)

A British tradition — although it's less common than it once was — is to start drinking at lunchtime, stumble back into the office for a few hours, then sprint to the pub at 5 pm-on-the-dot to down as many pints as possible before the bell, and — if you're in London — stumble to catch the last tube home, kebab in hand. Thus Britain has a big binge-drinking problem. The government has been talking for years about rethinking pub opening hours, but it's very low on its agenda.

Some pubs and bars get around the liquor laws by hosting a lock-in. At 11 pm the landlord locks the doors and continues drinking with his or her, er, 'friends'. Theoretically no one else is allowed in, but that sometimes depends on whether the authorities are looking. Lock-ins are especially good fun in friendly small towns in the North.

It's incongruous that despite the 11 pm closing, the laws about where you can buy alcohol in the UK are liberal. Local stores — called off-licences or 'offies' — sell beer by the can or bottle and keep a bottle opener behind the counter so you can drink it while you walk or travel. They also sell wines and spirits.

The Big OE Companion

Pub crawls

There are dozens of themed pub crawls in UK cities. They can be a lot of fun, but most require a bit of travel. In London you'll end up spending a lot of the day on the Tube. Because of the early pub closing and the travelling time, most pub crawls start when the pubs open at 11 am. You spend about 30 minutes in each pub, and you'll be lucky if you make the last pub by 11 pm. It's sensible to have half pints at each stop rather than pints. You'll probably lose people on the way, but you're just as likely to gain some. You can try the famous pub crawls listed below, or devise your own based on a local area or a theme — pubs with animals in the name, pubs with nautical themes, etc.

Notable pub crawls

- As the name suggests, the Circle Line crawl follows the route of the Circle Line. The idea is to stop at every station and find a local pub. There are 27 stations, so pace yourself. *See 'Getting your Kiwi fix' for details of a Waitangi Day pub crawl.*
- The Monopoly crawl can be pretty complicated so it requires a bit of planning. The idea is to have a drink at every street, square and station that's on the Monopoly board. You can't follow the board from beginning to end because you'd end up going all over the place — from east to north to east to south to north to west . . . Eager pub-crawlers have devised routes that you'll find by searching the internet.
- The Glasgow Sub Crawl. This one follows the route of the Glasgow Underground Railway. You pop up for a drink at each of the stops.

Food

British food doesn't have a good reputation — soggy chips with vinegar, mushy peas, baked beans, uninspiring jacket potatoes, gristly steak-and-ale pies, black pudding, bangers and mash (sausages and mashed potatoes). You'll still find plenty of pubs that serve up some very unappetising versions of this fare, but it's more common to find a pub that takes pride in its food, and serves gourmet interpretations of the

Enjoying the UK

above or decent Thai food. Gastro-pubs take it a step further and serve food worthy of a good restaurant. And the cultural diversity of the UK has introduced plenty of ethnic options — curry houses are said to be more common than chippies (fish and chip shops), and you'll frequently get chips served with your korma. The best places for cheap curry in the UK are in the north of England and in Brick Lane in east London.

Best places to soak up culture
- Edinburgh Festival
- Cambridge and Oxford
- The National Gallery, the Victoria and Albert Museum, and the Tate Modern in London
- Bath
- Liverpool
- York
- Hampton Court Palace
- Canterbury, Salisbury or Westminster Cathedrals
- Leeds, Windsor or Stirling Castles
- Avebury prehistoric remains
- Cornwall's seaside open-air Minack Theatre (summer only)

Takeaways

THE CHIPPIE

In the UK a fish and chip shop is called a chippie. When you order chips you'll be asked if you want them served open or closed. If you choose open, you'll get them served on a paper tray or in a paper cone with a wooden fork. Closed means wrapped up in paper.

If you're used to slathering your chips with tomato sauce, you might baulk at the vinegar and mayonnaise that English people prefer. Another strange use of chips is in chip butties (chip sandwiches).

Incidentally, the chips that come in packets are known as crisps.

The Big OE Companion

KEBABS

Late-night kebabs are as essential to the pub culture as ale. Most kebab shops wrap them ingeniously so you can rip off the paper while you eat, but you'll get kebab juice everywhere anyway.

Cost of going out	£
Kebab	3.50
Can of Coke from a vending machine	0.50
Big Mac	1.94
Battered fish with chips	3.10
Movie ticket	
— Odeon Leicester Square, best seats	12.00
— Odeon Sheffield, standard seat	3.20
Pint of lager at a pub	
— national average	2.17
— London average	2.34
Glass of wine at a pub, national average	1.57

Sources: Fish Fryers' Association, Odeon cinemas, McDonald's, Campaign for Real Ale, The Publican.

Café culture

The café culture in the UK is not nearly as well developed as in New Zealand. Most cafés are chains — Starbucks, Costa, Coffee Republic — and few would entice you to stay longer than it takes to drink a cup of coffee.

Restaurants

At least once in your stay, treat yourself to a meal at a Michelin-rated restaurant. This is considered the height of fine dining in Europe. A chef once committed suicide when he lost one of his Michelin stars. It won't be cheap, but it should set a standard for your palate that you'll be hard-pressed to beat. You can find Michelin-starred restaurants on the Michelin website www.viamichelin.com.

Some of the most talked-about (and often derided) restaurants in London are The Ivy in Covent Garden — famous for its celebrities — The

> **Best places to chill**
> - Snowdonia National Park
> - The Lakes District
> - Devon and Cornwall
> - Richmond, southwest London
> - A London park in summer
> - The Scottish Highlands
> - Royal Botanic Gardens, Kew, southwest London
> - Surfing the Severn Bore, near Bristol
> - Any remote island off the Scottish coast
> - The Yorkshire Dales
>
> *A National Trust Membership can be a good investment if you intend to see a bit of the countryside and you're partial to historic houses, castles and gardens. Phone 0870 458 4000, email enquiries@nationaltrust.org.uk, website www.nationaltrust.org.uk.*

River Café near Hammersmith, Jamie Oliver's Fifteen the Restaurant (near Old Street tube), Gordon Ramsay's self-titled restaurants in Chelsea and at Claridge's in Mayfair, Nobu at the Metropolitan Hotel in Old Park Lane, Marco Pierre White's Criterion Brasserie in Piccadilly, and anything to do with design and restaurant mogul Terence Conran. In the West End, you can get cheap pre-show dinner deals, sometimes for as little as £5. Also, some of the best restaurants offer a reasonable set-price lunch menu. If there's no service charge listed on the bill, it's standard practice to tip about 10–15 percent.

Taking tea

Sitting down for a three-course afternoon tea while playing ladies and gents in grand surroundings is a very English pastime and another thing you should do at least once. In London the epitome of afternoon tea is served at Claridge's in Mayfair, Fortnum & Mason in Piccadilly, the Savoy on The Strand, and the Ritz in Piccadilly. Expect to pay £17–28. To go to the Ritz for tea on a weekend you might have to book months in advance.

You don't have to pay a fortune for afternoon tea, of course. The best place for a Devonshire tea is, naturally, in Devon, where tea is served with scones, jam and clotted cream.

Royal events

Each year the New Zealand High Commission in London gets an allocation of tickets — some free — for certain royal events and passes them on via a ballot to New Zealand passport holders visiting Britain. The events are always popular — especially Royal Ascot and the Queen's Garden Parties — so keep an eye on the High Commission website www.nzembassy.com/uk early in the year. Applications usually have to be in to the High Commission by early March and there are dress codes for all events, including compulsory hats for ladies at Ascot. The dressing up is at least half the fun.

The events are:
- Trooping the Colour: the Colonel's Review (final dress rehearsal), usually held early June, free standing tickets, about £8 seated.
- The Queen's Birthday Parade, June, free standing tickets, about £16 seated.
- Royal Ascot, mid-June, £75 for a day's entry.
- Queen's Garden Parties, June/July in the Palace of Holyroodhouse, Edinburgh (for New Zealanders staying in Scotland) and at Buckingham Palace. Free.

Best places to spot royalty
- Remembrance Day at the Cenotaph, London, November 11
- Last Night of the Proms, Royal Albert Hall, September
- Any event that starts with 'Royal'
- A polo match
- West End premieres
- Search royal events diaries on www.royal.gov.uk
- From the route of a procession. (For the big events, such as weddings and funerals, fanatical royal watchers will spend the night before camped on the route to ensure a good spot. Watching the watchers is half the attraction.)

Enjoyng the UK

National Trust Working Holidays

If you're conservation-minded and don't mind a bit of hard work, you can apply for a National Trust Working Holiday. You pick your activity and decide how much time you can spare. Activities include outdoor conservation work, working on archaeological sites, recording botanical species, and building and repairing stone walls. You pay a small fee for accommodation and meals. Contacts: phone 0870 4292 429, website www.nationaltrust.org.uk/volunteering.

Live and armchair sport

Like them or hate them, the big team sports in the UK are football, football, rugby union, cricket and football.

Football

The pitfall of having English male flatmates is that they'll forbid you from watching television when the football's on. The thing is, the football's ALWAYS on, because there is a bewildering number of competitions. If you can't beat 'em, join 'em . . .

Football tournaments explained

World Cup
The biggie, won once by England (1966). Contested every four years (2006 in Germany, 2010 in South Africa)

The European Championships (called Euro2008, Euro2012, etc.)
Next in importance, has been contested every four years since 1960. The UK teams have dire records.

The UEFA Champions League
For Europe's big clubs — the top four English Premiership teams and the top Scottish Premier League team qualify.

The UEFA Cup
The next tier down from the Champions League, with the next best teams competing.

> **The English Premiership**
> The English club competition. Dominated in the past decade by Manchester United and Arsenal.
>
> **Nationwide Football League**
> The dozens of teams that don't make the Premiership make up English divisions one, two and three.
>
> **The Scottish Premier League**
> Just as incestuous as the English Premiership, with Glaswegian giants Rangers and Celtic dominating.
>
> **The FA Cup**
> Historic competition open to every English team no matter how lowly, and a few Welsh teams.
>
> **The League Cup**
> Contested by sides in the four top UK divisions. Confusing, since the word 'League' is replaced every few years by a different sponsor, which has included Milk, Littlewoods, Rumbalows, Coca-Cola, Worthington and Carling.

The football World Cup is England's be-all and end-all. They won once in 1966, and no future representative is allowed to forget this, the media deeming the competition England's birthright. English sport will wallow in underdog status until they win something, and then they'll consider themselves the world's best. It's a vicious and unrelenting circle which hinders development.

– Lyndon Hogg

Cricket

If you're a cricket fan, you won't want to come home until you've seen a match at the famous Lord's and Oval cricket grounds, home to Middlesex and Surrey counties respectively. In addition to the details below, you can often buy tickets for big matches through the website www.ticketmaster.co.uk.

- Foster's Oval, Kennington, phone 020 7582 6660, website www.surreycricket.com. To get advance tickets to international

matches at the Oval, you can apply in writing to the Surrey County Cricket Club, which manages the Oval. Download application forms from the website. Leftover tickets are put on sale through their credit card booking line, 020 7582 7764, and the ticket office at the Oval.
- Lord's, St John's Wood, phone 020 7289 1611, website www.lords.org. Book tickets online, or by calling 020 7432 1000.

Rugby

To get tickets to the matches of the big European rugby tournament, the Six Nations, you have to apply through affiliated clubs in each country. To find your local club, contact the Rugby Football Union in England, Scotland, Wales or Ireland, through websites www.rfu.com, www.scottishrugby.org, www.wru.co.uk, www.irishrugby.ie, respectively.
For information on tickets to All Blacks games, see 'Getting your Kiwi fix'.

Tennis

Wimbledon is the big tennis event in the UK. Tickets are allocated by ballot — you have to apply by December 31 of the year before — or you can queue on the actual day, as an allocation is always reserved for sale on the day. After 4 pm daily in the first week of competitions you can buy ultra-cheap returned tickets for the evening sessions, as those who have been there all day go home. Eat BYO strawberries and cream and soak up the atmosphere.

Contact: the All England Lawn Tennis Club, ticket office phone 020 8971 2473, website www.wimbledon.org.
For information about playing sport in the UK, see 'Health, fitness and sport'.

Music festivals

The famous Glastonbury Festival is the granddaddy of music festivals in the UK, attracting some of the world's biggest names — some merely as spectators in the mosh pits. But if you can't get there, there's always the V Festival, the Reading Festival, the Leeds Festival, Guilfest in Surrey, T in the Park in Scotland, The Isle of Wight Festival — and for the clubbers, Homelands in Hampshire and Creamfields in Liverpool. Check the calendar later in this chapter for details of dates and contacts. An informative website is efestivals.co.uk.

The Big OE Companion

Going out in London

Theatre

London is deservedly renowned for its thriving theatre industry. The West End is the British theatre capital, rivalled only by Broadway in New York. On any night there can be dozens of shows, from Andrew Lloyd Webber showstoppers to offbeat interpretations of Shakespeare, and there's often a Hollywood star or two slumming it on the boards for the sake of credibility. The theatres are unexpectedly intimate and some are downright shabby.

> **Best places to party**
> - Clubs in Brixton and Farringdon, London
> - The northern cities — Manchester, Liverpool and Newcastle
> - Any music festival
> - Soho, London
> - Notting Hill Carnival
> - Cardiff after an All Blacks game
> - Edinburgh's New Year Hogmanay Festival

BEYOND THE WEST END

But the West End is only a fraction of the entertainment on offer, and you will often find more adventurous theatre elsewhere. The National Theatre in South Bank (www.nt-online.org), the Old Vic in Waterloo (www.oldvictheatre.com) and the Barbican (www.barbican.org.uk) offer consistently classy productions, while the Young Vic in Waterloo (www.youngvic.org), the Tricycle Theatre in Kilburn (www.tricycle.co.uk), the Royal College of Music (www.rcm.ac.uk) and Trinity College of Music (www.tcm.ac.uk) offer good cheap productions by up-and-comers.

The Comedy Store (www.thecomedystore.co.uk) in Soho is renowned as the birthplace of the country's best comics — and there's the famous Jongleurs near Clapham Junction (there are other Jongleurs clubs in London and the UK, www.jongleurs.com).

In summer Shakespeare's Globe Theatre at London Bridge produces superb Shakespearean plays for as little as £5 for a standing ticket (www.shakespeares-globe.org), and there are productions under the stars in Regent's Park (www.openairtheatre.org). The best guide to theatre in London is *Time Out* magazine, which has reviews and exhaustive listings.

THEATRE TICKETS

It's cheaper to buy tickets at the theatre, but you can also buy through Ticketmaster (phone 0870 4000 700, website www.ticketmaster.co.uk) and First Call (phone 0870 906 3838, website www.firstcalltickets.com). The half-price ticket booth on Leicester Square, called tkts, and others around the square have discounted tickets on the day of the show. It's a good idea to sign up for free membership to a cheap tickets network, such as www.theatrenet.co.uk. You'll get weekly emails listing some good deals. Some theatres offer last-minute deals a few hours before curtain-up.

Music

The live music scene in the UK is colossal. In London, you're best to start with *Time Out* magazine, *TNT Magazine* and the *Evening Standard* newspaper. It's usually cheaper to buy tickets from the concert venue, but you can also get tickets from ticket agencies. The biggest ones are Ticketmaster (phone 0870 4000 700, website www.ticketmaster.co.uk) and Ticketweb (phone 08700 600 100, website www.ticketweb.co.uk). Nationwide, start by looking on the above websites, the British tourist authority website www.visitbritain.com, and www.gigsandtours.com. Book way in advance for anything popular.

Among the most famous musical offerings in London are:

- Ronnie Scott's jazz club, 47 Frith Street, Soho; phone 020 7439 0747; website www.ronniescotts.co.uk.
- Wigmore Hall (for classical music), 36 Wigmore Street, W1; phone 020 7935 2141; website www.wigmore-hall.org.uk.
- The summer classical Proms at the Royal Albert Hall, website www.bbc.co.uk/proms.
- For opera, the English National Opera (Coliseum, St Martin's Lane WC2; phone 020 7632 8300; website www.eno.org) is cheaper than the Royal Opera House (Bow Street, Covent Garden, WC2; phone 020 7304 4000; website www.royaloperahouse.org).
- Notting Hill Arts Club, 21 Notting Hill Gate; phone 020 7460 4459; website www.nottinghillartsclub.com.

The most popular rock venues in London are:
- The Wembley Arena, phone 0870 060 0870, website www.whatsonwembley.com.
- The London Arena in Docklands, phone 020 7538 1212, website www.londonarena.co.uk.
- The Earl's Court Exhibition Centre, phone 020 7385 1200, website www.eco.co.uk.
- The Astoria on Charing Cross Road, phone 020 7344 0044, website www.meanfiddler.com.
- The Brixton Academy, phone 020 7771 3000, website www.brixton-academy.co.uk.
- The Forum in Kentish Town, phone 020 7284 1001, website www.meanfiddler.com.
- The Shepherd's Bush Empire, phone 0870 771 2000, website www.shepherds-bush-empire.co.uk.

Cinema

Movie Mecca in the UK is Leicester Square, where they roll out the red carpet and bring in the limos for premieres. The mainstream cinemas there can be pretty expensive, but there are a couple of great places thereabouts.

The Prince Charles cinema, just off the Square on Leicester Place, is a vibrant independent cinema with a policy of keeping the tickets cheap and the films interesting — if not always new. The Curzon cinemas at 99 Shaftesbury Avenue, Soho and 38 Curzon Street, Mayfair also offer good art-house flicks and cosy, cheap Sunday matinée double-bills, from Katherine Hepburn movies to kung fu classics; look on the website www.curzoncinemas.com. Clapham Picture House is a favourite of southwesters. The National Film Theatre on the South Bank is a haven for film buffs; website www.bfi.org.uk. The annual London Film Festival is held in October and November; website www.lff.org.uk.

Clubbing

London's clubbing scene is one of the world's best. *Time Out* and *TNT Magazine* are good places to find out what's on. Plan ahead if you can, and get your name onto guest lists to avoid queuing and get discounted entry — or arrive early in the evening. The Fevah Records label (www.fevah.net) has Kiwi DJs on its books and they perform in clubs throughout the UK.

Clubbing by nature is a fickle pastime, but there are some clubs that are survivors:

- Camden Palace, 1A Camden High Street, NW1.
- Cargo, Kingsland Viaduct, 83 Rivington Street, Shoreditch, EC2; phone 020 7739 3440; website www.cargo-london.com.
- Electric Ballroom, 184 Camden High Street, NW1; phone 020 7485 9006; website www.electric-ballroom.co.uk.
- The End, 18 West Central Street, WC1; phone 020 7419 9199; website www.the-end.co.uk.
- Fabric, 77a Charterhouse Street, EC1; phone 020 7336 8898; website www.fabriclondon.com.
- Ministry of Sound, 103 Gaunt Street, SE1; phone 020 7378 6528; website www.ministryofsound.com.
- Turnmills, 63 Clerkenwell Rd, EC1; phone 020 7250 3409; website www.turnmills.co.uk.

Celebrity spotting

There are often early evening movie premieres in Leicester Square — check with the cinemas on the square. Arrive a few hours before (or even a day before if it's a cult movie) and get a spot with a good view of the red carpet. It's fun — limos, stars in their finery, paparazzi, screaming fans . . .

Other good spots for celeb spotting are the cafés and bars in Primrose Hill, the Carnaby Street shopping area, and indeed the whole of the West End.

The big music shops in the West End (Virgin Megastore and HMV on Oxford Street, Tower Records in Piccadilly Circus) often have free album-promoting gigs featuring stars as big as Madonna — be prepared to queue for several hours.

The bookshops in the centre of London attract the world's most popular authors for book signings and talks.

An Ecstasy pill in London costs about the same as a pint of lager. When I left New Zealand they cost up to $100, so if you were doing one, it was a serious investment and frankly too much of a big deal to justify the effort. In London I once bought 100 for £170. Bargain. Don't be daft enough to do any dealing. They're not for everyone, of course, but they're safer than the mainstream press might lead you to believe. The safety tips read like a guidebook to common sense: don't take too many at once; don't mix them with too much booze, and get in as many hugs as you can. Cocaine is another matter. I've never had any beef with it myself — the confidence and rush it induces along with the general coolness of snorting it up a tenner make it my drug of choice. But I've got a good mate — an English lad — who hoovers it up like a demented lab rat if there's ever any in his vicinity. Turns him from a good bloke to an annoying wanker in a hurry. You would have to be certifiable to do heroin.

— Anonymous

Sightseeing in London on the cheap

- Pick out a few of London's many museums and galleries to wander through — all public collections and many private ones are free, although some temporary exhibitions have entrance fees. The extensive National Gallery in Trafalgar Square is one of the only places in the world where you can see the masters for free — da Vinci, Monet, Cézanne and dozens more. The National Portrait Gallery next door is also well worth a look — it has some good contemporary work. The Tate Modern in Bankside is one of the world's best contemporary art galleries. Wealthy South Kensington hosts the Science Museum, the National History Museum and the fascinating Victoria and Albert Museum. The Imperial War Museum (Lambeth) and the British Museum (Bloomsbury) could each absorb a couple of days of your time. The Museum of London (the City) is a good one to visit early on to learn about your new city.
- Have a leisurely lunch in an English pub while reading a Saturday or Sunday newspaper. Make sure you allow plenty of time — they're whopping tomes.
- Go to St Paul's Cathedral and/or Westminster Cathedral for public services, which are free. St Paul's has daily evensong (evening services). Sit under the dome and listen to the pure voices of the

Enjoyng the UK

choirboys echoing around it. The disadvantage to going when it is free is that you won't be able to climb up to the famous whispering wall.

- Queue outside St Stephen's Gate of the Houses of Parliament to get into the public gallery (called the Stranger's Gallery) of the rowdy House of Commons or the far more demure House of Lords — a relic of upper-crust England. Check first if Parliament is sitting, and for times, on www.parliament.uk. The best show is the surprisingly juvenile Prime Minister's Question Time on a Wednesday, but you'll have to arrange (free) tickets in advance. You can do this through the New Zealand High Commission in Haymarket. Having a ticket doesn't guarantee you a spot, so you'll still have to get there early and queue. *For High Commission contact details, see 'New Zealand government in the UK and Europe'.*

- Go to the antipodean Redback Tavern in Acton with some friends on a Sunday afternoon in summer for a free barbecue and £1 Kiwi beers. It's far from the most sophisticated day out, but it is a good-value, good-fun time, and a good way to meet people. If you stay late enough you'll see the messy side of antipodean life in London, especially after the Churchgoers arrive (*see 'Getting your Kiwi fix'*).

- Retreat into a cheap weekend matinée double-bill at the Curzon cinemas in Soho and Mayfair (see 'Cinema' above).

- Get a cheap ticket to a West End show or go to an off-West End show (see 'Theatre' above).

- Check if there's a free or cheap lunchtime concert in St Martin-in-the-Fields church near Trafalgar Square, www.stmartin-in-the-fields.org; the Royal Academy of Music in Marylebone Road (www.ram.ac.uk); the Royal College of Music, Kensington (www.rcm.ac.uk); the Barbican (www.barbican.org.uk); St John's Church, Smith Square SW1 (www.sjss.org.uk); the South Bank's Royal National Theatre (www.nt-online.org) or the Hayward Gallery, www.hayward.org.uk.

- Watch the street performers at Covent Garden.

- In summer, a riverside outdoor stage at the Royal National Theatre on the South Bank hosts free performances every evening.

- Another summer pastime is getting a few friends, a few beers and a rugby ball and heading to one of London's many great parks for an afternoon — Regent's Park, St James' Park, Hyde Park, etc. The parks are London's equivalent of beaches — you'll see plenty of sunburnt

Worth the money
- Tower of London
- Hampton Court Palace
- Buckingham Palace summer opening
- Cabinet War Rooms
- Saatchi Gallery
- Kew Gardens on a sunny day

Overrated and overrun
- Stratford-upon-Avon
- Stonehenge
- Madame Tussaud's
- Any big free outdoor event in London (they attract too many people)
- Brighton Pier
- Blackpool

bodies in bikinis and, if you're unlucky, Speedos. The big downfall is that there's no swimmable water to cool off in if it gets hot.
- Window-shop at Harrods, the famous department store in Knightsbridge.
- Queue for the Proms at the Royal Albert Hall in South Kensington in summer. If you're time-rich and money-poor, take a good book and/or a good friend and get a spot in the queue on a sunny afternoon for £5 standing tickets to that night's Proms.
- Pop into the historic Old Bailey Central Criminal Court, Old Bailey, EC4, and watch a trial in the country's most famous court.
- Watch Tower Bridge open for a boat. To find out when the bridge will be next lifted, phone 020 7940 3984 or go to the website www.towerbridge.org.uk.
- Save money on entrance to royal palaces by buying a combined ticket. There are decent discounts for buying a pass (valid for three months) that will get you into two of the following: Tower of London, Hampton Court Palace and Kensington Palace. At least the first two should be on your must-do list while you're in the UK. Buy

Enjoyng the UK

at the gate or online at www.hrp.org.uk.

- Sit in the studio audience at a free taping of a telly show. For BBC shows, phone 020 8576 1227, or apply online at www.bbc.co.uk/tv. For ITV shows, try www.itv.com. Other options are Granada Media, phone 020 7261 3261, email granada.tickets@granadamedia.com, website www.tickets.granadamedia.com; and TV Recordings, website www.tvrecordings.com. A ticket doesn't always guarantee a place — because they're free the ticket companies overbook to ensure they still have a full house if half the audience finds something better to do — so you might still have to arrive early and queue.

Christmas in the UK can be fun, as long as you're not alone. With no family obligations — other than to ring home on the day — for once in your life you can decide what you want to do. You can take advantage of cheap skiing in France or Austria, or head to Morocco or Egypt, which you'll have mostly to yourself. Failing that, there are always a few other Kiwis in London with whom to have an orphans' Christmas after your English friends clear out.

— Anonymous

Highlights of the UK calendar

January
- Barbican International Theatre Event (BITE), www.barbican.org.uk
- London International Mime Festival, www.mimefest.co.uk

February
- Chinese New Year. Best seen in Chinatown, London W1
- Leicester Comedy Festival, www.comedy-festival.co.uk
- City of Love festival, Glasgow, www.cityoflove.co.uk
- London Fashion Week, www.londonfashionweek.co.uk
- Bath Literature Festival (until early March), www.bathlitfest.org.uk
- Six Nations Rugby Tournament (until March), www.6nations.net
- Pancake racing (on Shrove Tuesday), Olney, Buckinghamshire
- Great Spitalfields Pancake Day Race (also on Shrove Tuesday), Spitalfields markets, London

March
- Cornwall's Festival of Spring Gardens (until mid-May), www.gardensincornwall.co.uk
- London Drinker Beer and Cider Festival, www.camra.org.uk
- Head of the River Race, River Thames, London, www.horr.co.uk
- Oxford and Cambridge Boat Race, River Thames, London, www.theboatrace.org

April
- Grand National, Aintree, Liverpool, www.aintree.co.uk
- bristolive festival, Bristol, www.bristolive.co.uk
- London marathon, www.london-marathon.co.uk

May
- Brighton Arts Festival, www.brighton-festival.org.uk
- Bath International Festival, www.bathmusicfest.org.uk
- Glyndebourne Festival Opera (until August), www.glyndebourne.com
- Chelsea Flower Show, London, www.rhs.org.uk
- Hay Literary Festival, Hay-on-Wye, Wales, www.hayfestival.co.uk
- Homelands Music Festival, Matterley Estate, Hampshire, www.homelands.co.uk
- Coin Street Festival, South Bank (until September), www.coinstreetfestival.org
- Royal Windsor Horse Show, Windsor, www.royal-windsor-horse-show.co.uk
- FA Cup Final, www.the-fa.org
- Badminton Horse Trials, Badminton, www.badminton-horse.co.uk

June
- Trooping the Colour, London, www.royal.gov.uk
- Glastonbury Festival, Somerset, www.glastonburyfestivals.co.uk
- Royal Highland Show, Edinburgh, www.rhass.org.uk
- City of London Festival (until mid-July), www.colf.org
- Royal Ascot, Berkshire, www.ascot.co.uk
- Isle of Wight Festival, www.isleofwightfestival.com
- May Week, Cambridge
- The Queen's Garden Parties, London and Edinburgh (sometimes in July). For details see 'Royal events', earlier this chapter

Enjoyng the UK

- Hampton Court Palace Festival, www.hamptoncourtfestival.com
- Fleadh Music Festival, Finsbury Park, London (until July), www.meanfiddler.com
- Derby Meeting, Epsom, www.epsomderby.co.uk
- Wimbledon Tennis Championship, London (until early July), www.wimbledon.org
- Henley Royal Regatta, Henley-upon-Thames (late June/early July), www.hrr.co.uk
- Stonehenge Summer Solstice, Wiltshire, www.stonehengesolsticecelebration.org

July

- Birmingham International Jazz Festival, www.birminghamjazzfestival.com
- Hampton Court Palace Flower Show, www.rhs.org.uk
- The Proms, Royal Albert Hall, London (until early September), www.bbc.co.uk/proms
- Party in the Park, London, www.capitalfm.com
- T in the Park, Scotland, www.tinthepark.com
- Guilfest, Surrey, www.guilfest.co.uk
- Womad, Rivermead, Reading, www.womad.org

August

- Edinburgh Festival and Edinburgh Tattoo, www.edinburghfestivals.co.uk
- Creamfields, Liverpool, www.cream.co.uk
- Notting Hill Carnival, London, www.lnhc.org.uk
- Reading Festival, www.readingfestival.com
- Leeds Festival, www.leedsfestival.com
- Royal National Eisteddfod of Wales, www.eisteddfod.org.uk
- V Festival, www.vfestival.com
- Cowes Week, Isle of Wight, www.cowesweek.co.uk
- Cowal Highland Gathering, Dunoon, Argyll, www.cowalgathering.com

September

- Braemar Gathering, Aberdeenshire, Scotland, www.braemargathering.org
- London Open House Weekend, www.londonopenhouse.org

The Big OE Companion

- Great British Cheese Festival, Blenheim Palace, Woodstock, Oxfordshire, www.thecheeseweb.com
- The Great River Race, Richmond to Island Garden, London, www.greatriverrace.co.uk

October
- Glenfiddich Piping Championship, Blair Castle, Perthshire, www.blair-castle.co.uk

November
- Remembrance Day, November 11, Cenotaph, Whitehall, London
- State Opening of Parliament, www.parliament.uk
- London Film Festival, www.bfi.org.uk
- Lord Mayor's Show, City of London, www.lordmayorsshow.org.

December
- Hogmanay, Edinburgh, www.edinburghfestivals.co.uk/hogmanay

For New Zealand events, see 'Getting your Kiwi fix'.

It may not be a huge cultural leap from New Zealand to the UK but there are dozens of subtleties to adjust to. Packing your own groceries, for a start. Chips have become crisps, soccer is football. I buy my wine at the offie, not a wholesaler, and my newspaper from the newsagent, not the dairy. I now know that pumpkin is for pigs not people so there is no point in trying to find it at Safeways. Marmite lives in the gravy section, not with the jams and spreads. I now know that 'yer right' is a rhetorical question, and the time is 'half twelve' not 'huppast'. Asian cuisine means vindaloo, not sweet and sour pork; while shopping on the High Street involves basic chain stores, not designer shops.

— Christine Sheehy

5.
Transport and orientation

Around the UK

Information

Traveline (phone 0870 608 2 608, www.traveline.org.uk) offers impartial information to help you plan a journey on all public transport in England, Wales and Scotland.

Trains

If you are travelling off-peak and there are no delays, trains can be great. Not only do you get to your destination relatively quickly, but you can muse over nice views of rolling British countryside while stretching out in a more comfortable seat than you'll get in most cars, coaches and aeroplanes. It can be less inspiring if you're forced to stand in the smoking section on a long, overbooked, delayed trip on a public holiday in summer.

DISCOUNT PASSES

If you're under 26, get a Young Person's Railcard from a mainline station as soon as you arrive in the UK. You'll get a very nice one-third discount off most standard rail fares. You'll need to provide a passport photo, some ID showing proof of age, and pay an application fee (currently £18).

The Big OE Companion

You are also eligible if you are a full-time student aged 26 or older.

Another discount card worth considering is the Network Railcard, available to anyone over 16. It currently costs £20 for a year and is valid for up to four people. You save one-third off journeys made after 10 am weekdays, and all day at weekends. Buy from any mainline station.

For more information on discount passes, go to www.railcard.co.uk.

Tips on catching trains
- Timetables can be downloaded from the National Rail website, www.nationalrail.co.uk (you can also check fares, but you can't book on the site), or call the National Rail enquiry line, 08457 48 49 50.
- Book ahead. You can get considerable advance booking discounts, and you can book a seat on longer journeys so you won't get stuck facing backwards in the smoking carriage. There are more than twenty different railway companies covering different areas of the UK, but you can book for any of them at National Rail stations or online. Commercial websites offer bookings across the network: www.thetrainline.com and www.qjump.co.uk (now merged) offer online bookings. For a phone booking, call the appropriate railway company direct. To find out which one you need, call National Rail enquiries on 08457 48 49 50, or look on www.nationalrail.co.uk. You can also book rail journeys at some travel agents.
- Buy a return ticket rather than two one-way tickets. Return tickets are far cheaper, and you can get an open return, so you can come back any time.
- Travelling at peak times is more expensive than off-peak, especially over shorter distances. Off-peak is after 9.30 am Monday to Friday and all day Saturday and Sunday.
- Check the number of stops before your destination — the more stops, the longer the trip will take. There may be a quicker express train.
- Avoid having to change trains as much as possible, as this can be time-consuming, and you could miss connections if your train is late.

Transport and orientation

- Stations in the big cities can be hectic. Every big station has a board on which all the trains are listed, usually — but not always — left to right. If you don't have a booked seat, you'll have to wait in the station until a platform is announced — and then the race for a seat begins. It pays to double-check once on the platform that it's the right train, and that you're in the right part of it — sometimes only the doors of the front carriages will open at a particular station, or the train will split in half during the journey.
- There are ten mainline rail stations in London, so double-check which one you need to get to before you leave home. Generally, Victoria Station, Charing Cross and London Bridge serve the south and southeast, Paddington serves the southwest and southeast, Waterloo the southwest, Liverpool Street the northeast, King's Cross the north and northeast, Marylebone the west, and St Pancras the Midlands. Euston is Virgin Rail's main station, so its trains go all over the place.
- Conductors patrol the trains and you'll be expected to have a ticket unless you came from a tiny station where the office was closed. If you don't have an excuse for having no ticket, they can charge you for the missing ticket, and/or charge a penalty fare.
- First-class seats aren't usually worth the extra money, although at weekends you can sometimes get cheap upgrades so you can try it out for yourself.

Coaches

Long-distance buses are called coaches in the UK. They're usually pretty cheap — sometimes ridiculously so — but they take longer than trains, and are, of course, at the mercy of traffic. If you are aged 16–25 or over 50, or if you're a full-time student, you are eligible for a Discount Coachcard. You can buy online at the addresses below.

THE BIG COACH COMPANIES

National Express, phone 0870 580 8080, website www.nationalexpress.com
Scottish Citylink, phone 08705 50 50 50, website www.citylink.co.uk

Most coaches leave London from the Victoria Coach Station — a good five- to ten-minute walk from Victoria train and tube stations.

Postbus

Here's a quaint way to get to some really out-of-the-way places without your own transport: hitch a ride in a Royal Mail van. Passenger fares are cheap, and in most places the Postbus visits twice each weekday, which means you can be dropped off in the morning and picked up in the afternoon. In more remote places the Postbus comes by once a day. You can hail the bus anywhere on its route. For details, phone 08457 740 740, website www.royalmail.com/postbus.

Driving

NAVIGATING BRITAIN

You'll want a car if you are going to explore remote places, although it's common to meet Brits who have never learned to drive, especially in London.

THE ROADS

Britain's roads are pretty well maintained. All roads are numbered. The motorways are designated by the letter M and a number, the highways by the letter A and a number. The fewer the numbers, the bigger the road. Thus the M1 is one of the biggest roads out of London, while the B674 is probably a tiny country lane bordered by hedgerows which links a couple of obscure villages.

MAPS AND ROUTE PLANNERS

You can buy a road atlas from any service station or stationery shop. The British Automobile Association has a free route planner on its website, www.theaa.com, as does the RAC, a company offering similar services, www.rac.co.uk. It's astounding. You type in your starting point and your destination and it will give you frighteningly detailed instructions. Best you also have a road atlas with you though, in case you miss a turn or hit a detour.

PUBLIC HOLIDAYS

Driving on public holiday weekends can be frustrating, especially around the big cities, so try to outwit the traffic by timing your departure wisely. It can pay to stick to highways rather than joining every other motorist on the packed motorways.

ROAD RULES

Britain doesn't have a give-way-to-your-right rule. Otherwise the road rules are much the same as in New Zealand. The speed limits for cars are: 30 miles per hour in built-up areas, 60 mph on single carriageways, and 70 mph (a generous 112 km/h) on dual carriageways and motorways. It is illegal to use mobile phones while driving.

DRIVER'S LICENCES

Your New Zealand licence is valid for a year in the UK. After that year is up, you're driving illegally, and an insurance company can refuse to honour a claim. To avoid problems you can exchange your licence for a UK one. (You'll be able to exchange it for a New Zealand one when you get home.) Start the process at a UK post office or a local branch of the Driver and Vehicle Licensing Agency (DVLA), by asking for application form D1. You'll have to post the form and fee (currently £29) to the DVLA head office. For details contact the DVLA, phone 0870 240 0009, website www.dvla.gov.uk.

LOST OR STOLEN NEW ZEALAND LICENCES

If your New Zealand licence is lost or stolen while you're in the UK you can apply to the Land Transport Safety Authority (LTSA) in New Zealand for a replacement. (You can't get a replacement licence outside New Zealand if it expires.) It will take about a month. In the meantime you can have the details of your driver licence record (a Certificate of Particulars) sent to you by fax, mail or email.

Contact: LTSA Transport Registry Centre, phone +64 6 356 5150, fax +64 6 350 2347, email info@ltsa.govt.nz (for general enquiries) or cert@ltsa.govt.nz (for Certificate of Particulars enquiries), website www.ltsa.govt.nz.

See 'Travel on the Continent and beyond' for information on International Driving Permits.

The Big OE Companion

Buying a vehicle

THE PAPERWORK

If you buy a vehicle, you'll need:

- a Ministry of Transport (MOT) vehicle test certificate from a licensed garage (the equivalent of a Warrant of Fitness in New Zealand);
- full third-party insurance (check how much this will cost before you buy the car); and
- a registration document signed by both buyer and seller. A section is torn off and sent to the DVLA.

Once you have these, you'll need to present proof of all three at a post office or DVLA local office to pay Vehicle Excise Duty in order to get a Motor Vehicle Licence. You'll get a tax disc to prove you have paid.

MOT certificates and discs remain with the vehicle through a change of ownership, so if the car comes with them you can save yourself the hassle. For more information, ring the DVLA on 0870 240 0010, or go to www.dvla.gov.uk, which also has advice on buying a car. For other online advice, go to the government portal www.motoring.gov.uk, the Automobile Association site www.theaa.com, the Office of Fair Trading www.oft.gov.uk/consumer, or BBCi www.bbc.co.uk/motoring.

SEARCHING

Popular places to start searching for a car are the *Autotrader* magazine (from newsstands or online at www.autotrader.co.uk) and *Loot* newspaper (from newsstands or online at www.loot.com).

For advice on car rental, see 'Travel on the Continent and beyond'.

Air

Flying around Britain used to be unheard of for anyone but business travellers or people with siderodronophobia (fear of trains). But with budget airlines Ryanair (www.ryanair.com), British Midland Airways (www.flybmi.com) and easyJet (www.easyjet.com) offering cheap flights within Britain, and British Airways (www.britishairways.com) bringing out cheap deals to match, it's worth considering for longer hauls. Just remember that it will take you twice as long to get to an airport in London as it will take for the flight itself, so shorter trips might be quicker by train.

Transport and orientation

In London

Finding your way around

If you decide to live in London, transport may be the single biggest frustration of your time in the UK. It's probably the second most discussed aspect of London life after the weather. When the public transport system works well, it's good. When it's bad it's terrible.

ORIENTATION AND PLANNING YOUR JOURNEY

Although it's not at all straight, the Thames divides London into north and south. So while Lambeth is actually further north than Chelsea, it's considered to be in South London (nicknamed Saaf London because that's how the locals say it), while residents of exclusive Chelsea would be horrified to be called South Londoners. 'The City', with St Paul's Cathedral in its heart, is considered to be the traditional centre of London, flanked by the West End — where most of London's sights are — and the colourful East End.

ORIENTATION BY POSTCODE

London is cleverly divided into very specific postcodes, which can be very handy for finding your way around. (See the list at the end of this chapter.) You'll find that in some areas people talk postcodes rather than suburbs, especially in the West End and the City, as in, 'We're going for lunch in SW1.'

If you have an address and want to find the postcode, use the postcode finder on the website www.royalmail.com. Then type the postcode of your destination into the search facility on an online map — www.multimap.co.uk or www.streetmap.co.uk — and it will give you a detailed map. If you want to make things really easy, use the journey planner on the Transport for London website www.tfl.gov.uk. Type in your start and end points and it will tell you how to get there using public transport.

London postcodes

West Central
WC1 Bloomsbury, Gray's Inn
WC2 Covent Garden, Holborn, Strand

East Central
EC1 Clerkenwell, Finsbury, Barbican
EC2 Moorgate, Liverpool Street
EC3 Monument, Tower Hill, Aldgate
EC4 Fleet Street, St Paul's

East
E1 Whitechapel, Stepney, Mile End
E2 Bethnal Green, Shoreditch
E3 Bow, Bromley-by-Bow
E4 Chingford, Highams Park
E5 Clapton
E6 East Ham
E7 Forest Gate, Upton Park
E8 Hackney, Dalston
E9 Hackney, Homerton
E10 Leyton
E11 Leytonstone
E12 Manor Park
E13 Plaistow
E14 Poplar, Millwall, Isle of Dogs
E15 Stratford, West Ham
E16 Canning Town, North Woolwich
E17 Walthamstow
E18 South Woodford

North
N1 Islington, Barnsbury, Canonbury
N2 East Finchley
N3 Finchley Central
N4 Finsbury Park, Manor House
N5 Highbury
N6 Highgate
N7 Holloway
N8 Hornsey, Crouch End
N9 Lower Edmonton
N10 Muswell Hill
N11 Friern Barnet, New Southgate
N12 North Finchley, Woodside Park
N13 Palmers Green
N14 Southgate
N15 Seven Sisters
N16 Stoke Newington, Stamford Hill
N17 Tottenham
N18 Upper Edmonton
N19 Archway, Tufnell Park
N20 Whetstone, Totteridge
N21 Winchmore Hill
N22 Wood Green, Alexandra Palace

Northwest
NW1 Regent's Park, Camden Town
NW2 Cricklewood, Neasden
NW3 Hampstead, Swiss Cottage
NW4 Hendon, Brent Cross
NW5 Kentish Town
NW6 West Hampstead, Kilburn, Queens Park
NW7 Mill Hill
NW8 St John's Wood
NW9 Kinsbury, Colindale
NW10 Willesden, Harlesden, Kensal Green
NW11 Golders Green, Hampstead Gdn Suburb

Transport and orientation

Southeast
SE1 Waterloo, Bermondsey, Southwark, Borough
SE2 Abbey Wood
SE3 Blackheath, Westcombe Park
SE4 Brockley, Crofton Park, Honor Oak Park
SE5 Camberwell
SE6 Catford, Hither Green, Bellingham
SE7 Charlton
SE8 Deptford
SE9 Eltham, Mottingham
SE10 Greenwich
SE11 Lambeth
SE12 Lee, Grove Park
SE13 Lewisham, Hither Green
SE14 New Cross, New Cross Gate
SE15 Peckham, Nunhead
SE16 Rotherhithe, South Bermondsey, Surrey Docks
SE17 Walworth, Elephant & Castle
SE18 Woolwich, Plumstead
SE19 Upper Norwood, Crystal Palace
SE20 Penge, Anerley
SE21 Dulwich
SE22 East Dulwich
SE23 Forest Hill
SE24 Herne Hill
SE25 South Norwood
SE26 Sydenham
SE27 West Norwood, Tulse Hill
SE28 Thamesmead

Southwest
SW1 Westminster, Belgravia, Pimlico
SW2 Brixton, Streatham Hill
SW3 Chelsea, Brompton
SW4 Clapham
SW5 Earl's Court
SW6 Fulham, Parson's Green
SW7 South Kensington
SW8 South Lambeth, Nine Elms
SW9 Stockwell, Brixton
SW10 West Brompton, World's End
SW11 Battersea, Clapham Junction
SW12 Balham
SW13 Barnes, Castelnau
SW14 Mortlake, East Sheen
SW15 Putney, Roehampton
SW16 Streatham, Norbury
SW17 Tooting
SW18 Wandsworth, Earlsfield
SW19 Wimbledon, Merton
SW20 South Wimbledon, Raynes Park

West
W1 Mayfair, Marylebone, Soho
W2 Bayswater, Paddington
W3 Acton
W4 Chiswick
W5 Ealing
W6 Hammersmith
W7 Hanwell
W8 Kensington
W9 Maida Vale, Warwick Avenue
W10 Ladbroke Grove, North Kensington
W11 Notting Hill, Holland Park
W12 Shepherd's Bush
W13 West Ealing
W14 West Kensington

The Big OE Companion

STREET NUMBERS

There's not a lot of logic in the street numbering in the UK. Along some streets the house numbers are consecutive, others have odd numbers on one side and even numbers on the other. Buildings on a square are usually numbered according to their place on the square rather than on the road they're on.

Public transport

Allow plenty of time for any journeys on public transport in London, especially if you're going to something important, such as a job interview. And don't be ambitious and commit yourself to popping into three parties in different places on the same night — you'll end up spending most of the night on public transport. Because of the time it takes to get anywhere, London is a bit of a one-hit town. The constant Tube and train delays do have their advantages — if you sleep in and get to work late you need only mutter something about Tube delays and everyone nods in sympathy.

INFORMATION

Transport for London provides detailed information on London's public transport on its website www.tfl.gov.uk or by phone 020 7222 1234.

Public transport survival kit

- A *London A–Z* map book.
- An integrated London Tube and train map (available at all train stations).
- A bus map.
- A good book or newspaper.
- Patience.
- A good deodorant.
- A bottle of water (in summer).

Transport and orientation

ZONES

London is divided into six train/Tube zones. Zone 1 takes in the West End and Central City. The other zones form concentric circles around Zone 1, with Heathrow at one end of Zone 6 and Upminster at the other. Fares are calculated according to how many zones you pass through.

PASSES AND DISCOUNTS

Train and Tube travelcards come by day, weekend, week, month and year, and can save you a lot of money.

You buy according to the zones you travel in. A Zone 1 pass gets you unlimited travel in Zone 1, a Zone 1 and 2 pass gets unlimited travel in Zones 1 and 2, etc. Daily passes come as peak or off-peak (after 9.30 am) but for the other passes it doesn't matter. Passes are valid for all tubes and trains within the zones indicated. Any train or Tube pass is valid for buses throughout London, regardless of zones. Bus-only passes are far cheaper. You can buy bus, train and Tube passes from stations and some newsagents.

An Oyster card is a rechargeable prepaid smartcard for public transport in London. It saves you having to deal with dog-eared paper tickets, and you can load a weekly or monthly pass onto it. You can buy and recharge it at Tube stations, online at www.oystercard.com or by phoning the Oyster helpline 0845 330 9876.

A student photocard gets you a 30 percent discount on travelcards and bus passes valid for a week or longer.

Carnet tickets are discounted single Tube-only tickets that are valid for Tube trips within Zone 1, sold in lots of ten; they can be handy if your travel pass doesn't cover Zone 1.

There are other passes and discounts — ask at a station or look on www.tfl.gov.uk.

THE TUBE

Along with double-decker buses and black cabs, the Tube sign is a symbol of London. The Tube — more formally London Underground — is great for a newcomer to London. You can get almost anywhere without really paying attention to where you're going. But the longer you stay in London, the more you'll avoid using the Tube, which can get crowded, smelly, dirty, hot, stuck and delayed.

The Tube map is not to scale and can really skew your impressions of London's geography. Some keen Tube-spotter designed a to-scale Tube map that looks a bit like a pile of spaghetti compared with the orderly official map (find a copy of the to-scale map by doing an internet search for 'the real Underground').

Some stations that look close together on the official map are miles apart, and vice versa. For example, there are two Shepherd's Bush stations — one on the Hammersmith and City Line, the other on the Central Line — and they're a good half a kilometre apart.

Several of the stations in the West End and central city are so close together that it's not worth taking a Tube between them. Charing Cross and Embankments stations, for example, are so close they may as well be one station. And you don't want to be hauling heavy bags down the long tunnels between lines at Green Park or King's Cross. The platforms are so far apart they may as well be separate stations.

Bill Bryson lists Tube tricks to play on newcomers to London in his very funny 1995 book *Notes from a Small Island* (recommended reading). One is to take them to Bank Station and tell them to find their way to Mansion House. Using the Tube map they'll probably take the Central Line to Liverpool Street, change to an eastward Central Line train and trundle along five stops to Mansion House. They'll emerge to find they're 200 metres down the road from where they began.

OVERLAND TRAINS

Trains can be much more use than the Tube in some areas, particularly south London. They're operated by different companies from the Tube and have their own single and return tickets, but they accept the same travel passes. Tube and train stations with the same name aren't always integrated — or even in the same places. For example, there are huge walks between Clapham Junction train station and the Clapham stations on the Northern line of the Tube system, and at Hampstead Heath there are two train stations and one Tube stop down the street from each other.

DOCKLANDS LIGHT RAILWAY (DLR)

This is a privately owned, above-ground driverless train line that operates in east London. Travelcards are valid on board, or you can get single tickets from the stations.

Famous Tube announcements

Tube drivers can be hilariously laconic — maybe that's what you get from being stuck in a little box underground for hours every day. Here is a famous list of Tube announcements reputed to have been made by drivers:

- 'Ladies and gentlemen, I do apologise for the delay to your service. I know you're all dying to get home, unless, of course, you happen to be married to my ex-wife, in which case you'll want to cross over to the westbound and go in the opposite direction.'
- 'Your delay this evening is caused by the line controller suffering from E and B syndrome, not knowing his elbow from his backside.'
- 'Do you want the good news first or the bad news? The good news is that last Friday was my birthday and I hit the town and had a great time. The bad news is that there is a points failure somewhere between Stratford and East Ham, which means we probably won't reach our destination.'
- 'Ladies and gentlemen, we apologise for the delay, but there is a security alert at Victoria Station and we are therefore stuck here for the foreseeable future, so let's take our minds off it and pass some time together. All together now, "Ten green bottles, hanging on a wall . . . " '
- 'We are now travelling through Baker Street. As you can see, Baker Street is closed. It would have been nice if they had actually told me so I could tell you earlier, but no, they don't think about things like that.'
- 'Let the passengers off the train FIRST! (Pause.) Oh go on then, stuff yourselves in like sardines, see if I care — I'm going home.'
- 'Please allow the doors to close. Try not to confuse this with "Please hold the doors open." The two are distinct and separate instructions.'
- 'To the gentleman wearing the long grey coat trying to get on the second carriage — what part of "Stand clear of the doors" don't you understand?'
- 'May I remind all passengers that there is strictly no smoking allowed on any part of the Underground. However, if you are smoking a joint, it's only fair that you pass it round the rest of the carriage.'

The Big OE Companion

Tips for Tube and train travel

- On escalators, stand on the right and walk up on the left.
- Avoid changing lines wherever possible, as this can take more time than passing through extra stations.
- Watch for big walks between Tube platforms, denoted by more than one circle marking the station.
- Check the time of your last tube or train home before you go out on a night on the town.
- There are very few garbage bags at Tube stations, because of the chance that a terrorist could leave a bomb in one, so you'll have to carry your rubbish with you.
- Take some reading material with you. Burying your nose in a newspaper can be far more pleasant than spending half an hour trying to avoid catching the eye of the person opposite you.
- Don't crush onto a packed tube if there is another one a minute away. Chances are it'll be half empty and well worth the extra minute on the platform. Most people don't seem to have figured this out.
- Tubes are usually less packed at peak times at the front or back.
- Make sure your belongings are secure and never leave them unattended.
- No matter how drunk you may be, never venture onto the tracks — they're electrified.
- You'll hear the words 'Mind the gap' almost every time you take the Tube. They're talking about the step between the platform and the train, which can be big enough to swallow a man. Get into the habit of watching where you're going.
- On a packed tube, get to the doors before your stop. Don't be scared to push through people.
- This sounds really geeky, but it has been done. If you have a tendency to sleep on trains, and thus keep missing your stop, carry some Post-It notes. Write, 'Please wake me up at (station)' on one and stick it to yourself before you nod off. Some kind person will probably be so amused that they will.

Transport and orientation

> ▸ There's a Transport for London lost-property office at 200 Baker Street, London NW1 (near Baker Street Tube) for Tube and black cab losses. If you turn up and ask for a black umbrella they'll probably roll their eyes. (If you've lost a wallet with your New Zealand driver's licence in it, or your New Zealand passport, or something similarly Kiwi, there's a slight possibility it might end up at the New Zealand High Commission in Haymarket.)

Buy a 50-cc scooter. You don't need a motorbike licence, it will pay for itself within nine months from saved Tube passes, you will get to know London better than your Tube-bound friends who have been here ten years, your choice of flats won't be restricted to those within a ten-minute walk of a Tube station, and it's heaps of fun. Most importantly, you will massively cut your travel times and triple the things you can do every day. My scooter changed my London life — I can't recommend it highly enough.

— Reuben Woods

BUSES

London buses can take ages to get between destinations and can get hot in summer, but they are otherwise underrated as a form of public transport. Since congestion charging was introduced in central London, buses have had a bit more space on the roads and journeys are quicker. Buses are also much cheaper than tubes or trains.

Buy a London bus map from a stationery shop or corner store for a good overall picture — they can be hard to find, but are very useful. Otherwise check the maps on bus stops.

The drawback of buses is that stops aren't announced, as they are in trains and tubes, so you can end up lost. Sit downstairs in a left-hand window seat if you're not sure where you are — from there you should be able to read the location signs at the bus stops. You can also ask the driver or conductor to let you know when it's your stop — they are usually pretty good at remembering.

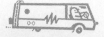

You can buy tickets from the driver, but see also 'Passes and discounts' above. With older double-deckers that have the entry at the back, just hop on and the conductor will come to you. There is an increasing number of routes in the central city for which you need a ticket before boarding, conductor or no conductor. These are clearly identified at the bus stops, and there are vending machines there.

NIGHT BUSES
Night buses are the stuff of legends in London. They run from midnight to 6am and have an 'N' in front of the route number. You will come to pity people who have to take them to get to or from night jobs. They operate after the tubes and trains and other buses have shut down for the night, transporting the dregs of London home. At their best, they're a cheap option, you'll occasionally find a party on board, and it can be entertaining overhearing the drunken conversations. At their worst they can take hours when you're feeling least able to cope with a long trip, they can be filled with drunks, they can smell of vomit and there can be fights on board.

It pays to figure out early on in your London experience which night bus takes you home, where it leaves from (usually around Trafalgar Square) and when it leaves (there can be long waits between buses). You don't want to be rolling drunk around the West End in the middle of the night trying to find your bus.

> The night bus takes on an odour of vomit before it even leaves the bus garage, picks up several football chants on the way and seems to drag out a 15-minute ride home into a Nelson to Invercargill marathon with less scenic views and no whitebait fritters.
>
> — Al Pitcher

BOATS
River boats are more a tourist gimmick than a viable commuter transport option, but they're worth trying out on at least one nice summer's afternoon. There are routes between Hampton Court in the west and Woolwich in the east, stopping at — among other places — Richmond, Westminster, the Tower of London, St Katherine's Dock and Greenwich.

Taxis

BLACK CABS

Because of the cost, you'll usually take the famous black cab option only when the boss is paying, for shorter distances around the central city, and/or when there are a few of you to split the cost (black cabs seat five, which is more than the average car taxi). The drivers expect a tip. You can hail one from the street if the yellow light on its roof is on, or from a taxi rank. You can look up fares and tariffs on www.tfl.gov.uk/pco.

You can order a cab from one of half a dozen taxi service providers:

- Call-A-Cab, phone 020 8901 4444.
- Computer Cab, phone 020 7432 1432, website www.computercab.co.uk.
- DataCab, phone 020 7432 1540.
- Dial-a-Cab, phone 020 7253 5000 (credit) or 020 7908 0207 (cash), website www.dialacab.co.uk.
- Radio Taxis, phone 020 7272 0272, website www.radiotaxis.co.uk.
- Xeta, phone 08451 083 000.
- Zingo, phone 08700 700 700, website www.zingotaxi.co.uk.

If you can afford it, there is something reassuring about a London cab that gives you a sense of security and comfort that's missing from a minicab (see below) in which the driver stops every ten minutes to consult his *London A–Z* and mutters to himself in an unidentifiable dialect.

THE KNOWLEDGE

London's cabs are licensed by Hackney Carriage. Drivers must complete what is known as the 'Knowledge'. Drivers who have the Knowledge have spent three years studying the streets of London within a six-mile radius of Charing Cross. You can easily spot drivers in training for the Knowledge — they ride around the city on scooters and small motorcycles with a large perspex clipboard with a list of destinations on it attached to the windshield. You will often see them stopped in strange places consulting a map and looking confused. What this means is that you can flag down a black cab and mention to the driver any of about 17,000 streets within six miles of Charing Cross and countless places of interest, and he or she will instantly know the quickest way of getting there. Test your own knowledge with the Knowledge game on www.radiotaxis.co.uk.

MINICABS

The word 'minicab' is most often preceded by 'dodgy'. They are usually unmarked and can be far cheaper than ordinary taxis, especially if you are dividing the costs, and they'll give you the chance to have a most fascinating chat you probably won't remember in the morning.

Minicab drivers and firms must be licensed. Don't accept an offer of a minicab off the street. To book one, in advance or for immediate travel, call or pop into a minicab office — there are dozens throughout London.

Ladycabs, phone 020 7254 3501, website www.ladycabslondon.com, uses only women drivers. Many clubs have their own fleets of drivers, and bouncers arrange the cabs for you.

Agree the price before you get in — make sure you have the cash, and feel free to barter. If they ask for more money at the destination, give them what you agreed on and no more.

KERB CRAWLERS

A scourge of London in the early hours is kerb crawlers. These are private citizens in their own vehicles who have come from God-knows-where to offer you a lift home. They obviously think it's a good idea to supplement their income by driving into the city and charging you whatever they think they can negotiate in your inebriated haze to give you a ride. There have been incidents of women being driven to secluded spots and sexually assaulted. Police constantly warn people never to accept an offer of a lift off the street.

Driving

Driving in London can be pretty scary the first time, but once you get used to it you'll discover a few major arteries which link up the city. The M25 London Orbital is a circular 120-mile road that goes right around the city, but it's not always a quick option. (It's sometimes called 'The World's Biggest Parking Lot' because of the congestion.) As you'd expect, London's roads can get ridiculously clogged and parking can be stupidly expensive — some parking meters in central London earn more an hour than a poor schmuck on the minimum wage — so you might be better off taking public transport for trips into particularly busy areas.

Transport and orientation

CONGESTION CHARGE

You'll also have to pay a £5-a-day congestion charge if you drive in central London on weekdays between 7 am and 6.30 pm. Traffic signs will warn you if you are heading into a charging area. You have to pay before 10 pm on the day or incur extra charges and penalties. You can pay online at some shops, petrol stations and car parks, at BT internet kiosks, by text message (once you're registered) or by calling 0845 900 1234. To pay online, or for more information, go to www.cclondon.com.

Cycling

Buy a second-hand bike early on in your time in London. Not only will you save money on transport, but you'll get to know London far better than your Tube-bound mates, and you'll get some exercise — which can be hard to come by in London. A bike can sometimes get you around quicker than public transport or a car. A Transport for London study found the average journey time for a cyclist travelling four miles in central London was 22 minutes, compared with 30 minutes by Tube, 40 minutes by car, 62 minutes by bus and 90 minutes on foot.

> Driving is expensive and impractical in London, the Tube is crowded, overland trains are usually late, and buses get stuck in traffic. Okay, this is a little pessimistic, but it all points to cycling being a top way of getting around London. Most traffic travels at low speeds, drivers are well behaved, and more and more cycle lanes are being built. Best of all, if you cycle you don't have to chance your luck with London's antiquated public transport.
>
> — Adam Ray

BUYING A BIKE

There are loads of second-hand bikes for sale in London, at markets and on websites like the Gumtree (www.thegumtree.com) and *Loot* newspaper (www.loot.com). Be wary of paying too much, as plenty of bikes get nicked. You'll need a good coat against the rain and cold in the winter, and good, bright lights. Make sure you also buy a helmet and a very, very, very good lock. (If your bike gets stolen there's a good chance you'll find it again at the Brick Lane markets; *see 'Shopping'*.)

The Big OE Companion

NAVIGATING
Get a free cycle route map (order from www.tfl.gov.uk or by calling 020 7222 1234), which will show you how to navigate the city without gassing yourself on the main driving routes. It will also tell you in what circumstances you can take a bike on the Tube and trains.

BIKES ON TRAINS
Bikes can be taken on some trains and tubes, but you might have to pay a supplement. Train companies have varying policies. Call the National Rail 24-hour enquiry line 08457 48 49 50 for more information. To check where and when you can take a bike on the Tube, go to tube.tfl.gov.uk, or pick up a map at a Tube station. (You can't take a bike anywhere on the Tube from 7.30 am to 9.30 am and 4 pm to 7 pm weekdays.) You can also take your bike on some trains heading out of London — there are some scenic bike routes in Kent and Surrey — and you can take it to Europe (see 'Travel on the Continent and beyond').

> If you depend on the Tube to commute to work, it becomes a daily vexation. It is noisy, packed and subject to its own laws of physics. There are random inexplicable delays and unannounced cancellations. There's an unwritten law that passengers must not talk or interact. Even when the carriages are packed during rush hour and the next person is inches away from your face, eye contact is forbidden. Don't try and say hello to anyone on the Tube or they may try to have you arrested. If you are female, expect the occasional grope from anonymous strangers in a crowded carriage. A friend once had such an experience; she immediately grabbed the offender's hand from her posterior and held it in the air, announcing in a loud voice, 'Does this belong to anyone? I just found it on my arse.'
>
> In a PR exercise gone wrong, British Prime Minister Tony Blair once took a ride on the Tube to show that he was in touch with common people. He sat next to an unsuspecting young woman. He tried in vain to strike up a conversation with her, but she shuffled away and buried her face deeper into her book. The press printed a photo of the two of them, with a look akin to disgust on the woman's face.
>
> — Andrew Knight

6. Accommodation

Your accommodation can really make or break your OE. Find a decent place with good flatmates and a fair landlord and you have got a cosy haven in a cold winter, guaranteed good company without the expense and hassle of going out, and an antidote for the inevitable down times.

Temporary accommodation

There are two options for the budget-conscious new Kiwi in town: dossing or a hostel.

Dossing

If you're lucky you'll have a good friend or distant great-aunt by marriage living somewhere handy, who has a spare room and delights in having Kiwi visitors. Or at least a friend living in a dodgy dive with a lumpy couch. If you think you'd feel comfortable taking advantage of his or her hospitality, ask very nicely if you can stay for a couple of weeks. Legends abound about serial dossers — people who spend their entire OE going from couch to couch.

> **Dossing etiquette**
>
> Dossing is a great OE tradition. Kiwis established in London who dossed on arrival will repay the karmic debt by hosting someone else. If you are lucky enough to have friends who are happy to lend you the spare bed, the couch, the VW Kombi or even the lawn (it's been known), keep the tradition healthy by observing a few rules:
> - Dossers do dishes. And every other bit of housework. And keep their belongings tidy, especially if there are flatmates they don't know.

- Many established antipodean flats will have a Dosser Policy, and will charge dossers a token rent — the standard rate is £5 a night. If your hosts don't ask for it, offer it.
- If your hosts are Kiwis, the best way to ingratiate yourself is to bring over a stash of Minties, Jaffas, Pineapple Lumps and the like. If your host is English, consider getting them a greenstone pendant or bone carving or something. *See 'Getting your Kiwi fix' to find out where to buy New Zealand food and gifts in the UK.*
- Treat your hosts to a roast. Ring your mum and ask how to cook it if necessary. Kiwis in London miss roasts.
- Don't overstay your welcome. Agree a time period with your hosts and stick to it.

Hostels

A dorm bed in a hostel can be a good, cheap option, especially if you don't know many people in your chosen port of disembarkation. If you strike a good bunch of fellow-hostellers in the same situation as you, you could find your next flatmates among them, or at least some friends who'll be feeling the same mixture of excitement and apprehension. There are hundreds of hostels in London, and dozens in other big cities.

In London, a different take on the hostel option is an outfit called Accommodation London. Instead of a bed in a dorm you'll get a bed or room in a kitted-out flat, or a studio apartment to yourself. Contact: phone 0800 028 3636 (from the UK) or +44 20 8459 6203 (from overseas), email info@accommodationlondon.net, website www.accommodationlondon.net.

FINDING A HOSTEL

See if you can get a friend to recommend a hostel, or trawl through accommodation websites, reading reviews from people who have stayed there. Budget on paying £10–20 a night for a bed in a dorm room, depending on the city. To get an idea where your hostel is, look up its postcode or address on www.multimap.com or www.streetmap.co.uk. *For a list of London postcodes, see 'Transport and orientation'.*

Accommodation

Some sites:
www.hostelworld.com
www.hostellondon.com
www.hostels.com
www.yha.org.uk
www.visitbritain.com
www.backpackers.co.uk
www.astorhostels.com

Where to live in London

Almost every New Zealander in London waxes lyrical about his or her own suburb, but there is no golden area of London. It depends on what you want. If you want to flat with antipodeans, walk to a touch rugby field, booze up at an antipodean local and buy Pineapple Lumps at your corner shop, you'll probably be happiest in Acton, Clapham Junction, Fulham or Willesden Green.

Unless you've got a job in London's extremities you'll probably want to live in the Zone 2 transport area — near enough to where it's happening, but cheaper than Zone 1. Generally, the closer you get to Zone 1 the more upmarket and expensive the housing. (If you can afford to live in Zone 1 then go for your life.) Flats get cheaper further out, but your transport costs and commuting times increase — check the distance and travelling times before you move in. Also keep in mind that it's a pain to be too far from your friends.

Areas of London

This is a basic guide to the pros and cons of some of the most popular areas for antipodeans. It is by no means an exhaustive list. You might well find your Eden elsewhere. A good website to check out your prospective neighbourhood and find services in your area is www.upmystreet.co.uk.

For a list of London postcodes, see 'Transport and orientation'.

Northwest

There are popular and cheap antipodean enclaves in Willesden, Dollis Hill, Kilburn, Kensal Green, Queen's Park, Neasden, Cricklewood and Finchley Road. You'll find few English people living here — it's an area of mostly New Zealand, Australian and Caribbean immigrants. Zadie Smith's brilliant novel *White Teeth* is set here. You'll like it if you want a reasonably quiet area with some of the comforts of home and you want to flat with three or more (sometimes many more) antipodeans. The nightlife is predominantly antipodean. More upmarket and expensive are Hampstead Heath, Highgate, West Hampstead, Swiss Cottage and Maida Vale.

Northeast

Camden, Angel and Islington are among the most popular neighbourhoods for London's young professionals. They are trendy areas with good restaurants and a lively nightlife, and you can find affordable accommodation, although in Islington it's getting scarce. Further out, Golders Green, Finsbury Park and Kentish Town are cheap and liveable, and the former dives of Hoxton and Shoreditch are now far more stylish — and have the bonus of being close to Spitalfields markets and London curry heaven, aka Brick Lane.

East

A lot of these places were ignored before the Jubilee Line extension was opened in the late 1990s, so some parts are still underdeveloped and affordable, yet accessible to the West End and city. Canary Wharf and Docklands hold the upmarket ground. Docklands used to be an East End dive, but it's been gentrified since a city of skyscrapers, finance executives and the latter-day Fleet Street was built at Canary Wharf. Bermondsey has come a long way, while Bethnal Green is towards the dodgier end of the scale, but is cheap, lively and popular with antipodeans.

Southeast

New Zealanders who have lived in Brixton swear it's the UK capital of cool. It's got a reputation for being dangerous and drug-ridden, but it has a legendary nightlife, is still reasonably cheap and is pretty close to the city. Be prepared to have clubbing friends crashing on your couch every weekend. Also worth trying are London Bridge and Lewisham. Borough has a good smattering of Kiwis and has the excellent Borough markets to recommend it.

Southwest

The southwest is probably the most popular area for young New Zealand professionals. It has good transport links, is affordable and most areas have lively cafés and pubs. Earl's Court used to be synonymous with antipodeans, but in recent years the rents have begun to reflect the privilege of its Zone 1 status, and the antipodeans have been pushed out to West Kensington and Baron's Court. Further south, towards the Thames, Fulham and Parson's Green are popular choices, with quiet streets, lively pubs and good parks. On the south side of the Thames are the extremely popular areas of Clapham (great park), Battersea and Wandsworth, with Balham and Tooting up-and-coming options. Further west is leafy, upmarket Putney, and Southfields and Wimbledon, the latter a well-established antipodean haunt, although you're more likely to hear a South African accent than any other. An exception to the don't-live-out-of-Zone-2 rule is Richmond, which has the Thames flowing through it, boasts fantastic parks and feels more like a quaint, if overpopulated, village than part of London. What you lose in more expensive rent and travelling time you'll gain in atmosphere.

West

Notting Hill is famous for its annual carnival and bohemian atmosphere, a certain Hugh Grant/Julia Roberts movie and the Portobello Road markets. And all those attractions are now reflected in the rents, as they are in Bayswater. Failing that, still-affordable options are Paddington and Westbourne Green. Hammersmith boasts some great riverside pubs. Ugly but cheap Shepherd's Bush, Acton and the leafy Ealing have long had a hold over young antipodeans. You'll find a lot of 16-to-a-flat houses here, plenty of touch games, the infamous Redback Tavern and generally cheap rent.

The Big OE Companion

Flatting

It'll be far easier at first to rent a room in an established flat than to set up your own flat. It's much less hassle, you'll have less initial outlay and landlords, agents and utility companies might be a bit sceptical about someone without a UK renting history. That's not to say it's impossible to get a lease (see below).

Costs

Expect to pay about £60 to £100 for a single room and £80 to £150 for a double. Naturally, the cost varies wildly according to how nice the place is, where it is and how many people live there. On top of that, you'll usually have to pay for power, phone, gas, council tax, television licence, sometimes water, and perhaps pay-TV. If you're sharing with a few people, budget on paying an extra £10–20 a week. When you move in, you'll normally be asked to pay a deposit equivalent to four weeks' rent and four weeks' rent in advance. (This is why you had to save so much money in New Zealand.)

Where to look

If you're living outside London, try the advertisements in your local paper or www.flat-sharer.com (which also covers London). In Edinburgh try http://edinburgh.gumtree.com.

If in London, start with the antipodean websites and publications (see 'Getting your Kiwi fix') and *Loot* newspaper, available from newspaper sellers or online at www.loot.com.

What to look for

- The first consideration is location. You want to feel safe, you'll probably want to be close to a Tube or train station and shops, and you'd be a fool to be more than an hour's journey from work.
- Naturally, you'll also want to get on with your flatmates.
- Ask how much utility bills and council tax cost, and check if any of the appliances are leased.
- If you value a good shower, check it — in many places it's a hand-held nozzle above a bath that releases water drip by drip.
- Make sure there's central heating, and preferably double-glazed windows — winters will be miserable and expensive without them.

- Flats generally come fully furnished, which is a bonus for travellers — but check what you get.
- Don't overlook the curtains. In the height of summer London gets sun from about 4 am to 10 pm, so if you're a light sleeper you'll want dark curtains. In winter, you'll want heavy curtains that cover the entire length of the window frame to keep the draughts out.
- Make sure there are deadlocks on outside doors and locks on the windows.
- Check that there's a washing machine. If not, make sure there's a laundromat nearby.
- Check the flat policy on dossers — if you want to be able to have friends to stay — and on subletting your room if you decide to spend a summer in Europe.

Culture and flatmates

Some people — New Zealanders and Brits alike — get a bit sniffy about the tendency of antipodeans to flat together in enclaves. They think it's a cop-out on having an authentic British experience. There's merit in that opinion, but there are also sound reasons it happens. For starters, your fellow antipodeans are more likely to be living similar lifestyles — working hard, going out regularly, travelling a lot, having mates over to watch rugby, playing touch rugby, letting friends stay on the couch for a week. Brits can be understandably intolerant of dossers, which are a common feature of antipodean flats. They're not always understanding if you want to sublet your room while you spend the summer in Europe, and they might be worried that you're going to decide to go home at any minute and leave them in the lurch. Also, it can be comforting when you're feeling homesick or at times like Christmas to be surrounded by people who are as far from home as you, and understand what that's like.

If you flat with Brits you'll find a hundred subtle differences between the house-sharing habits of Brits and the flatting habits of New Zealanders. For a reason that no British person seems to be able to explain, they do their dishes in a bucket in the sink. They watch *EastEnders*, *Coronation Street* and/or soccer. Religiously. And they might not be amenable to missing a *Big Brother* eviction just because there's some quaint colonial grudge match called a Bledisloe Cup test on the other channel. They tend to get possessive of the contents of the fridge.

The Big OE Companion

You're best to take a big breath and do things their way, rather than try and change the habits of two millennia.

> I've asked many English people since I've lived here why they do their dishes in a bucket and the most common response is a shrug.
> The only two coherent answers I've managed to get are:
> — Because the water is 'heavy' and lime-scale is a problem, people don't want unsightly stains that build up in their sinks and are difficult to clean.
> — When your sink is full of water, there is nowhere to tip the water out of a saucepan you've been soaking, which makes it easier to clean. In New Zealand, tipping it out the kitchen window is the usual answer. In the UK that may get you evicted, depending on whom it lands on. With a plastic bucket, you can still tip it down the side and it drains away.
> — Andrew Knight

The educational option — but one demanding even more patience and cooperation — is to flat with a bunch of people of different nationalities. You'll need to be very laid-back, and it's not a good idea to put the lease and all the utility bills in your name — you might find it tricky to track down your ex-flatmate in a Sicilian back street or the plains of Kenya. If it works out, you'll have good friends to stay with all over the world.

> You might think living with ten or sometimes twelve people would get claustrophobic but the good thing was there was always something happening — like staying at a hostel. It only felt weird when there were less than five people in the house. As soon as I moved in I had ten new instant best mates, which was a big relief as I knew hardly a soul in the city. My first week was great, but not for my bank balance — going out every night and getting home in the wee hours. I started to see why everyone raved about London. The place was huge and everyone had their own room — I was glad I wouldn't have to sleep in the lounge with six other blokes. I'll never forget my time in my London flat — the nights sitting around the dining table having a good laugh with a bottle of wine from the offie or having our mates round for a barbie in the backyard. It was a great place to start out an OE.
> — Ben Watson

Accommodation

Some peculiarities of flatting in the UK

- You might find yourself sleeping in a single bed for the first time since you left home, and you might even find yourself sharing a room for the first time since you were a kid in a bunk. Both are common for penny-pinching antipodeans in London.
- It's common for young antipodeans to share a large house in London with a few dozen people — two to four in each room, an indeterminate number of dossers in the lounge, a guy in the cupboard under the stairs and others in Kombi vans parked outside. There will be rosters for the shower and, unless it's a complete dump, some very strict rules on housework. Just sorting the mail can be a challenge. These quasi-hostels can be fun if you're not wealthy and not fussy. You get a guaranteed party every night — whether you like it or not — you'll meet lots of people, and it's probably a pretty flexible arrangement. But you'd be crazy to stay long-term.
- In the UK shared rental accommodation is most often called flatshare or houseshare.
- You're usually expected to find your own replacement when you move out.
- The washing machine is usually in the kitchen, as houses don't tend to have laundries. It'll be a front loader, and will probably take twice as long as the top-loaders you're used to.
- You'll be warmer inside in winter than in summer, since central heating is pretty cheap. (Australians are renowned for pumping up their heating to 30 degrees or more.)

Taking on a lease

Whether you have an easy or a hard time securing the lease on a flat can come down to how desperate the landlord or agent is to fill it. You might get one on the strength of the honest look in your eyes, but more likely the least you'll have to provide is proof of your income and/or finances and references from former landlords. They might also do a credit check on you.

You can register with local real estate offices. Registration is free, but they'll usually charge you the equivalent of a week's rent if they find you a place.

If you're successful, you'll get an Assured Shorthold Tenancy Agreement, for a minimum of six or twelve months. Make sure you read the fine print on the lease and any conditions, and be pedantic about doing an inventory of contents, which lists everything the flat comes with and what condition it's all in. You don't want to give your landlord any excuse for withholding your deposit (usually four weeks' bond). It is not unusual for tenants in the UK who don't trust their landlords to withhold their last rent payment before they move out.

Why live in London when you can live in...

- Backside
- Beeswing
- Blubberhouses
- Broadbottom
- Carrot
- Cold Blow
- Doddiscomsleigh
- Dog Village
- Donkey Town
- Dorking
- Drunkendub
- Duffus
- Farleigh Wallop
- Fattahead
- Fishnish
- Fladdabister
- Foulbog
- Frisby on the Weake
- Great Snoring
- Kettlesing Bottom
- Knabbygates
- Lickey End
- Little Snoring
- Lower Down
- Maggieknockater
- Muddleswood
- Nether End
- North Piddle
- Pity Me
- Playing Place
- Pratt's Bottom
- Puddletown
- Seething
- Sheepy Magna
- Snishival
- Stain
- Stuck
- Swell
- Swine
- The Bog
- The Shoe
- Tiptoe
- Tongue
- Twatt
- Upper Dicker
- Upper Slaughter
- Washaway
- Whale
- Wham
- Wide Open
- Wookey Hole
- Wootten Wawen
- Wormhill

Accommodation

Utilities, etc.

If possible, ask the existing tenants if you can take over their utility and council tax accounts and put them into your name. It can be cheaper and far less hassle to merely change the name at the top of the bill.

Otherwise, take readings on the gas and power meters, and call the power, gas and water companies immediately to notify them of the change of resident. A useful tool for finding your local utility providers and comparing prices is the website www.uswitch.com. You will have to pay connection fees and a deposit for each utility. If your prospective flatmates have sound utilities histories in the UK, ask if they mind taking on the responsibility.

Some flats have an electricity meter which you have to keep recharging at the local store. This can be a pain in the neck, especially when you arrive home at midnight in winter to find you have no power.

COUNCIL TAX

Ring your local council to get the council tax bill put in your name. This is the equivalent of rates in New Zealand — in the UK it's the tenant's responsibility. The cost varies according to the area in which you live. Council tax is usually paid monthly and utility bills are paid quarterly. To track down your local council, go to www.gov.uk.

LANDLINES

Don't assume you'll need a landline phone connection if you've got a good deal on your mobile phone. You'll often meet New Zealanders in the UK who have never used their home phones and have no idea of the number. If you want one, you'll have to pay to connect it, as well as paying a deposit.

TELEVISION LICENCES

If you have a television in your flat, you or your landlord must pay a television licence — about £120 a year. If the landlord supplies it, he or she must pay the fee, unless it's otherwise stated in your rental agreement — but you share the responsibility of ensuring it's covered. One licence covers all the television sets in your flat. There are checks by detector vans, and if you get caught without a licence you could be fined £1000.

Contact TV Licensing, phone 0870 241 6468, email vlcsc@capita.co.uk, website www.tvlicensing.co.uk.
For information on pay TV and broadband internet, see 'Communications and media'.

Contents insurance

A lot of New Zealanders don't bother getting contents insurance for the simple reason that they don't have anything worth insuring. However, if your flat comes fully furnished, you may be responsible for the furniture if your landlord hasn't already insured it.

Some catches in the fine print of contents insurance policies:
- Contents policies don't usually cover your belongings if you take them out of the house. You'll have to take out an extra all-risks cover policy if you want to carry possessions like laptops and cameras around the UK. Your possessions should be covered by your travel insurance while you're in Europe.
- The policy might exclude cover for your mobile phone. *See 'Communications and media' for advice on mobile phone insurance.*
- If you have flatmates, your possessions might only be covered if they are locked in your room. Check the small print.

Moving in and kitting out

Unless you've just arrived and own only what's in your backpack, it's a bitch to move flats in London without a car. Easycar rentals (www.easycar.com) has cheap daily and even hourly rentals.

The Argos chain is a popular one-stop for kitting out a flat on a budget; website www.argos.co.uk. There are branches throughout the UK. The cheap Swedish furniture store IKEA (website www.ikea.co.uk) has a dozen stores in the UK and you can get things home-delivered if you don't have transport. Also, have a look in the classified advertisements on antipodean websites (*see 'Getting your Kiwi fix'*) and in *Loot* newspaper (www.loot.com). With the constant ebb and flow of antipodeans in London, you can usually pick up some bargains.

Accommodation

Tenancy advice and your rights

Your basic rights as a leaseholder with an assured shorthold tenancy are to security of tenure, to have the place repaired and maintained in good working order, and to have the rent increased only in certain circumstances.

If you run into problems or want to know more about your rights as a tenant, you can contact a Citizens Advice Bureau. Their website, www.adviceguide.org.uk, has advice and links to other good advisory sites.

The terminology
You might come across these unfamiliar abbreviations in flatmate-wanted advertisements.

bedsit — a small studio flat
BR — British Rail
ch — central heating
council tax — the equivalent of rates
gch — gas central heating
dep — deposit
detached — a stand-alone house (rare in London)
dg — double glazing
ff — fully furnished
flatshare/houseshare (sometimes abbreviated to fs or hs) — a rental property shared between flatmates
ns — non-smoker
o/r — own room (not always something you can take for granted)
osp — off-street parking
pf — partly furnished
pppcm — per person per calendar month
pppw (or pppm) — per person per week (or month)
semi-detached — a house that's joined to another house on one side
terraced house — a house that's joined to houses on both sides
uf — unfurnished
w/d — washer and dryer

The Big OE Companion

There are advantages to living in the smaller, quainter towns and cities in the UK. You get to experience British life and culture close-up. You get to know the local homeless lad who sits outside the Indian restaurant. You won't see other antipodeans for days on end and you won't end up feeling like you haven't left home. You can offer your friends in London a place to stay when they want a break from the city. It's cheaper than London and the air is fresher. You have easy access to the outdoors and great cycling and walking, and it's easier to keep up your fitness and sports. You're more likely to be able to walk or ride to work, so you can avoid infected manky seats and handles on the Tube and trains, and sweaty armpits and the feeling that you are a sardine — and if you're not travelling the same distances as in London you get an extra few hours in your day. For all this, you have to put up with missing midweek social events with your mates in London, and you don't have easy access to cheaper midweek tickets to things such as West End productions.

— Angela Lash

7.

Work

If you waltz into your dream job on arrival in the UK you're a very lucky aberration. Even the most educated and experienced New Zealanders can wait six months for a decent job offer. It's an astonishingly competitive market so employers in most industries can afford to be very picky — and it's frustratingly common for employers to insist you have UK work experience. Try not to get discouraged. You do have something very valuable in your favour — over the years New Zealanders have developed a reputation for being hard-working, flexible and reliable.

Searching

You'll have to do a bit of research into your job market to find out where the job advertisements are, as every industry has its idiosyncrasies when it comes to recruitment. They don't all advertise in the same place.

If you're in an in-demand occupation such as nursing or teaching then it's likely you'll be courted by potential employers and agencies — mostly through the antipodean publications and websites (*for a list, see 'Getting your Kiwi fix'*).

Familiarise yourself with the British newspapers. As well as general job advertisement sections they print regular industry-specific recruitment sections. Jobs advertised in national British papers can attract thousands of applications, and many employers will advertise in more selective media.

If you know people who are working in your industry in the UK, pick their brains. If you know what companies you'd like to work for, ring their human resources departments.

Websites

The internet is a good start. Search the job advertisements on these newspaper websites: www.guardian.co.uk, www.timesonline.co.uk, www.independent.co.uk, www.telegraph.co.uk. Some large general sites are: www.worktrain.gov.uk, www.reed.co.uk, www.monster.co.uk, www.jobs.co.uk and www.fish4jobs.co.uk. For government jobs: civil service, www.civil-service.gov.uk; health sector, www.nhscareers.nhs.uk; academic jobs, www.jobs.ac.uk.

Search for professional and trade associations in your field (some are listed under 'Registration' below, and others can be located on www.certoffice.org). There are hundreds of industry-specific job websites that you should be able to find in a web search.

Recruitment agencies

As well as using your own initiative, it doesn't hurt to sign up to two or three recruitment agencies dealing in your industry. Some high-demand industries always use agencies if they don't have the resources to filter through thousands of applicants themselves.

It can be as hard to sign up with a recruitment agency as it is to land a job — often you have to do some quick talking just to get past the switchboard operator. You can email dozens of CVs and not hear back. You need to develop a very good pitch and be persistent — call them every few days once you're listed.

Temping work

Agency or temping work can be a good place to start, as you get a chance to look around before making a big commitment. But temp recruitment agents are a mixed bunch, and you have to be wary that your agent is not just trying to get you into any old job in order get a nice little commission as soon as possible. They will hire you out at an exorbitant rate and pay you far less. They might not care if you are doing work that's far below your qualifications, as long as they're filling their orders. If you're canny you'll try to get work without them by undercutting their rates, but they can make things much easier. Always keep on the best of terms with your agent, and go to any social functions the agency organises. If they like you, trust you — and most importantly, remember you — they'll give you the good jobs.

Work

Finding an agent

The Recruitment and Employment Confederation's website www.jobseekers-uk.com allows you to search for recruitment agents in your industry, as does www.agencycentral.co.uk.

> The Kiwi Agency is a recruitment agency specialising in dealing with New Zealanders. It has been running since 1987 and deals in the following industries:
> - medical (locum doctors, personal assistants, secretaries, clerical and admin, reception);
> - commercial (secretaries, audio typists, administration);
> - teaching (primary, secondary and special needs).
>
> Contact: phone 020 7629 1666, email sales@barnettgroup.biz, website www.barnettgroup.biz, address 28 South Molton Street, London, W1K.

Selling yourself

Because of the sheer number of job seekers in the UK, the recruitment process can be merciless. If an employer has a hundred CVs sitting on his or her desk, at least fifty are going to be discarded after a very quick glance at the first page.

Naturally, the attributes an employer looks for vary wildly between industries. The best advice is to keep your pitch succinct and finely targeted, be it in a CV, covering letter, email or phone call. An exhaustive list of the companies you worked for in New Zealand and the institutes at which you studied is going to mean very little to a UK employer, so keep that part short. Focus on a concise explanation of your qualifications, skills and experience, and outline what you can offer. On a CV, list these on the first page. If you're applying for a specific job, keep to the job description, and answer all the requirements. Do not waffle in a covering letter or CV. Stick to a two-page CV and provide phone referees.

The Big OE Companion

Filling in time

If after a few weeks your money is getting low and your dream job hasn't presented itself, consider taking any old job. Having a temporary, casual and/or part-time job while you look for something better can boost your confidence as well as tide you over financially. And who knows? You might find yourself having a bit of fun and meeting people. If it's summer, take off to a beach resort town and knock on doors — cafés, restaurants, bars, shops and tourist attractions might need casual staff. If you can type, try to blag your way into secretarial temping work. If it's winter, the ski resorts in Europe might need staff for their slopes, hotels, restaurants, cafés and bars (although you might need a visa).

> **Tips for staying sane when you're looking for work**
> - Join a library. Free books, free CDs and DVDs, free internet, and surprisingly interesting people.
> - Approach job-hunting like you would a job. Set aside part of the day to do it, and consider the rest time off.
> - Amuse yourself at London's free attractions (see 'Enjoying the UK').
> - Treat yourself to a cheap weekend in Europe, to remind yourself why you're here.
> - Don't be too hard on yourself. It can be difficult to get a job, but keep at it and you'll get one. Don't take it personally and don't give up.
> - Go on a National Trust Working Holiday — you volunteer your time to help with conservation projects in the UK (see 'Enjoying the UK').
> - Take any old job in the meantime, just to keep your spirits and finances up.

Live-in jobs

Live-in work can be handy, especially when you first arrive. You have the chance to settle in a bit without committing to the cost and responsibility of a flat.

Work

It can also be a trap. If you're living and working in a pub you might have a good time, but you probably won't pocket much money — which might make it hard to save a rent deposit. And if you're doing split shifts and working into the early hours, you might not have much time or energy left for anything else, including job-hunting. If you're a live-in carer or nanny choose your situation carefully — you might find it tiring if you can't escape your charges.

Playing rugby

This is where boys get lucky. If you've got a half-decent rugby-playing record in New Zealand, you could land yourself a deal whereby you get shared accommodation, a basic job and a car sorted for you in return for playing for a local side, usually somewhere outside London. You may tire of it fairly quickly, but it's an easy introduction to the UK, you'll probably end up in a town or city you wouldn't otherwise go to (for better or worse), and you only have to stick it out for a season. Ask your rugby associates at home whether they have any contacts in the UK, or know anyone who has gone down that route. You could also try the website www.rugbyclub-connect.com and check the advertisements in the New Zealand magazine *Rugby News*, www.rugby.co.nz.

Registration and certification

In addition to being qualified in your profession or trade, you might have to be registered or certified to work in the UK. This might involve sitting a test. In other cases registration is optional but might smooth your way to work.

Some professions and trades which require or recommend you to be registered are listed below. If your profession is not listed and you suspect you'll need certification, or you want to know if your qualification is recognised, contact the National Academic Recognition Information Centre (Naric), phone 0870 990 4088, email info@naric.org.uk, website www.naric.org.uk.

There are some New Zealand professional groups in the UK that might be able to give advice. *For listings, see 'Getting your Kiwi fix'.*

If you have a vocational qualification, such as a trades certificate,

The Big OE Companion

Advice from a Kiwi human resources manager in London

Recruiters and agencies

- Ask friends to refer good agencies/recruiters they've used and don't be afraid to use that friend's name to get you in the door.
- When hunting for jobs call every day. Don't worry about seeming pushy; if you don't, they'll forget you.
- Have a good idea about what sort of role and industry you'd like to be in and/or are qualified for. Most recruiters are just that — recruiters — not career advisers, and they aren't going to look for something you might like but rather something that you can actually do.

CVs

- Before leaving New Zealand get your current manager to have a look at your CV. New Zealanders have a tendency to be modest about their achievements and you'll need to sell yourself once you're in the UK.
- Layout of CV: don't have pages and pages of irrelevant information. Include the information you think is important, but an entire page for your name, address and visa status is a bit over the top. Have key contact and visa information at the start, then move into recent experience through to schooling at the end. Make sure you include your key skills and qualifications, and what the UK equivalents are, if necessary.
- Once you are in the UK keep a note of the experience and skills you're gaining as you go along. Don't wait until it's time to update your CV for the next role.
- Don't be worried about gaps in your CV due to travelling. Recruiters and employers expect that you'll have come to do some travelling. But make sure when you're in an interview that what you're saying about travelling matches what's in your CV.
- Tailor your CV for the role. Highlight the IT/project management/leadership/banking/sole charge, etc. aspects if they are particular to the desired role. There's more competition in the UK in particular sectors, so you need to come across better on paper than the people you're competing with.

Other tips

- Be aware of what your visa restrictions are. You need to be more conscious of this than the recruiter does. You have more to lose if you contravene your visa conditions.
- Prepare for an interview by thinking of actual examples to support your CV. Recruiters don't want to hear hypothetical answers — 'I would do this' — they want to hear real examples — 'When this happened, this is what I did and this was the outcome . . .'
- Where is the role you are considering based? That two-hour commute might seem okay in June, but wait until November when there are leaves on the line and only seven hours of daylight.
- Consider how you're being paid. Are you contracting through a company and set up in the right way? Are you considering taking a permanent job? Although a salary might be lower for permanent employment you also need to consider benefits such as holiday pay, sick pay, medical insurance and pension contributions (pretty much standard in the UK).

contact the National Reference Point for Vocational Qualifications, phone 012 4226 0225, email vq@ecctis.co.uk, website www.uknrp.org.uk.

Health and social work

Doctors must register with the General Medical Council; phone 020 7915 3630, email registrationhelp@gmc-uk.org, website www.gmc-uk.org.

Dentists and dental hygienists must register with the General Dental Council; phone 020 7887 3800, email gdcregistration@gdc-uk.org, website www.gdc-uk.org.

Nurses and midwives must register with the Nursing and Midwifery Council; phone 020 7333 6600, email overseasreg@nmc-uk.org, website www.nmc-uk.org.

Other health professionals, including occupational therapists, podiatrists, paramedics, laboratory technicians, clinical scientists, physiotherapists, radiographers and speech therapists, must register with the Health Professionals Council; phone 020 7840 9804, email international@hpc-uk.org (with your profession in the subject line), website www.hpc-uk.org.

Veterinarians and veterinarian nurses must register with the Royal College of Veterinary Surgeons; phone 020 7202 0739, email membership@rcvs.org.uk, website www.rcvs.org.uk.

Pharmacists should contact the Royal Pharmaceutical Society of Great Britain; phone 020 7572 2317, email overseas@rpsgb.org.uk, website www.rpsgb.org.uk.

Other health professionals can find links to the organisations that regulate their professions in the UK at the National Health Service careers website, www.nhscareers.nhs.uk.

Most health professionals need to be covered by Professional Indemnity insurance — you might automatically be covered, but it's best to make sure.

Social workers must get clearance from the General Social Care Council; phone 020 7397 5100 or 0845 070 0630, email registration@gscc.org.uk, website www.gscc.org.uk.

Teaching

If you're a teacher, your employer or agency is responsible for checking your qualifications and police record, but you can help by having all the paperwork in order, and getting a copy of your New Zealand criminal record. Qualifications requirements differ slightly between countries, so check the links below.

For more information, contact:

- The Department for Education and Skills, phone 0870 000 2288, email info@dfes.gsi.gov.uk, websites www.dfes.gov.uk and www.teachernet.gov.uk.
- General Teaching Council for England, phone 0870 0010 308, email info@gtce.org.uk, website www.gtce.org.uk.
- General Teaching Council for Wales, phone 029 2055 0350, email registration@gtcw.org.uk, website www.gtcw.org.uk.
- General Teaching Council for Scotland, phone 0131 314 6036, email registration@gtcs.org.uk, website www.gtcs.org.uk.
- General Teaching Council for Northern Ireland, phone 028 9033 3390, email info@gtcni.org.uk, website www.gtcni.org.uk.

Tempering people's expectations is very important as it seems like there just isn't the same volume of work around that there used to be a few years ago. If people's expectations are high about their OE (which generally they are) the initial few months might be harder going than first expected — a common experience. Nobody ever really told me about the crap times. I suppose people returning from OE don't dwell on those, but it would have been good to know that it wasn't all going to be a bed of roses and Park Lane apartments.

— Anonymous

Law and finance

Although lawyers can work with just a New Zealand qualification, the Law Society will not allow you to hold yourself up as a solicitor until you have passed the Qualified Lawyer Transfer Test (QLTT). This involves two exams — accounts and ethics. Once you have passed, you can be admitted to the Roll of Solicitors.

For more information, contact:
- The Law Society of England and Wales, phone 020 7242 1222, email legaled@lawsociety.org.uk, website www.lawsoc.org.uk.
- The Law Society of Scotland, phone 013 1226 7411, email lawscot@lawscot.org.uk, website www.lawscot.org.uk.
- The Law Society of Northern Ireland, phone 028 9023 1614, email info@lawsoc-ni.org, website www.lawsoc-ni.org.
- One World Studies (administers exams), www.onewstudies.com.

Barristers should contact the Bar Council; phone 020 7440 0082, website www.barcouncil.org.uk.

Chartered accountants and auditors can contact the Association of Chartered Certified Accountants; phone 014 1582 2000, email info@accaglobal.com, website www.accaglobal.com.

Engineering and trades

Trades increasingly require some kind of accreditation. In some cases, this isn't compulsory, but it can help you get work.

For information, contact:
- The Construction Skills Certification Scheme, phone 014 8557 8777, website www.cscs.uk.com.

- Engineering Services Skill Card, phone 017 6886 0406, email skillcard@welplan.co.uk, website www.skillcard.org.uk.
- The Construction Industry Training Board, phone 014 8557 7577, email information.centre@citb.co.uk, website www.citb.co.uk.
- Smarter Builder, phone 016 8588 8700, email info@smarter-builder.co.uk, website www.smarter-builder.co.uk.

Electricians can get certification from the Joint Industry Board for the Electrical Contracting Industry; phone 020 8302 0031, email administration@jib.org.uk, website www.jib.org.uk.

Engineers may have to register with the UK institute that covers their field. Contact the UK Engineering Council, phone 020 7240 7891, email staff@engc.org.uk, website www.engc.org.uk.

Plumbers can register with the Institute of Plumbing, phone 017 0847 2791, email info@plumbers.org.uk, website www.plumbers.org.uk.

Police checks

If you work with children or as a social worker or carer, you will probably be asked for a Criminal Records Disclosure — effectively a police check. Of course, if you're new to the UK, a UK police check will be inadequate and you'll need the New Zealand equivalent. You can download a form from www.courts.govt.nz/privacy then you'll have to fax it to the Department for Courts, +64 4 918 8974. Allow a few weeks for the report to arrive.

Unions

Trade unions are pretty strong in the UK. It's worth joining if there's one for your industry. You'll get advice, professional support, and legal support if you get into trouble with your employer. More information from the Trade Unions Council, phone 020 7636 4030, email info@tuc.org.uk, website www.tuc.org.uk.

British working attitudes

You'll hear many jokes about the laziness of British workers, but make up your own mind. Of course plenty of Brits slack off — as do plenty of New Zealanders — but studies have credited them with working far longer hours on average than most nationalities in Continental Europe. The tradition of spending Friday afternoons at the pub is not as prevalent as it might once have been, but it does still happen. Employees of many companies and government departments in London start the working day at 9.30 or 10 am for the very good reason of relieving pressure on the public transport system at peak times.

> For many Kiwis it seems the nature of the Big OE is changing. No longer content to pull pints, more and more of us come to London in search of the next career move. We're prepared to sacrifice travel in favour of a deposit on a house, contenting ourselves with European city breaks in place of long van tours, or spending half our holidays tripping home for weddings. I find myself torn between my roles as young, ambitious professional and restless wanderer. In these materialistic times, maybe it takes more courage to pick up the hippy trail and fruit-pick our way around the world.
>
> — Christine Sheehy

8.
Money matters

the topics in this chapter — banking, national insurance and tax — are potentially the most, er, taxing matters you'll deal with in the UK. But you'll find matters a lot easier if you understand how the systems work, and how to work within their limitations.

Banking in the UK — the basics

Opening an account

If you didn't open an account before you arrived, you might have a bit of a mission ahead of you. You'd think you would be able to walk into a bank, pull out £100 and say, 'I want you to have my money,' and they'd be only too glad to take it. Not in the UK. But if you have arrived without a bank account, you'll just have to try your luck. Go into your local branch with as much documentation as you can rustle up proving your identity, your address, your financial standing, your employment situation, etc.

The very least you'll want is a savings account with a Switch (ATM) card, but ask for a chequebook as well. Solo cards are often given to people with no banking records, but they are less widely accepted and don't provide a cheque guarantee, as Switch cards do.

If the bank turns you down, or if you want to take a shortcut, there is a burgeoning market for agencies that will open an account for you for a fee. You'll find advertisements in the antipodean publications and

Money matters

websites (see *'Getting your Kiwi fix'*).

For information on opening an account from New Zealand, see *'Groundwork'*.

For information on sending money to New Zealand, see *'What next?'*.

Fees

Standard accounts tend to be a lot cheaper in the UK than in New Zealand, although the interest is laughable. With most basic accounts you won't be charged for withdrawals from ATM machines within the UK (there are a few exceptions, but they should be clearly marked on the machines) and the fees will be small or non-existent.

ATM cards

Make sure your ATM card (usually called a Switch card) has a Cirrus or Maestro logo on the back, so you can use it at ATMs all over the world.

Chequebook

You'll need a chequebook, mainly for paying rent and utility bills.

Credit cards

You are unlikely to be able to get a credit card until you have established a good record with your bank, although there are tales of people getting one straight away. Once you have been a good little customer for six months or so, ring your bank and sweet-talk them. Once you've got a card, the bank is prone to extending your credit limit without asking you. You don't want to be stuck with paying off a £6000 debt once you're back in New Zealand, so be careful. Note the number to call to report a lost or stolen card.

Internet banking

Get set up for internet banking. You can pay many bills this way, and it's useful for accessing your funds while you're travelling.

Cashback

You can get money out on your card when you're purchasing goods and services at some shops — it's called cashback.

Eftpos

The UK banking system lags behind New Zealand in terms of Eftpos, but it finally introduced a comparable system in 2004, called 'chip and pin'.

Getting a National Insurance number

Applying for a permanent National Insurance number can be the single most frustrating experience of your OE. Some people don't even bother, but you should. It's the number your employer will use to deduct tax and National Insurance contributions, and will make dealing with Inland Revenue much easier when it comes to claiming your tax returns.

When you arrive, your recruitment agency or employer will automatically start you on a temporary number (called an Emergency number). While you're on this, you'll be taxed at a higher rate than when you get issued a permanent number (you'll be able to claim the difference back in your annual tax return — see below).

To apply, you'll have to get an appointment for an interview at your local Jobcentre Plus office. If you're living in a smaller city or town the process can be pretty smooth. But in built-up areas with a high number of immigrants it can take months to even get an interview. To further frustrate the process, some of the busier offices only take calls to make appointments over the phone, but they rarely answer their appointments phone line or return calls — especially to mobile phones. If you don't get an answer, try sending them a fax. You may find they phone you back straight away. Be persistent. Some offices offer appointments on the weekends, but take what you can get, and organise the time off work later.

Once you get the appointment, you'll have to show up with a load of documentation and a frazzled Department of Work and Pensions (DWP) worker will help you fill in the form. It will be sent away to head office, and you might have to wait another three months to get your card in the mail.

The process is simple, at least in theory.
1. Ring the DWP public enquiry office, 020 7712 2171, or go to website www.jobcentreplus.gov.uk to find out the number for your local Jobcentre Plus office.

Money matters

Tips for conserving money (while still having a life)

- Make a point of ending your nights out while public transport is still running, rather than taking a cab home or staying up 'til dawn.
- Choose your travel buddies wisely. It's easy to be coaxed into spending more money than you have.
- Get addicted to *EastEnders*. That way you'll always want to go straight home after work (although admittedly you won't have a life).
- If you go clubbing, make it a night of dancing and drinking just water. Alcohol costs a bomb in clubs.
- Get to clubs early so you don't have to pay entrance charges.
- Don't take your ATM or credit card on a night out — just take as much money as you want to spend.
- If your friends are going for dinner and drinks, join them for just the drinks, or just the meal.
- If you're catching up with friends, the first instinct is usually to meet at a pub, bar or restaurant. There are cheaper alternatives. In summer, meet them at a park, perhaps for a touch rugby game; or make plans to go for a walk. In winter, meet one or two friends at one of Britain's many free museums and galleries.
- Take day trips into the countryside, rather than going for the whole weekend. Same-day return rail fares can be very cheap and you won't have to pay for accommodation.
- Join a library. As well as books, you can hire videos and DVDs.
- It can be tempting to go to the pub every day. If you tend to drink a lot of alcohol, develop a policy of drinking only on certain days of the week.
- In London, many West End restaurants offer cheap early dinners, from about 5 pm.

For a list of things to do in London on the cheap, see 'Enjoying the UK'.

2. Ring your local office for an appointment. Double-check the documentation you'll need.
3. Take to the interview proof of: your identification; your eligibility to work in the UK; your address; your employment or efforts to find work. For details, go to www.dwp.gov.uk.

Tax

As in New Zealand, if you're an employee your employer or agency will deduct tax and National Insurance from your earnings under the Pay As You Earn (PAYE) system. If you have tax problems or questions, contact Inland Revenue. They don't always answer the phone immediately, but they're usually surprisingly cheerful.

> Inland Revenue UK
> Helpline: 0845 9000 444
> From overseas: +44 870 1555 445
> Orderline (to get forms): phone 0845 9000 404,
> or email saorderline.ir@gtnet.gov.uk
> Website: www.inlandrevenue.gov.uk
> (many forms are available to download)

Arrival

When you arrive in the UK you will have to fill out an Inland Revenue P86 — Arrival in the United Kingdom form. Your agency or employer will probably provide this, or you can get the form from Inland Revenue and fill it in yourself.

Tax rebates

There is one advantage to paying tax in the UK — tax rebates. Call it an additional savings plan.

The main reasons you might be due a rebate are:
- you've been working with a temporary National Insurance number;
- you've worked for only part of the tax year (April 6 to April 5);
- you've changed jobs;
- your company has had you on the wrong rate;

- you've had periods of unemployment or unpaid holidays and travels.

If that's you, you'd be a mug not to send in a tax claim. Each time you leave a job you'll get a P45 form from your employer, and at the end of the tax year you'll get a P60 from your employer. Keep these documents, as they are your path to tax refunds.

Personal tax rates Rates for the 2004/2005 year		Note: Most New Zealanders in the UK can also claim the personal allowance, which allows you to earn £4745 each year tax free, thus the first tax bracket doesn't apply.
Earnings up to £2020	10 percent	
£2021 to £31,400	22 percent	
Over £31,400	40 percent	

Claiming a personal tax return

It's easy to do your own tax return — you don't even need to do any calculations. Fill in a couple of forms, attach your tax statements, send it in and wait for your windfall. And wait. And wait. Sometimes you could be waiting three weeks, other times five months — depends how busy Inland Revenue is. You can make claims for any year within the last six.

You can get forms from Inland Revenue. You will need a Tax Return form and an additional Employment Pages form for each job you have had in the UK in the tax year. Your employer will give you a P60 statement at the end of each financial year, which you will have to send in. Also, if you have left a job during the year, that employer should have given you a P45 statement, which you will also need to send in. Keep photocopies of these statements. You can also file a tax return over the internet at the Inland Revenue site.

You'll need to send your tax return to the office that deals with your tax, which is determined by the area your employer is based in. Your employer should be able to tell you, otherwise you can find out from Inland Revenue.

If you change jobs in the UK, show your new employer your P45, so they can calculate where you're up to with paying tax for the year.

For information about claiming a tax rebate when you leave the UK, look in 'What next?'.

Being self-employed

If you are self-employed — as distinct from having a limited company (see below) — you have to register with Inland Revenue within three months of the end of your first month of work. You are responsible for paying your own tax and National Insurance contributions.

The Inland Revenue test for determining self-employment is as follows: if you can answer 'Yes' to the following questions, it will usually mean you are self-employed.

- Do you have the final say in how the business is run?
- Do you risk your own money in the business?
- Are you responsible for meeting the losses as well as taking the profits?
- Do you provide the main items of equipment you need to do your job, not just the small tools many employees provide for themselves?
- Are you free to hire other people on your own terms to do the work you have taken on? Do you pay them out of your own pocket?
- Do you have to correct unsatisfactory work in your own time and at your own expense?

If you're not sure about your status you can look on the Inland Revenue website or call their self-employed helpline 08459 15 45 15. You can make an appointment to get free advice and help from the Inland Revenue business support teams.

Setting up a limited company

You may be able to set up a limited company if you're working through an agency or on a temporary or contract basis. There can be financial benefits in turning yourself into a company. You may find yourself on a lower company tax rate, and you will be able to claim back certain work-related expenses.

If you want to do it yourself, you can start by getting a guide from Inland Revenue, either online or by calling the self-employed helpline 08459 15 45 15. The Inland Revenue business support teams offer free advice and help with the basics of forming a limited company, and can advise you how to register with Companies House, Inland Revenue and Customs and Excise. If you are working through an agency, the staff there may also be able to help you.

Money matters

It's common for New Zealanders in the UK to enlist the services of a company to set them up with an 'off-the-shelf' limited company and administer it. If you want to go down this route, read on.

National Insurance taxback

Part of your National Insurance contributions goes towards your pension. You can transfer this money to a private pension fund, which you can access when you retire. To do this, contact an independent financial adviser (find one on the Association of Independent Financial Advisers website www.aifa.net) or try some of the companies listed below (not all offer the service).

Getting professional help

If you don't want to do your own tax return, or you're bewildered at the prospect of setting up your own company or being self-employed, there are a lot of companies that will help you.

Some companies targeting the antipodean market are:
- 1st Contact, website www.1stcontact.co.uk; for tax return enquiries phone 0800 039 3098 or email taxrefunds@1stcontact.co.uk; for limited company enquiries phone 0800 039 3082 or email ltdcompanies@1stcontact.co.uk
- Ambler Collins, phone 020 7736 6060, email theservices@amblercollins.com, website www.amblercollins.com
- Dynamic Management Solutions, phone 020 7562 7900, email info@dms-london.co.uk, website www.dms-london.co.uk
- Rapid Refunds, phone 0800 071 2222, email info@rapidrefunds.co.uk, website www.rapidrefunds.co.uk
- Safe Solutions, phone 020 8742 6000, email info@safesolutions.co.uk, website www.safesolutions.co.uk
- Taxback, phone 0207 244 6666, email info@taxback.co.uk, website www.taxback.co.uk

You'll find others in the antipodean publications and websites (see 'Getting your Kiwi fix').

Individual Savings Account (ISA)

If you want to do some serious saving in the UK, consider getting an ISA. It's a tax-free investment account that's open to anyone who is a UK resident for tax purposes. You can choose if you want to keep your investment in cash — which makes it just a tax-free savings account — or in stocks and shares — a greater risk, but potentially a higher return. The maximum amount you can invest in an ISA is limited — currently to £3000 a year in cash and £7000 a year in stocks and shares. Any returns you get are tax-free.

You can get ISAs in all sorts of strange places — even some supermarkets. But a good starting point is your bank. For more advice, go to the Financial Services Authority website, www.fsa.gov.uk/consumer.

9. Health, fitness and sport

the long UK winter, the pub culture, the temptation to overindulge in the gastronomic delights of Europe, the endless socialising, long working hours and commuting all conspire to part you from your health and fitness. And the bureaucratic inefficiency of the National Health Service (NHS) can take your sanity. But there are ways to hold onto your health, fitness and sanity.

Health

Emergency number: 999

NHS Direct
This is a telephone advisory service staffed by nurses, who can offer advice or refer you elsewhere. There is also a website loaded with health advice and information. Phone 0845 4647, website www.nhsdirect.nhs.uk.

GPs
Seeing a GP is free in the UK (you pay for it through the National Insurance contributions in your tax). You should register with a local GP

as soon as you find accommodation in the UK. Don't wait until you're sick, because it can take weeks to register if your local surgeries are busy. For a list of GPs in your area, contact NHS Direct (see above). You might have to ring around a few surgeries until you find one that can take you. You'll have to pop down to fill in a few forms, and they might give you an initial medical exam. After that, you can book an appointment. If you have a choice, find a surgery that opens in the weekends or after working hours.

You're not supposed to register with a doctor outside your local area (defined by the NHS), but some GPs will refuse to register you if they're at full capacity. If all the GPs in your area turn you away, contact your Local Health Authority, which might force a GP to take you on. Find your local authority through NHS Direct.

There's a walk-in NHS surgery near Tottenham Court Road in London. It's the Great Chapel Street Medical Centre, 13 Great Chapel Street, W1; phone 020 7437 9360. Opening hours are limited.

> I was living in Willesden Green and rang around the local doctors' surgeries to register. The first two or three wouldn't take me because they were full, and a lady at the next one very helpfully advised me, 'We take the first three callers on a Thursday morning.' When I finally found one willing to take me, I rocked on up with my passport, but they wouldn't sign me up because I had less than six months left on my Working Holiday Visa. I moved to southwest London shortly afterwards and was registered straight away. It just depends on where you live.
> — Anonymous

Dentists

NHS dentists can be cheap but hard to find. Recently an NHS dentist opened for business in one of England's northern towns and there was a queue of people around the block who waited all day simply to register. It's a good idea to register before you need a dentist as it can take a while, and private clinics can be budget-breaking. Locate your nearest clinic through NHS Direct (see above). In an emergency, you can get free treatment at Guy's Hospital Dental Services, St Thomas Street, SE1; phone 020 7955 4317, website www.guysandstthomas.nhs.uk.

Walk-in centres

If you have a minor complaint for which you don't need prescription medicine or a blood test, you can go to a free NHS walk-in centre, staffed by nurses. Locate your nearest centre through NHS Direct (see above).

Hospitals

Treatment in hospital Accident and Emergency departments is free to all, and New Zealand citizens also do not have to pay for any hospital treatment for conditions that arise during their stay in the UK.

Prescriptions

Prescriptions aren't free (except for the contraceptive pill). There's a set price for prescriptions, currently £6.20. The chemists Boots and Superdrug, which you can find on almost any high street, offer very cheap generic shop-brand drugs, such as paracetamol — far cheaper than name brands.

Contraception, etc.

Contraception and STD treatments are free, through your doctor or local Family Planning Clinic (www.fpa.org.uk, helpline 0845 310 1334). You can also buy the morning-after pill over the counter at pharmacies. If you need an abortion, you can get a referral from your GP to a hospital or clinic, or you can go directly to a clinic as a private patient. For advice and referrals on contraception, pregnancy and abortion, contact the British Pregnancy Advice Service, 08457 304 030, website www.bpas.org.

Student clinics

You can often get free or very cheap additional health care, such as physiotherapy, osteopathy, optometry and homeopathy from student clinics at training colleges and universities. The students are supervised by people who know what they're doing. Locate them by doing a Yellow Pages or internet search.

Winter survival strategies

It's not so much the cold of winter in the UK that'll get to you, but the bleakness — the 4 pm sunsets (if the sun comes out at all), the feeling that it's never going to end. On the darkest day of the year — the winter solstice (December 22) — there is only seven hours and fifty minutes of daylight and the maximum elevation of the sun is just 15 degrees, which means it sits close to the horizon even at midday. The average UK temperature in the 2003/2004 winter was a measly 4°C, according to the Met Office.

There's even a medical condition to describe the winter blues — Seasonal Affective Disorder, or SAD. It's often joked about, but it's a very real problem.

Tips for winter survival

- Buy a coat so thick it stands up by itself . . .
- . . . and gloves and a hat and a scarf.
- Dress in layers that you can easily pull on or off as you go from home to the street to the Tube to work to the pub and back again.
- Get a few people together to rent a country cottage or castle for a weekend.
- Have an orphans' Christmas with a big group of friends.
- Get addicted to *Pop Idol/Survivor/Big Brother*.
- Holiday in Morocco, the Middle East or the Marlborough Sounds.
- Wrap up warm and go to a really cold place, like Stockholm. The UK will feel comparatively tropical.
- Spend a stormy afternoon in an absorbing museum or gallery.
- Go ice-skating at Somerset House, London.
- Get some exercise and eat healthily.
- Move to a flat closer to a Tube line.
- Move into a more sociable flat so you are happy to spend more time cosied up at home.
- Crank up the central heating.
- Do a session on a sunbed.
- Spend a Sunday afternoon watching old movies at the Curzon cinema in Mayfair or Soho.

Health, fitness and sport

Fitness and sport
Playing sport
TOUCH RUGBY

There are touch rugby competitions from spring to autumn all over the UK. You can play socially or competitively, you can assemble your own team, put your name down to join someone else's team or, in some competitions, you can join as a ring-in player. Keep an eye on the antipodean publications and websites (see 'Getting your Kiwi fix') or follow the links below to find out when competitions start.

LONDON AND THE SOUTHEAST

There are more than twenty touch competitions in Greater London and the southeast, operated by several clubs and companies:

- In2touch (locations include Cambridge, Canada Water, Clapham, Fulham/Putney, Maidenhead, Milton Keynes, Oxford, Reading, Slough, Surrey Quays, Wandsworth, Wimbledon, Wood Green). Phone 020 8487 8230 or 07 905 976 935, email info@in2touch.com, website www.in2touch.com.
- Old Actonians (Acton). Phone 020 8896 6072, email info@londontouchrugby.com, website www.londontouchrugby.com.
- Touchrugby.com (locations include Acton, Blackheath, Ealing, Fulham, Islington (see also the website www.sanza.co.uk), Kingston, Leytonstone, Merton, Richmond, Southwark, Teddington, Tonbridge, Wimbledon). Email [location]@touchrugby.com (e.g. acton@touchrugby.com), website www.touchrugby.com.
- Willesden Green. Contact Down Under Centre, phone 020 8451 8976, email downundercentre@hotmail.com.

IF YOU LIVE ELSEWHERE

- Check the Kiwi-run portal website www.touchrugby.com, email admin@touchrugby.com.
- Check the website www.in2touch.com/uk.
- Contact your nearest rugby or rugby league club (see 'Rugby', below).
- In Scotland, try Scottish Touch, email contact@scottishtouch.com, website www.scottishtouch.com.

> ### Avoiding the Heathrow injection
> The much-discussed Heathrow injection is the name for the weight New Zealanders tend to put on when they get to the UK — usually because of the sedentary lifestyle and beer-drinking. Here are some tips to avoid it:
> - Buy a bike *(see 'Transport and orientation')*.
> - Join a sports team or gym (see below).
> - Don't catch public transport if you can walk.
> - If you're drinking alcohol, drink wine rather than the more fattening beer.
> - Cook for yourself as often as you can (you can cheat by buying low-fat ready meals from supermarkets).
> - Go on an active holiday — biking, skiing, climbing, walking.

NETBALL

British women don't seem to play as much sport as New Zealand women, but netball is big. You wouldn't catch many British men playing, but plenty of antipodean blokes do. It's more popular among antipodeans as a summer sport, but a few hardy souls brave outdoor netball in winter.

If you're outside London, locate a competition through:
- England Netball, phone 014 6244 2344, email info@englandnetball.co.uk, website www.england-netball.co.uk.
- Netball Scotland, phone 014 1572 0114, email tellus@netballscotland.com, website www.netballscotland.com.
- Welsh Netball Association, phone 029 2023 7048, email info@welshnetball.com, website www.welshnetball.co.uk.
- Northern Ireland Netball Association, phone 028 9038 1222.

In London, some of the more established competitions catering to antipodeans are:
- Commonwealth Netball UK. Locations: Pimlico and St John's Wood. Phone 020 7834 0979, email info@commonwealthnetballuk.com, website www.commonwealthnetballuk.com.
- Downunder Centre competition. Location: Willesden Green. Contact Downunder Centre, phone 020 8451 8976, email downundercentre@hotmail.com.

Health, fitness and sport

- Old Actonians. Location: Acton. Phone 020 8896 6072, email info@londontouchrugby.com, website www.londontouchrugby.com.
- Sanza competitions. Locations: Islington, Acton and Wimbledon/Southfields. Email sanzanetball@hotmail.com, website www.sanza.co.uk.
- Social Sports. Locations: Paddington, Docklands, Shepherd's Bush and Stratford. Phone 020 8534 8444, email netball@socialsports.co.uk, website www.socialsports.co.uk.

RUGBY

Once you've spent a season playing rugby in the damp, dreary, cold UK winter, you might figure that England deserved to win the 2003 Rugby World Cup. If you don't mind playing on frozen paddocks, or up to your knees in mud, playing rugby is a fun way to ward off a winter beer belly. There are a few rugby sevens tournaments in summer.

Locate your local rugby club through the national unions:

- England: phone 020 8892 2000, email reception@rfu.com, website www.rfu.com.
- Scotland: phone 013 1346 5000, email feedback@sru.org.uk, website www.scottishrugby.org.uk.
- Wales: phone 0870 013 8600, website www.wru.co.uk.
- Ireland: phone +353 1 647 3800, website www.irishrugby.ie.

For Kiwi clubs based in London, see 'Getting your Kiwi fix'.

CRICKET

There are very few things more English than the thwack of willow, the smell of fresh strawberries and the taste of Pimm's.

In England and Wales locate your nearest club through:

- The England and Wales Cricket Board, phone 020 7432 1200, website www.ecb.co.uk.
- Cricket Scotland, phone 013 1313 7420, email admin@cricketscotland.co.uk, website www.scottishcricket.org.

For details of the London New Zealand Cricket Club, see 'Getting your Kiwi fix'.

SOCCER

Called football in the UK. Since it's the national grassroots sport, the standard is high. Many companies have corporate teams, so ask around the office. There's a hotline for women players, 0845 310 8555. In London, SANZA runs a competition in Islington; email sanzasoccer@hotmail.com, website www.sanza.co.uk.

Locate your local County Football Association through:
- Football Association (England), website www.thefa.com/grassroots.
- Football Association of Wales, phone 029 2037 2325, email info@faw.org.uk, website www.faw.org.uk.
- Scottish Football Association, phone 0141 616 6000, email info@scottishfa.co.uk, website www.scottishfa.co.uk.
- Irish Football Association (for Northern Ireland), phone 028 9066 9458, email enquiries@irishfa.com, website www.irishfa.com.

BASKETBALL

The ANZSAC Basketball Association organises women's, men's and mixed competitions in Elephant and Castle, London, aimed at antipodeans. You can register a team or as an individual player. Phone 020 7562 7900, email info@anzsacbasketball.com, website www.anzsacbasketball.com.

OTHER SPORTS

Find links to other sports organisations through:
- Government agency UK Sport, phone 020 7211 5100, email info@uksport.gov.uk, website www.uksport.gov.uk.
- Sport England, phone 020 7273 1500, email info@sportengland.org, website www.sportengland.org.
- Sports Council for Wales, phone 029 2030 0500, email publicity@scw.co.uk, website www.sports-council-wales.co.uk.
- Sport Scotland, phone 0131 317 7200, email library@sportscotland.org.uk, website www.sportscotland.org.uk.
- Sports Council for Northern Ireland, phone 028 9038 1222, email info@sportni.net, website www.sportni.net.

For information about watching sport, see 'Enjoying the UK'.

Health, fitness and sport

Gyms and pools

Councils usually own fitness centres. Some of them are very good, with fully kitted-out gyms and Olympic pools. The best ones aren't dirt cheap, but they're usually less expensive than private health clubs. To find the one nearest to you, contact your local council.

10.
Communications and media

home phone numbers are so 20th century. If you're living in London there's a good chance you'll never get around to learning your home number, because you'll hardly ever be there. Hell, an 11-digit mobile is enough of a challenge for the memory. Consequently, it's extremely rare to meet a Kiwi in the UK who doesn't have a mobile phone. We tend to live such transitory lifestyles that we wonder how people who travelled back in the 1980s lived without mobiles — or email, for that matter. Email, text messaging and cheap international phone accounts leave you with no excuse to neglect your family and friends back home (but if you don't tell them how cheap it is to phone home, they'll never know).

Phones
Finding numbers

Directory services have been deregulated, so there are about a dozen companies vying for your business. Directory enquiry services begin with 118. The BT number is 118 500, and its website, www.bt.com, has a free online directory service. Its most prominent directory services competitor is The Number, 118 118. Businesses are listed in the Yellow Pages, which are delivered free, or you can search the website www.yellowpages.co.uk.

Your mobile phone provider might have its own directory service, and will text numbers to your phone. It usually costs about 50p for a number.

Communications and media

Call rates

BT local calls are charged at 5p minimum, and then per minute after that. National calls (including to Northern Ireland) are about 8p a minute. To check what's in your local area, go to www.bt.com. In London all 020 numbers are in the local calling area, as well as some numbers starting with 01 in areas on the outskirts.

Calling numbers with an 0500, 0800, 0899 or 0808 prefix is free from a landline (but you'll pay if you call from a mobile). If you dial an 0845 number you'll pay the standard local call rate, and if you dial an 0870 or 0871 number you'll pay the standard national call rate. Numbers beginning with 05, 06, 07, 08, 09 or 12 are charged at a variety of rates. You can find out how much a call will cost on www.bt.com or the Office of Communications website, www.oftel.org.uk.

International calls

Dialling overseas from the UK is the same as dialling from New Zealand — dial 00 then the country code, area code (dropping the initial zero) and the phone number. The area code for New Zealand is 64, thus, to call the prime minister in New Zealand you'd dial 0064 4 471 9999.

> **Calling the operator**
> UK operator: phone 100
> For international operator (to make collect calls): phone 155
> Telecom New Zealand direct (collect calls to New Zealand):
>   phone 0800 890 064
> International directory enquiries: phone 118 505

Money savers

With a calling card or international calling account it's incredibly cheap to phone New Zealand — as little as 3p a minute. With these, you call a local number which will patch you through to New Zealand. If you use your mobile phone's free minutes to call you'll avoid paying local call charges from your landline.

You can buy calling cards from newsagents, supermarkets and corner stores, or sign up for an account. Accounts can work out cheaper because calling cards often have expensive minimum call charges — sometimes £1, which can be frustrating if you're trying to get through to someone whose answerphone keeps coming on.

Popular sign-up accounts are Alpha (phone 0800 279 3205, email info@alphatelecom.com, website www.alphatelecom.co.uk) and Swiftcall (phone 0800 769 0022, website www.swiftcall.co.uk) but there are heaps more. Check the antipodean publications and websites in the UK for those targeting New Zealanders *(see 'Getting your Kiwi fix')*.

Alternatively, you can use a telecommunications shop. You'll find these in most high streets, and they're often run in tandem with internet outlets. You'll get cheap calling rates and a booth to sit in.

Time difference

New Zealand standard time is 12 hours ahead of the UK. However, there are actually only a few weeks in the year when it's that easy. Both countries switch to daylight saving time in summer. Thus, when the UK is in daylight saving time, New Zealand is 11 hours ahead. When New Zealand is in daylight saving time, it is 13 hours ahead.

Mobile phones

IF YOU HAVE A HANDSET

If you've brought a mobile phone from home, you'll need a new SIM card and a UK power adaptor for your phone charger to get it working. You might also need to unlock it, as some phones are locked to a network. If you haven't done this already, you can contact your last network in New Zealand and ask them to do it, or there are hundreds of dodgy street vendors and corner stores who will do it for you for a few pounds.

THE NETWORKS

Most mobile phone shops are aligned with a particular network. The big networks are Vodafone, Orange, T-Mobile, Virgin and O2. Plans that come with free minutes and free texts will sometimes restrict them to the company's own network and to calls to landlines. Either find a plan that specifies free cross-networking minutes, or find out which network most of your friends are on and consider signing up with that one — that way you'll be able to use the free minutes.

Unlike New Zealand numbers, you can't tell immediately which network a mobile is on from the prefix.

BUYING A HANDSET

You can usually get a cheap handset as part of a contract deal — and there are also some cheapies available with prepaid deals. Most mobile phone shops are aligned with a particular network — and there's usually no mistaking which one, the logos will be emblazoned everywhere. Independent retailers, such as the Carphone Warehouse, offer a range of phones and deals across networks. You can do a price comparison of handsets and networks on its website, www.carphonewarehouse.com.

Most phones can be used with any network, but note that some Orange phones — the ones emblazoned with Orange logos — can only be used on that network.

PREPAID OR CONTRACT?

Contract If you use your phone for more than three minutes a day, you'll be better off on a contract than on a prepaid deal. Most contracts tie you in for a year.

Because applying for a contract is effectively an application for credit, you might find it difficult until you have proof of your address and a bank account. Having said that, the competition is such that if a pedantic salesperson in one shop turns you down, you can try your luck with the next shop. Some will figure that if you're creditworthy enough to have a credit card, then that's good enough security. Or they could be satisfied if you sign up to pay by direct debit from your bank account on the spot.

Which tariff? The more you pay in line rental, the less you pay in calls and the more free minutes you'll get. The basic line rentals are about

£15–30. If you're not sure how much you'll end up using your phone, sign up for the cheapest line rental — you can change the tariff later. Shop around, and compare the deals with free minutes and free texts.

Prepaid If you're a very light user, or you don't feel comfortable committing to a year's contract, you'll be better off with a prepaid deal. You can buy the phone and SIM card together or separately, and can recharge by buying a recharge card, or applying to recharge online or over the phone with a credit or debit card — useful if you travel overseas a lot.

There are two types of tariff. A traditional tariff is cheaper on the weekends and evenings and more expensive during the day. A stepped tariff makes no distinctions between peak and off-peak, but gives you cheaper calls after you have used your phone for a minimum period each day — usually a few minutes.

ROAMING

If you want to use your phone overseas — and you probably will — you might need permission from your network. Call your phone provider to check. Before you go, find out how much it will cost to use your phone overseas — your network should be able to give you a brochure, telling you which network to choose in each country, and outlining the call and text costs. Even texting is expensive in some countries — in Croatia, for

---

Things to check
- Cost of peak and off-peak calls and texts.
- Definition of peak and off-peak.
- Cost of calls to a different network.
- Cost of text messages.
- Cost of making and receiving calls and text messages overseas.
- Cost of voicemail retrieval.
- Cost of roaming.
- Period of the contract.
- Free minutes.

example, it can cost £1 a text. You'll pay to receive calls while overseas, so if someone rings your mobile from the UK and it's patched through to you in Europe, they only pay the standard charge to call a mobile — you pay for the international part, which can be very expensive. You won't be able to use a standard UK phone in the United States or Canada because the systems are incompatible.

SECURITY

Mobile phone theft is a big problem in the UK — police statistics show that a mobile phone is stolen every three minutes. However, false claims for insurance purposes are thought to account for some phone theft complaints.

When you buy a phone, make a note of your handset's unique 15-digit registration number, called an IMEI. You can find this by dialling *#06# from your mobile, or it'll be listed on a sticker beneath the battery. Keep a note of this number, and your network's customer service number, in your bag and at home. If your handset is lost or stolen, call your network immediately, and they will be able to immobilise it, then contact the police. Lock the keypad when you're not using it.

The UK police advise that you avoid using your mobile phone in public. This rather defies the point of having one, but certainly use it discreetly, especially on the street after dark if you're alone, keep it hidden while it's not in use and turn off the ring in public.

It's a good idea to copy numbers from your mobile phonebook into your diary, and leave a photocopy of the list at home, or you'll be lost if you lose your phone. Also, memorise the mobile numbers of a couple of your friends, so you can call in an emergency.

INSURANCE

Mobile phone insurance might sound like a good idea, but it can be a bit of a have. Read the fine print before you sign up — it could be that you're only covered if the phone is taken by force or if it's stolen from your locked house in a break-in. If you merely lose or drop it, you're not covered. The proliferation of phone theft notwithstanding, the chances of either of these things happening are slim. And if you've taken a note of the IMEI number (see 'Security' above) you'll be able to stop anyone clocking up calls on your account.

SWITCHING NETWORKS

You can use any SIM card in your phone unless the handset is SIM-locked — which means your network has locked the phone. Your network can give you the code to unlock it, but they might charge for it. The alternative is to use a dodgy street vendor or corner store.

To keep your phone number when you switch networks, you'll have to ask your current network for a PAC (porting authorisation code) to give to your new provider.

Post

As well as the official post offices, many newsagents and corner stores have dingy little counters that double as a mini post office. See the websites www.royalmail.com or www.postoffice.co.uk for more information on postage in the UK or to locate your nearest post office.

Postage costs

Postage stamps (for letters up to 20 g):	£
— 1st class (next-day delivery) letter within UK	0.28
— 2nd class (about two days) letter within UK	0.20
— Surface mail letter to New Zealand	0.37
— Airmail letter to New Zealand, 10 g	0.47

The cost of posting a package to New Zealand airmail is determined by its weight, starting at about £1.20 for 100 g. A 500-g package will cost about £5, a 1-kg package about £10, and a 2-kg package about £20. Posting printed material only is a bit cheaper. Surface mail is at least half the cost but takes up to eight weeks to get to New Zealand.

If you're expecting a bulky parcel, it might be wise to get it mailed to your work, as the small mail slots in most British houses don't accommodate much, and you'll end up traipsing down to your nearest post-holding centre — which could be quite a distance away by public transport — to pick it up.

If you want to send Christmas gifts to New Zealand, Royal Mail recommends you post them by about December 6.

Communications and media

Cyberspace

Accessing the internet

LIBRARIES

You can usually get free internet access at public libraries, although you might have to book a slot, and there are usually limits on the time you can spend online.

INTERNET CAFÉS

There's no shortage of internet cafés in the UK, and prices in areas where there's a bit of competition are pretty reasonable. You might pay a premium in the middle of nowhere. The prices often vary between peak and off-peak time.

Easyeverything is the market leader, with stores all over the UK and Europe, some open 24 hours. They offer reasonable daily, weekly and monthly all-you-can-surf offers, which are good value, although they encourage some over-eager internet addicts to spend entire days online. The 24-hour stores attract a strange clientele in the early hours of the morning. You can locate your nearest store online at www.easyeverything.co.uk (which of course is not much use to you if you're walking the streets trying to find one). Some of the big stores in London are: on Oxford Street near the Bond Street Tube station; on The Strand near Trafalgar Square, and on the Oxford Street end of Tottenham Court Road. In Edinburgh the store is on Rose Street.

For information on internet email accounts, see 'Groundwork'.

INTERNET AT HOME

As in New Zealand, you have a choice between dial-up and broadband internet connections. Dial-up connections are slower and cheaper and use your phone line. Broadband connections are faster and more reliable, give you a higher bandwidth, and are more expensive.

Your telephone or cable company might limit your choice of internet Service Providers (ISPs). It's better to sign up with a company with a freephone number so you don't get stung with local calling charges as well as your internet charges.

Some ISPs will tie you into a year's contract; others will allow you to cancel the contract at any time.

Dial-up: You can pay a flat fee — usually about £8–16 a month — for unlimited access, or choose a metered plan in which you pay per minute — usually from 1p to 4p a minute. You can get deals in which you pay a metered rate during peak times and get free calls off-peak.

In 2004, *Which?* magazine (www.which.net) judged Claranet's Unlimited Free Trial, Firenet's Pay As You Go, Freeserves's No Ties, NDO's HomeDial and Supanet's Classic as their best-buy pay-as-you-go services. For unmetered services, they chose Firenet's LitePlus package and Supanet's Supahighway service.

Broadband: Broadband will cost £20–30 a month, and there will probably be installation and equipment charges — these can total as much as £160. Most UK broadband connections involve an upgrade of your standard line to a Digital Subscriber Line (DSL) — offered through BT — or cable modem connection from the cable companies. Broadband is not available in some areas. For more information about broadband and for a list of ISPs, look on www.bt.com/broadband.

Media

The British media is one of the best and the worst things about Britain. The UK press reaches the heights of intellectual debate and the depths of celebrity gossip. Celebrities are created and slain in the tabloids, and issues can be blown out of all recognisable proportion, especially in summer when not much is happening in politics and business.

Newspapers

The conservative national newspapers are *The Times*, the *Daily Telegraph*, the *Independent* and the *Guardian* (with its Sunday sister paper the *Observer*). They tend to figuratively nail their political colours to their mastheads. *The Times* and the *Telegraph* tend towards the right wing, and the *Independent*, the *Guardian* and the *Observer* to the left. Reading a Sunday paper front to back could take a week.

The red-top tabloids are fun, if sometimes infuriatingly inflammatory and lowbrow. At the bottom of the market the *Sun* and the *Daily Star* fight for the highly lucrative redneck market. The *Daily Sport* has no sport and a 'nipple count'. Slightly more upmarket are the *Daily Mail*, the

Daily Mirror and the *Daily Express*. The London evening daily the *Evening Standard* is a good read on the Tube on the way home, and the free *Metro* — available at Tube and train stations — is a rudimentary news digest that's published weekday mornings.

Most of the newspapers have very good websites. The best one is probably www.guardian.co.uk, which has screeds of information, from news to employment pages to advice on buying insurance.

> After travelling through South-east Asia and Europe before reaching London I was gagging to get some good updates on New Zealand domestic rugby. So on my first day in London I went out from my mate's place where I was dossing and went into a newsagent's, wondering which newspaper would be most likely to run an NPC scoreboard. I came away with the promisingly titled *Daily Sport*. Surely somewhere in a newspaper dedicated to nothing but sport I'll find a story about my beloved Waikato, I thought. No. The *Daily Sport* was wall-to-wall tits and phone sex ads. Funny headlines though.
>
> — Winston Aldworth

Television

Considering the size of its population, it's surprising that Britain has only five national free-to-air television channels. The ubiquitous BBC has two of the stations — BBC1 and BBC2 — and there are three commercial channels — ITV, Channel 4 and Channel 5. You don't need a TV guide to know what's on. At any given moment there will be a combination of the following screening: home and garden improvement programmes, reality TV shows, quiz shows, war documentaries, gritty British dramas, reruns of *Only Fools and Horses*, football and British soaps. Most weekend papers include a weekly TV guide.

There are hundreds of satellite and cable channels. The market leader is Sky, which you'll need if you want to watch most New Zealand sports games. It's not expensive if you have a few All Black fans in the flat to split the cost — especially if you consider how much you'll save in not having to go to the pub. To sign up, call Sky on 08702 40 40 40, email skydigital@sky.com, or go to the website www.sky.com.

For information on the antipodean television channel Right Side Up TV, see 'Getting your Kiwi fix'.

The Big OE Companion

Radio

If you're a devoted 95bFM or Radio Active listener in New Zealand, you'll have a hard time finding a good radio station in the UK. You're best to log onto www.95bfm.co.nz or www.radioactive.co.nz, for the music stations in the UK are mostly poppy and repetitive. On the other hand, if you like National Radio, you'll be in radio heaven with Radio Four.

The BBC is dominant. You can find frequencies or listen online at www.bbc.co.uk/radio.

- Radio One has some excellent new music shows among the bland Britpop and sometimes gratingly annoying hosts — and if you miss a show you can download it later from the website.
- Radio Two plays middle-of-the-road classics.
- Radio Three has classical music and plays.
- Radio Four, with its flagship morning Today programme, has an inspired and sometimes eclectic mix of news, current affairs, documentaries and drama.
- Radio Five Live carries news and sport.

The BBC website www.bbc.co.uk has a stack of useful news, community and consumer information.

11.

Shopping

Shop assistants in London have an uncanny ability to prevent work getting in the way of a good gossip. The professionals can process dozens of transactions without pausing in their conversation with colleagues to acknowledge a single customer. The lack of customer service is one of the first things a New Zealander will notice — and conversely you'll be bowled over by the sheer friendliness of it all when you go out of London or return to New Zealand. Still, it's something you're just going to have to get used to — and it won't keep you away from the shops.

The high street

It's strange that a country with such inclement weather has so few indoor shopping malls, or even awnings, so shopping can be a wet experience on a rainy day. A couple of exceptions are the massive 330-shop Bluewater mall in Kent and the Bullring in Birmingham — two of Europe's largest malls.

Instead, every town and suburb has a high street, where the main shops are gathered. The high street is easy to find because it's usually imaginatively titled High Street. This is where you'll get all the standard chain stores — and in the UK almost everything is a chain. There are benefits to the high-street competition — prices have been driven down. Books, for example, can be very cheap, and Boots and Superdrug (chemists) are constantly outdoing each other.

Chain-store heaven (or hell, depending on your point of view) is at Oxford Circus in London, where many of the chains have enormous stores. However, many small local shops have been forced out — for this reason it's a good policy to support local stores whenever you can.

Supermarkets

Nowhere is globalisation more apparent than in the fruit and vege sections of the supermarkets. The avocados are from South Africa, the oranges from Spain, the beans from Kenya, and of course, the kiwifruit from New Zealand.

The UK supermarkets have turned the corner on TV dinners. No longer the domain of trailer trash, the 'ready meals' of today are often fresh, nutritious and cheaper than the sum of their parts. Some of them are so good you could be tempted to pass them off as your own at a dinner party.

In fact, everything in the big UK supermarkets comes packaged for the single, busy person-about-town who doesn't have a car to lug groceries home in bulk — pre-cut vegetables, washed salads, complete gourmet curry meals.

The Asda supermarket chain is regularly judged the cheapest. A survey by *The Grocer* magazine found that from June 2002 to March 2003 a basket of basic groceries was, on average, cheapest at Asda. In order, from cheapest to most expensive, the ratings were: Asda, Morrisons (a northern England chain), Tesco, Sainsbury's, Safeway, Waitrose, Coop and Somerfield. Not included in the survey were Iceland, which sells cheap ambient goods, and Marks and Spencer, which tends towards the more gourmet — and expensive — food.

Department stores

UK department stores are like shopping malls without borders — an entire high street in one enormous shop. Harrods is the quintessential English department store, and it even has a dress code, but its Latin slogan, 'Omnia, omnibus, ubique' (everything for everyone, everywhere) could refer to any of the other big department stores — Debenhams, Fortnum & Mason, Harvey Nichols, John Lewis, Liberty and Selfridges. In London, you'll find Harrods in its famous Knightsbridge building, and most of the others are collected in and around Oxford Street — between Marble Arch and Oxford Circus — Regent Street and Piccadilly. Most also have stores in other UK cities.

Shopping

Markets

Most cities boast markets, and many towns and villages host traditional farmers' markets, selling produce, meat and local crafts. Notable active market towns are Salisbury in Wiltshire; Wells in Somerset; Totnes in Devon; Bury St Edmonds in Suffolk; Beverley, Thirsk and Helmsley in Yorkshire; Alnwick and Brampton in Northumberland; Perth in Perthshire, and Abergavenny in Wales.

In London, there are more than 300 markets, from the tacky to the bizarre. Even if you're not buying, wandering through a lively one can be a great way to spend a morning. Most are best at the weekends. *Time Out* has a good markets guide on its website www.timeout.com.

The London markets

- Borough market, Borough High Street/Southwark Street, SE1. A fabulous food market where you can buy something exotic for lunch, and shop for fruit and veges and gourmet foods. Open: Friday and Saturday. Tube: London Bridge.
- Brick Lane market, Brick Lane and surrounding streets, E1. Hundreds of people throw a tarpaulin on the street and spread out their offerings, from stolen bikes and produce to cosmetics and leather jackets. Open: Sunday. Tubes: Liverpool Street, Aldgate East.
- Brixton market, Electric Avenue, Atlantic Road, Pope's Road, Brixton Station Road, SW9. Atmospheric food, music and second-hand clothing market. Open: Monday to Saturday. Tube: Brixton.
- Camden markets, Camden Town, NW1. Hectic connecting markets selling clothes, food, antiques, records, etc. Open: daily, but weekends are best (if crowded). Tube: Camden Town.
- Columbia Road market, E2. A colourful flower and plant market that can't help but cheer you up. A good place for Sunday brunch. Open: Sunday. Tubes: Old Street, Bethnal Green, Shoreditch.
- Greenwich market, SE10. An arts and crafts market, also selling second-hand clothes. Open: weekends. DLR stations: Greenwich, Cutty Sark.

- Petticoat Lane market, Middlesex and Wentworth Streets, E1. A centuries-old market with thousands of stalls, many selling clothes. A bit touristy. Open: Monday to Friday and Sunday. Tubes: Liverpool Street, Aldgate, Aldgate East.
- The Piazza, Covent Garden, WC2E. The famous market where the fictitious Eliza Doolittle sold flowers in *My Fair Lady*. You won't find many bargains, but there are lots of little speciality stores and stalls, and usually several excellent buskers. Open: daily. Tube: Covent Garden.
- Portobello Road market, Notting Hill, W11. Think of the movie *Notting Hill*. It's famous for its antiques but sells clothes and all sorts of other things. Open: Monday to Saturday, but Saturday is best. Tubes: Ladbroke Grove, Notting Hill, Westbourne Park.
- Riverside Walk market, under Waterloo Bridge, South Bank, SE1. Second-hand book stalls. Open: weekends and some weekdays, especially in summer. Tubes: Waterloo, Embankment.
- Smithfield market, 300 Charterhouse Street, EC1M. London's famous meat market, on a site where witches and traitors were once burned alive. Open: Monday to Friday, early mornings only. Tubes: Farringdon, Barbican.
- Spitalfields market, 65 Brushfield Street, E1. Housed in an enormous Victorian building, the stalls sell mostly clothes, crafts, second-hand books, junk and organic food. Open: Monday to Friday and Sunday. Tube: Liverpool Street.

Speciality shopping areas

London

There are several areas in London where speciality shops are clustered. Bookshops line Charing Cross Road, electronics stores clutter Tottenham Court Road, there are antique enclaves in Islington, Notting Hill, Kensington and Chelsea, jewellery-makers vie for trade at Hatton Garden, there are shoe shops galore around Covent Garden and in South Molton Street, Denmark Street has sheet music and musical instruments,

Soho has funky clothes and music, Kings Road has boutiques, and several camping and travel shops fight for business along Kensington High Street.

Rest of UK

Dozens of UK towns market themselves as 'the UK capital of (insert name of product here)'. With the exception of Hay-on-Wye, most wouldn't warrant a trip purely for the sake of the shopping, but they are worth a look if you're nearby. Predominant are: Hay-on-Wye in Wales and Micklegate and Fossgate in York for second-hand books; Birmingham's jewellery quarter; Bath for fudge and Sally Lunn buns; Ludlow in Shropshire for gourmet Michelin-starred restaurants; Saffron Walden in Essex and Ledbury in Hereford for antiques; Worcester in Worcestershire and Stoke-on-Trent in Staffordshire for porcelain; Nottingham for lace; Glastonbury in Somerset for New Age paraphernalia; St Ives in Cornwall for galleries and crafts; Spalding in Lincolnshire for factory shops; Ambleside and Keswick in the Lakes District and Fort William in Scotland for sporting and outdoor equipment; Arran in Scotland for cheese; Dufftown in Scotland for whisky.

Elite shopping

Got £50,000 to spend on a pair of earrings? Whether you do or not, it's fun to browse through the elite shops of London. You don't see anything like this in New Zealand — £10,000 Conway and Stewart pens, £1500 Gucci handbags, £234,000 Piaget watches, £220 Swaine Adeny Brigg umbrellas.

It won't surprise any Monopoly player that Mayfair is a good place to look. It's the retail playground for the ultra-wealthy. Take a jaw-dropping walk through Mayfair and Piccadilly. Savile Row is where most of the men in the royal family get their suits made. In New Bond Street and South Molton Street you'll find nestled in sparkling stores jewellers Tiffany & Co, Bulgari, De Beers, Cartier and Asprey & Garrard, and designers Gucci, Dolce & Gabanna, Yves Saint Laurent, Armani, Chanel, Prada, Ralph Lauren, Hermes and Versace, and shoemaker Jimmy Choo. In Kensington, Harrods has a spectacular jewellery department, where you might find the aforementioned £234,000 Piaget watch. Sloane Street, Knightsbridge is the home of haute couture — Christian Lacroix, Hermes, Prada, Dior, etc.

Auction houses

Even if you're not buying, it's interesting to take a peek at London's great elite auction houses, where the world's treasures change hands.

Most famous are:
- Bonhams (Montpelier Street, Knightsbridge, website www.bonhams.com);
- Christie's (8 King Street, SW1, website www.christies.com);
- Sotheby's (34 New Bond Street, W1, website www.sothebys.com).

Loyalty programmes

There are grumbles that loyalty schemes invade people's privacy, but they are big business in the UK. You get a membership card from a chain of stores and use it to earn points when you purchase. The stores do it because they can keep track of what you buy and compare it with your profile, and to encourage you to choose them over the competition. You'll do it because you can build up your points to exchange them for goods in the shop. The big ones are the Tesco supermarket chain's Clubcard, the Boots Advantage Card, and the Nectar card — which covers Sainsbury's supermarkets, Debenham's, Vodafone, BP and more. If you're not too worried about Big Brother watching you it's worth joining up early on in your stay, especially since you'll end up spending a lot of money at those ubiquitous stores. You can get some nice little freebies every now and then. Pound for pound, the Boots card has been judged the most generous of the loyalty schemes.

Cost of basics (£)

At the supermarket

Cornflakes, 1 kg	2.05
Rice, 1 kg	0.75
Spaghetti, 1 kg	0.58
Cadbury Dairy Milk chocolate, 200 g	1.89
Free-range eggs, six pack	0.77
Milk, two-pint bottle	0.58
Anchor butter, 500 g	1.54
Beef mince, 1 kg	2.58
Sirloin steak, 1 kg	11.49
Chicken breast fillet, 1 kg	13.27
Leg of lamb, approx. 2 kg	13.50
Salmon fillet, 480 g	5.99
Vanilla ice cream, 1 l	2.29
Braeburn apples, 1 kg	1.59
Bananas, 1 kg	0.74
Oranges, each	0.25
Broccoli, 1 kg	1.39
Carrots, 1 kg	0.55
New potatoes, 1 kg	0.99
Tomatoes, 1 kg	1.28
Surf washing powder, 1.1 kg	1.90
Cif cleaning cream	1.17
Palmolive soap, four-pack	0.99
Sunsilk normal shampoo, 200 ml	1.99

Source: Sainsbury's; January 2004

At the chemist

Tampax tampons regular, 30 pack	2.99
Durex Gossamer condoms, 12 pack	7.99
Nurofen tablets, 16 pack	0.99

Source: Boots the Chemist; January 2004

Other

Kodak ultra 36-exposure film	5.29
The Sun newspaper	0.30
The Times newspaper	0.50
Loaded magazine	3.30
Latest-release paperback	6.99
Latest-release CD	9.99

Sources: Boots the Chemist, Sainsbury's, Waterstone's, HMV; January 2004

12.
Getting your Kiwi fix

You'd have to be a robot not to get homesick occasionally during your stay in the UK. It's usually in the dark of winter when your friends and family in New Zealand are taunting you with tales about barbecues on the beach and Christmas Day beside the pool. It is hard not to get wistful now and then. And sometimes you'll feel the urge to relax with people who share your history and understand you innately. Don't feel guilty about wanting to hang out with Kiwis, or having occasional feelings of gloom about the UK. You can still enjoy the UK and pine for home. It happens to the best of us.

> London winters are legendary so it's not as if I didn't know what to expect. It wasn't the cold that got to me either. It was the unanticipated impact on my spirits of the short daylight hours and the weakness of what little sun there was. It was the greyness, the bleakness of a seemingly interminable winter in a city devoid of evergreen trees.
> — Christine Sheehy

Katherine Mansfield, who left New Zealand for the UK at the age of 20, went through periods of hating it passionately. She once wrote in her journal, 'No, I don't want England. England is of no use to me . . . I would not care if I never saw the English country again. Even in its flowering I feel deeply antagonistic towards it, and I will never change.'

Kiri Te Kanawa told Melbourne's *Herald-Sun* newspaper in 2003 that she had very, very few friends left in New Zealand, and found that sad.

Getting your Kiwi fix

'I think, now, it's the saddest part of my life, to have left my country for so many years,' she said.

You're not alone. But if you know how to get the occasional Kiwi fix you might find it easier to get through the tough times.

Antipodean media

Newspapers and magazines

New Zealand News UK is a free weekly newspaper that's been doing the rounds for more than 75 years. It has news and sport from home, and news and features about the New Zealand community in the UK. You can pick it up from stands outside Tube stations, antipodean shops and the like. To find your nearest distribution site, look on the website www.nznewsuk.co.uk or call them on 020 7582 3910. You can also take out a subscription for the cost of the postage; email subs@landor.co.uk.

TNT Magazine is a popular free glossy magazine aimed at young New Zealand, Australian and South African travellers. You'll have no trouble finding it in London — it's on every third street corner, or you can subscribe. Phone 020 7373 3377, email enquiries@tntmag.co.uk, website www.tntmag.co.uk. Its sister publication *SX* has some New Zealand content, but is aimed more towards Canadians.

Recruitment UK is a free quarterly job-hunters' magazine aimed at New Zealanders and others heading to the UK to work. To locate your nearest distribution point in the UK, look on the website. Their office is in the arcade under New Zealand House. Phone 020 7930 7777, email contact@recruitmentuk.net, website www.recruitmentuk.net.

In London is a magazine targeting antipodeans in the UK, backed by Australian writer and broadcaster Clive James. Find your nearest distribution point on www.inlondon.com or call 020 7557 4700.

LAM (Living Abroad Magazine) is another freebie found at Tube stations, but it has a broader target audience than the other magazines, so you'll find less New Zealand content. Phone 020 7005 2000, website www.lam-online.com.

Websites

In just a few years, the Gumtree, www.thegumtree.com, has become an antipodean institution in the UK. It's a website with stacks of listings for all sorts of things — flats, jobs, events, travel, stuff for sale, etc.

Other websites targeting New Zealanders in the UK are:

www.1stcontact.co.uk
www.ebigoe.com
www.nzuk.com
www.southern-cross-group.org
www.workgateways.com.
www.anzsac.com
www.kiwikingdom.com
www.sanza.co.uk
www.thefullquid.com

Television

Right Side Up TV, a dedicated New Zealand, Australian and South African television channel, was due to launch in mid-2004 on BSkyB, promising news, current affairs, sport and entertainment shows from New Zealand. BSkyB is free to Sky subscribers. Which means it's not really free at all, but there you go. Contact: email info@rightsideup.tv, website www.rightsideup.tv.

For information on connecting to Sky, see 'Communications and media'.

New Zealand/UK history

If you're interested in finding out more about the historic links between the UK and New Zealand within Britain, county by county, get a copy of *Guide for the New Zealand Traveller in Britain* by John McLean, published in 2002. It details where former New Zealand governors, prime ministers, premiers and the like came from, explains the links between New Zealand and British place names, maps out where New Zealand soldiers trained and recuperated in the world wars, etc. Look in a library, or write to the publisher, Winter Productions, at 37b New Cavendish Street, London W1G 8JR or 27 Euston Road, Wadestown, Wellington, New Zealand.

New Zealand media

New Zealand House at 80 Haymarket has an information point run by Tourism New Zealand, which houses stacks of recent New Zealand newspapers — the *New Zealand Herald*, the *Dominion Post*, the *Press*, the *Otago Daily Times* and the *Sunday Star-Times*. The papers can be a week or two old by the time new batches arrive, but the High Commission

Getting your Kiwi fix

provides a daily news sheet that summarises the news from New Zealand. From time to time Tourism New Zealand leaves free posters of stunning New Zealand scenery in the information point.

On the web, the best New Zealand media sites are www.stuff.co.nz; www.nzherald.co.nz; www.listener.co.nz; and www.tvnz.co.nz. The government website New Zealand connection (www.nzconnection.govt.nz) is designed to keep New Zealanders informed of government and business initiatives in New Zealand. And the website New Zealand edge (www.nzedge.com) is an interesting, intelligent site for the global Kiwi community.

New Zealand events

Waitangi Day, February 6

For most people in New Zealand, Waitangi Day is just a welcome day off near the end of summer. You only know it's Waitangi Day when you switch the news on at 6 pm and see the inevitable scenes of protest. In the UK it has become an innocent toast to our nationality, uncomplicated by the controversies that haunt it in New Zealand. It's a sometimes riotous celebration that can last three or four days, and through thousands of drunken renditions of Dave Dobbyn's 'Loyal', the theme tune for New Zealanders in London.

It's the little things you miss

- Steak and cheese pies
- Flat whites
- Feijoas
- Pineapple Lumps
- Krispa chicken chips
- Reduced cream and onion soup dip
- Marshmallow Easter eggs
- Chocolate fish
- Caramello chocolate
- Good eggs Benedict
- Roast pumpkin
- Sunday brunch
- Space
- Your Mum (when you're sick)
- The *Listener*
- Decent potato peelers
- Top-loading washing machines

In London, the annual events are:
- The New Zealand Society's Waitangi Day Dinner, a classy but fun affair held in a posh hotel (see below for contact details).
- The Waitangi Day Circle Line Pub Crawl (held on the weekend closest to Waitangi Day). It's usually loosely organised by an outfit called the New Zealand Party Embassy, email nzpartyembassy@hotmail.com, which will give you a choice of starting points. The crawl winds up with a haka in Trafalgar Square. Keep an eye on the antipodean publications for details.
- Kiwi bands and singers will often cash in on the nationalistic fervour by timing a tour to coincide with Waitangi Day. Look for advertisements in the antipodean publications.
- Any of the antipodean pubs (listed later in this chapter) will go off on Waitangi Day, but get to them early to avoid queuing.

> Everyone was so homesick, they loved everything we did. There were some magic moments there. I got all glassy-eyed when the local iwi gave it heaps at the start. When you see that kind of patriotism offshore it kind of moves you to understand your New Zealandness on another level.
> — Dave Dobbyn speaks to *New Zealand News UK* about performing at a Waitangi Day concert in Brixton, London

Anzac Day, April 25

Anzac Day starts off fittingly sombre in the UK, with dawn and lunchtime services in many towns and cities, and ends in a mess of high-spirited young New Zealanders and Australians in the antipodean pubs. An exhaustive list of events and services nationwide appears each year on the High Commission website www.nzembassy.com/uk. Another site with events listings is www.gallipoli-association.org. *New Zealand News UK* usually lists the services too.

In London, the highlights are:
- A dawn service at the Australian War Memorial in Hyde Park. There are plans to build a New Zealand war memorial nearby by 2005.
- A morning service at St Paul's Cathedral.
- A mid-morning service at the Cenotaph in Whitehall.
- An afternoon service at Westminster Cathedral. You'll need a (free) ticket from the New Zealand High Commission to get into the service.

Getting your Kiwi fix

- *TNT Magazine* hosts an Anzac Ball at Chelsea Village Hotel, London on the weekend nearest Anzac Day.
- There are often antipodean concerts and other events around Anzac Day. Keep an eye on the antipodean media.

There are a couple of dozen Anzac services outside London, held on or around April 25. For details, see the websites listed above.
Notable among them are:

- Arbroath, Scotland, where there are the graves of four New Zealand servicemen who died flying operations in World War II.
- Edinburgh: a service at the Scottish National War Memorial, Edinburgh Castle.
- Brockenhurst, Hampshire, where the No. 1 New Zealand General Hospital was based in World War I. In his *Guide for the New Zealand Traveller in Britain* (details above) John McLean writes that 14 of the recuperating New Zealand soldiers married girls in the village, and 93 were buried in the local church, Saint Nicholas.
- Cannock Chase, Staffordshire, where tens of thousands of New Zealanders trained for World War I and 71 New Zealand soldiers were buried.
- Walton on Thames, Sussex, where thousands of wounded New Zealand soldiers were treated at Mount Felix, a country house converted into the No. 2 New Zealand General Hospital in World War I. There's a New Zealand Avenue in the town and a pub called the Wellington. Nineteen Kiwi soldiers died at the hospital and are buried in St Mary's churchyard.

For services in Europe, see 'Travel on the Continent and beyond'.

Toast Life

The Toast Life New Zealand food and wine festival is held around July in southwest London. It's a relaxing day, with the best of New Zealand food, wine, entertainment, clothing and crafts on offer. Details are on the website www.toastfestivals.co.uk.

New Zealand art and music

There is a constant flow of tours by New Zealand bands, DJs and other musicians in the UK. They're usually listed in the antipodean publications, but keep an eye on *Time Out* as well, as some artists trying to break into the UK will skirt the antipodean networks. There is usually an exhibition by a New Zealand artist in the mezzanine floor of New Zealand house — details are on the High Commission website www.nzembassy.com/uk.

Getting tickets to All Blacks games

To get tickets to All Blacks games in the UK and Europe, go through the ticketing arm of the New Zealand Rugby Football Union, website www.stilrugby.com. You'll have to provide New Zealand passport details for everyone who's going — names, numbers and dates of issue. You can join a mailing list on the website to ensure you are notified when tickets are released.

> They usually post a date on the website that the tickets are available from and you have to get in early as they sell out bl**dy fast! The England tickets always go within a day. Have the rest of your family's passport details on hand to get one for any non-Kiwis you want to go with. Tickets are usually around £50 but can cost quite a lot more.
> — Adrian McCloy

For information on getting tickets to other sporting events, see 'Enjoying the UK'.

New Zealand shops

The poor deprived Britons haven't heard of Pineapple Lumps, Peanut Slabs or Burger Rings. They're only stocked at speciality shops catering to antipodeans.

The best of these is Kiwifruits The New Zealand Shop, in the Opera Arcade under New Zealand House, Haymarket, SW1:
  phone 0207 930 4587, email theteam@kiwifruitsnzshop.com,
  website www.kiwifruitsnzshop.com.
As well as New Zealand food, it does a good line in New Zealand books, music, magazines, clothing and jewellery. You can also order by email.
  Other shops stocking Kiwi food and beer are:
- The Downunder Centre, 12A High Road, NW10, phone 020 8451 8976, email downundercentre@hotmail.com.

Getting your Kiwi fix

- New Zealand Shop, 26 Henrietta Street, Covent Garden, WC2, phone 020 7836 2292, email shop@newzealandshop.uk.com, website www.newzealandshop.uk.com. You can also order online.
- SANZA online shop, www.sanza.co.uk/shop.
- Beers of Europe, an online store that sells New Zealand beer; phone 01553 812 000, email sales@beersofeurope.co.uk, website www.beersofeurope.co.uk.
- The website www.kiwihomesickpack.co.nz does a good line in gift boxes of Kiwi foods — always well received by homesick Kiwis overseas.
- The website www.nzedge.com has an online shop with a wide range of New Zealand food, music and gifts.

New Zealand fashion

For a range of New Zealand designer fashion, try Dunedinite Charlotte Smith's self-titled boutique at 160 Walton Street, West Brompton, London SW3; phone 020 7584 3223.

Buying gifts for people at home

It can be easier and cheaper to shop for friends and family back home through New Zealand websites, rather than send them presents from the UK. Some good websites are www.allblacks.com; www.beer.co.nz; www.ikoiko.co.nz, and www.thepantryshop.com.

Note that Father's Day and Mother's Day in the UK are on different dates from those in New Zealand. In New Zealand, Father's Day is the first Sunday in September and Mother's Day is the second Sunday in May. (In the UK, Mother's Day is in March and Father's Day is in June, so buy your cards then to really impress the folks.)

New Zealand cafés and restaurants in London

Gourmet Burger Kitchen

Gourmet Burger Kitchen (GBK) is a popular chain of burger stores in the gourmet Kiwi tradition, with a Kiwi burger complete with egg and beetroot (which Britons think is crazy), and a great selection of other huge, yummy burgers, served with tomato sauce in the good old tomato-shaped plastic bottles. Website www.gbkinfo.co.uk. The restaurants are at 331 West End Lane, West Hampstead, NW6, phone 020 7794 5455; 44 Northcote Road, Battersea, SW11 (near Clapham Junction), phone 020 7228 3309; 333 Putney Bridge Road, Putney, SW15, phone 020 8789 1199; 49 Fulham Broadway, Fulham, SW6, phone 020 7381 4242; and 131 Chiswick High Road, Chiswick, W4, phone 020 8995 4548.

Sugar Club

Set up in the mid-1980s by Wellingtonian Vivienne Hayman and Dunedinite Ashley Sumner, the Sugar Club has an outstanding reputation for Pacific-style fusion food. There are usually a few Kiwi-ish things on the menu, and top New Zealand wines on offer. You'll find it at 21 Warwick Street, Soho, W1; phone 020 7437 7776, website www.thesugarclub.co.uk. Bali Sugar is a spin-off restaurant at 33a All Saints Road, Notting Hill, W11, phone 020 7221 4477.

Suze of Mayfair and Suze Wine Bar

Kiwi couple Susan and Tom Glynn have two fantastic places in London with New Zealand food on the menu: Suze of Mayfair, 41 North Audley Street, W1, phone 020 7491 3237, and Suze Wine Bar, 1 Glentworth Street, NW1, phone 020 7486 8216, website www.suzewinebar.com.

Tapa Room and The Providores

Canny New Zealanders in London know that the best place for a leisurely coffee or brunch is renowned Kiwi chef Peter Gordon's Tapa Room café at 109 Marylebone High Street, W1. With a huge tapa cloth on the wall, New Zealand magazines to read, flat whites and fantastic Pacific Rim fusion cooking on the menu — including Vegemite soldiers with boiled eggs — it feels like a home away from Ponsonby Road or Cuba Street. Above the Tapa Room is the highly praised The Providores restaurant, co-owned by Gordon.

Website for both is www.theprovidores.co.uk; phone 020 7935 6175.

Truc Vert

Next door to Suze of Mayfair is Truc Vert, a cafe and gourmet deli with a touch of Kiwi; 42 North Audley Street, Mayfair, London W1, phone 020 7491 9988. The place to get great Anzac biscuits.

Getting your Kiwi fix

Antipodean pubs

They're not usually the classiest of establishments, but the antipodean pubs offer hours of stupid fun.

Walkabout

The most ubiquitous antipodean pubs are those of the Australian-themed Walkabout chain, and the most infamous of them is probably the one at 58 Shepherd's Bush Green, Shepherd's Bush; phone 020 8740 4339.

The Redback

The Redback Tavern in Acton is another stalwart — its free barbecues on Sunday afternoons in summer attract a good-natured young antipodean crowd, and things usually get out of hand when the sun goes down. The Redback is at 264 High Street, Acton, W3; phone 020 8896 1458; website www.redbacktavern.com.

The Church

The most notorious of all antipodean drinking attractions is The Church, so named not for its beliefs but because it's held every Sunday afternoon. It's fun but it's not pretty, and the heavy drinking culture has led many a Kiwi into disgrace. If you find yourself there for the fourth weekend in a row, head out the door immediately, take a tube to Heathrow and catch the first flight home. For your poor mother's sake. The Church is held at The Forum, 9-17 Highgate Road, Kentish Town, London NW5; phone 0800 3283450; website www.thechurch.co.uk.

Others

You'll find an antipodean pub in every antipodean neighbourhood of London. (In fact, you'll probably find that every pub in those suburbs has an antipodean clientele propping up the bar.) Some of the most popular are:

- Backpacker, 126 York Way, King's Cross, N1; website www.thebackpacker.co.uk.
- The Crown, 152 Cricklewood, Cricklewood, NW2.
- The Elusive Camel, 121 Lower Marsh, Waterloo; 186 Tooley Street, London Bridge, London SE1; cnr Wilton Road & Gillingham Street, Victoria, SW1; 31 Duke Street, W1; website www.elusivecamel.com.

- Polar Bear, 30 Lisle Street, near Leicester Square, WC2.
- Prince of Teck, 161 Earl's Court Road, SW5.
- Slug and Lettuce, 474 Fulham Road, Fulham, SW6.
- Southside Bar, 125 Cleveland Street, W1.
- The Spotted Dog, 38 High Road, Willesden, NW10.
- The Swan, 215 Clapham Road, Stockwell, SW9.
- World's End, 174 Camden High Road, Camden, NW1.

New Zealand clubs and societies

The surprising number of New Zealand clubs and societies in the UK is probably testament to the desire of expat New Zealanders to seek like-minded society. A nice bonus to belonging to one of these associations is that many meet in the penthouse function room of New Zealand House, which offers almost unparalleled 360-degree views of London. Events run by the groups are often listed on www.nzembassy.com/uk and in *New Zealand News UK*.

Sporting

AUSSIE–KIWI RUGBY LEAGUE IN LONDON CLUB
For armchair sports fans and spectators. Contact: London Broncos, phone 0871 222 1132, website www.londonbroncos.co.uk.

LONDON KIWIS RUGBY FOOTBALL CLUB
The London Kiwis club enters two teams in the Canterbury Shield (sponsored by the New Zealand clothing company). It's an amateur club, established in 1998 as a place where Kiwi rugby lovers could 'feel at home away from home'.
 Contact: phone 020 7629 1666, email alan@londonkiwis.com, website www.londonkiwis.com, address 28 South Molton Street, London W1.
 Canterbury Shield website www.kiwismail.com/canterburyshield, email canterburyshield@yahoo.co.uk.

LONDON NEW ZEALAND CRICKET CLUB
A club for New Zealand cricketers in the UK, established in 1951. It's a wandering side with a full season of matches, and holds social functions in southeast England. Contact: website www.lnzcc.org.

Getting your Kiwi fix

> **Words to the All Blacks' haka**
>
> | | English translation |
> |---|---|
> | Ka Mate! Ka Mate! | It is death! It is death! |
> | Ka Ora! Ka Ora! | It is life! It is life! |
> | Tenei te ta ngata puhuru huru | This is the hairy person |
> | Nana nei i tiki mai | Who caused the sun to shine |
> | Whakawhiti te ra | Keep abreast! Keep abreast |
> | A upane ka upane! | The rank! Hold fast! |
> | A upane kaupane whiti te ra! | Into the sun that shines! |
> | Hi! | |

LONDON NEW ZEALAND RUGBY FOOTBALL CLUB

Here's your chance to wear the silver fern: the London New Zealand club is said to be the only team permitted to wear the fern aside from New Zealand national sides. Established in 1926, the club welcomes New Zealand players. It is based in southwest London.

Contact: Clubhouse, phone 0208 578 1930; address Birkbeck Sports Ground Birkbeck Avenue, Greenford, Middlesex; website www.Inzrugby.co.uk.

Social

NEW ZEALAND IRELAND ASSOCIATION

Set up in 1987, the New Zealand Ireland Association hosts regular social events for New Zealanders in Ireland and Irish people with an interest in New Zealand.

Contact: email info@nzireland.com, website www.nzireland.com, or c/- New Zealand Consulate, 37 Leeson Park, Dublin 6; phone +353 1 660 4233.

NEW ZEALAND LONDON CONNECTIONS

NZ London Connections is a social and business network forum for New Zealanders and people with an affinity with New Zealand. It revolves around regular social evenings, usually held in the penthouse of New Zealand House, with high-profile New Zealand guest speakers, often from the sporting or entertainment worlds. You can take out an annual membership or go along to the functions as a guest for £10. London Connections is associated with the Kiwi Expat Association (details below).

Contact: website www.nzlc.org.uk.

THE NEW ZEALAND SOCIETY

The New Zealand Society started in 1927 as a dinner club in London. It has evolved into a wider social and cultural association, which organises regular social events. The Waitangi Day dinner is its biggest event — a classy affair held on the Friday closest to Waitangi Day at the Dorchester Hotel in Mayfair. Membership is open to New Zealanders living in Britain and Brits with an association with New Zealand. The society is based in London and has a lively branch in Scotland.

Contact: email nzsociety@hotmail.com, website www.nzsociety.co.uk.

NEW ZEALAND WOMEN'S ASSOCIATION

The New Zealand Women's Association was formed in 1930, with the aim of promoting the interests of New Zealand. The association usually meets every month for lunch at the penthouse function room of New Zealand House, with a prominent guest speaker, and hosts other events. Membership is open to women born in New Zealand, married to a New Zealander, or women otherwise interested in New Zealand who have the support of two members.

Contact: website www.nzwa.co.uk.

Professional

AUSTRALIA NEW ZEALAND CHAMBER OF COMMERCE

A membership-based organisation that provides information and assistance to businesses wishing to raise their profile within the British Australasian business community. ANZCC has more than 200 member companies; it helps members with the practicalities of running and promoting their business, organises regular networking events and provides information.

Contact: phone 0870 8900 720, email enquiries@anzcc.org.uk, website www.anzcc.org.uk

KIWI EXPAT ASSOCIATION (KEA)

Kea UK is the largest chapter in what has been termed 'New Zealand's global network', which spans 64 countries. Kea members are expats and others with an interest in New Zealand, from a wide range of backgrounds. Kea was set up to help members share knowledge, establish connections and pursue entrepreneurship and opportunities, while keeping them in touch and involved with business, investment, research and developments in New Zealand.

UK contact: email uk@kiwiexpat.org.nz, website www.kiwiexpat.org.nz.

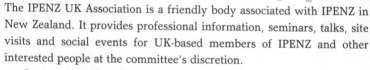

INSTITUTION OF PROFESSIONAL ENGINEERS NEW ZEALAND UNITED KINGDOM ASSOCIATION

The IPENZ UK Association is a friendly body associated with IPENZ in New Zealand. It provides professional information, seminars, talks, site visits and social events for UK-based members of IPENZ and other interested people at the committee's discretion.

Contact: email honsec@ipenz.org.uk, website www.ipenz.org.uk.

NEW ZEALAND DENTAL SOCIETY IN LONDON

The professional association for New Zealand dental professionals living and working in Europe. The society holds continuing professional education courses and occasional social events. Membership is open to graduates at any stage in their careers.

Contact: Kirsty Fiddes, phone 020 7680 1800 (work) or 07 788 413 188 (mobile), email nzdsl@hotmail.com or kirsty.fiddes@thedentalsurgery.co.uk, address The Dental Surgery, The Corn Exchange Building, 55 Mark Lane, London EC3R 7NE.

NEW ZEALAND INSTITUTE OF CHARTERED ACCOUNTANTS, UK BRANCH

The professional organisation for New Zealand accountants in Europe. It has around 2000 members — New Zealanders living permanently in the UK and Europe and those on working holidays. The branch offers professional development opportunities, various special interest group meetings, and hosts social events. There is also a Social Interest Group in Edinburgh, covering Scotland and the north of England.

Contact: email info@icanz.co.uk, website www.icanz.co.uk.

NEW ZEALAND LAWYER'S SOCIETY

The professional association for New Zealand lawyers in the UK. Meetings are held three to four times a year. Members' services are available to New Zealanders who need legal assistance in Britain and to British people who need legal assistance in New Zealand or with New Zealand law.

Contact: website www.nzls.co.uk.

NEW ZEALAND UNIVERSITIES GRADUATES ASSOCIATION

The association has more than 250 members and holds meetings attended by professional speakers.

Contact: for details, see the website www.nzembassy.com/uk.

Political

INTERNATIONALS

The UK branch of the New Zealand National Party. It hosts formal events and dinners with visiting National MPs.

Contact: for details, see the website www.nzembassy.com/uk.

Maori culture

TE KOHANGA REO O RANANA

A Maori language nest that meets every Saturday (excluding school holidays) at New Zealand House, London (4th floor), 10.30 am to 12.30 pm. It was established in 1997 by a group of New Zealanders who had settled in London and wanted their children to learn the Maori language. The focus of Te Kohanga Reo is te reo Maori, and activities include songs, stories, drama, games and art. They cater for children from birth to about ten years old. A koha of £2 per family each week is suggested as well as a plate of food to share at the end of the session. Everyone welcome.

Contact: Maina Thompson, phone 020 8777 6468,
email kohangareo_ranana@hotmail.com.

MARAMARA TOTARA

The London branch of Te Whare Tu Taua o Aotearoa, the New Zealand National School of Ancient Weaponry, founded in the 1980s by Dr Pita Sharples. Maramara Totara provides an innovative programme in physical fitness that encompasses Maori language, history, cultural values, Maori Atua, whakapapa, haka, karakia, waiata, and respect for all uses of Maori weaponry. It also promotes healthy lifestyles. The school teaches men, women and children of any age and ethnic background the use of the taiaha.

Contact: Kateia Burrows, 28 Alexandra Road, Wimbledon, London, phone 07 887 760 328, email kateiaburrows@yahoo.co.nz.

MATARIKI MAORI CULTURAL GROUP

A professional Maori dance troupe formed more than twenty years ago in New Zealand. Matariki works and entertains in the UK and Europe, 'sharing with respect and humility' all aspects of Maori music, song and dance, art, traditions and culture. Although it is a family-orientated cultural group, new members are welcome.

Contact: phone 020 8491 5889, email paniarose@hotmail.com.

NGATI RANANA LONDON MAORI CLUB

A non-profit organisation first created in the 1960s to give New Zealanders in the UK and other interested people the chance to teach, learn and participate in Maori culture: kapa haka, te reo, wananga and whanaungatanga. It also promotes New Zealand through Maori culture and language. Ngati Ranana has an average consistent membership of 40+ (including non-Kiwis), with new people coming to visit, participate and/or get a taste of home every week. Ngati Ranana meets each Wednesday from 6.30 pm on the 4th floor of New Zealand House for kapa haka followed by a brief welcome around 7.30 pm. There is also a kohanga reo (see above).

Contact: email ngatiranana@fsmail.net, website www.ngatiranana.org.uk, address Ngati Ranana, c/- New Zealand House, 80 Haymarket, London SW1Y 4TQ.

TE TAU (NEW SEASON)

A Maori performance group that aims to retain, enhance and promote Maori culture through song, dance and haka. Can also be hired for haka training sessions and to put down a hangi.

Contact: John, phone 07 949 029 622, email tetau@london.com, website www.tetau.com.

> ### Hinemihi marae
> The grounds of an 18th-century mansion in Surrey might seem an unlikely place to find a Maori marae. The Hinemihi marae, which survived the 1886 Mount Tarawera eruption, was shipped to the UK in 1892 by Lord Onslow, then outgoing New Zealand Governor-General. It's now in the gardens of Clandon House, a National Trust property in Guildford, Surrey. You can stroll through the mansion and the gardens for a small fee.
> Clandon House:
> phone 014 8322 2482
> email clandonpark@nationaltrust.org.uk
> website www.nationaltrust.org.uk/places/clandonpark.

Art and culture

NEW ZEALAND ARTS CLUB
An arts club for New Zealand artists, musicians and actors, which seeks to provide a permanent home for New Zealand arts in London.
Contact: Murray Rowlands, phone 020 7450 9235,
email murray.rowlands@morleycollege.ac.uk.

KAKAPO BOOKS
UK-based Kakapo Books supports and promotes research that seeks to examine, question and communicate developments in New Zealand culture. Published monographs and anthologies consider New Zealand literature, film, the media, music, art, theatre, lifestyles and consumer culture, sport, gender, race and ethnicity, identity, communities, history, tourism, globalisation, and the environment.
Contact: Ian Conrich, phone 0115 9846578,
email ian@ianconrich.co.uk, website www.kakapobooks.co.uk.

NEW ZEALAND STUDIES ASSOCIATION
The NZSA is an association for people interested in the social, cultural, political and economic study of New Zealand. It organises an annual conference in London, which attracts high-profile speakers. Research is published in a journal.

Contact: Ian Conrich, Chair NZSA, University of Surrey Roehampton, School of Humanities and Cultural Studies, Roehampton Lane, London SW15 5PH; phone 0115 9846578, email ian@ianconrich.co.uk, website www.richmond.ac.uk/nzsa.

ROYAL OVER-SEAS LEAGUE
The Royal Over-Seas League was founded in 1910 to foster international understanding and friendship. It has branches in London and Edinburgh. It organises Commonwealth art and music competitions.

Contact: phone 020 7408 0214, email info@rosl.org.uk, website www.rosl.org.uk, London base Over-Seas House, Park Place, St James's Street, SW1A 1LR.

> Some OEs had involved loneliness, homesickness, alienation, unemployment, job dissatisfaction, homelessness, poverty, relationship traumas, even muggings. Yet these were overwhelmed by the positives of OE and were typically described as 'growth experiences'.
> — Barbara Myers and Kerr Inkson, in *The Big OE: How it works and what it can do for New Zealand*

Homesickness remedies

Often the best way to deal with the inevitable homesickness is to do something to remind yourself why you've come all this way. Go sightseeing in London, go to Paris on Eurostar for a day, or take a cheap flight anywhere else on the Continent for a weekend. If you live in London sometimes just getting out can help. If loneliness is your problem, book an antipodean bus tour in Europe or the UK, or move into an enormous antipodean flat, where you can meet others who may not know many people in the UK.

Other remedies:
- Attend a function in the penthouse of New Zealand House (see 'New Zealand clubs and societies', above).
- Delve into the New Zealand newspapers at the Information Point at New Zealand House.
- Have a flat white and Vegemite soldiers at the Tapa Room (see 'New Zealand cafés and restaurants in London', above).

The Big OE Companion

- Spend a Sunday afternoon at the Redback Tavern *(see 'Antipodean pubs', above)*.
- Go to Europe with a friend for a city break.
- Play a game of touch rugby *(see 'Health, fitness and sport')*.
- Gorge yourself on a packet of Pineapple Lumps.
- Get a book of New Zealand poetry or short stories. Even if you've never appreciated it before, a poem by A. R. D. Fairburn or short story by Witi Ihimaera can epitomise New Zealand like nothing else.
- Take a one-way flight to New Zealand.
- Get the *Whale Rider* video out and wallow in a good cry.

> **ANZSAC/ANZSAF/SANZA explained**
>
> You'll probably come across these terms in London. It's a way of including South Africans and Canadians in the Kiwi and Australian club. ANZSAC means Australian, New Zealand, South African and Canadian. ANZSAF is Australian, New Zealand and South African. SANZA is South African, New Zealand and Australian. Antipodean tends to encompass everyone from the Southern Hemisphere.

13. New Zealand government in the UK and Europe

From time to time, you may need contact with official New Zealand agencies.

New Zealand House

New Zealand House, near Trafalgar Square, is home to several New Zealand government departments and agencies, including the New Zealand High Commission. It's not the most delicate building in the West End, but when it was built in the 1960s the 69-metre-high structure was considered a breakthrough in concrete and glass architecture. There's an enormous, stunning Maori carving by the late carver and singer Inia Te Wiata in the foyer — completed by his sons after his death — and a penthouse function room with great views over the Thames and the West End.

Tucked in the arcade behind the building are Kiwifruits The New Zealand Shop and the headquarters of the newspaper *Recruitment UK*.

The Big OE Companion

On the ground floor is an Information Point with recent New Zealand newspapers set up in a reading area (open 8 am to 6 pm weekdays), and an Air New Zealand office.

In the 1960s and 1970s New Zealand House was a real home away from home for New Zealanders, with a mail service, a cafeteria, a community notice board and a big library. It still holds a few attractions for New Zealanders — the newspaper room, regular New Zealand art exhibitions and the penthouse function room — but these days it's more of a functional New Zealand government building.

> New Zealand House
> 80 Haymarket
> London SW1Y 4TQ
> Nearest Tube station: Piccadilly

The New Zealand High Commission

Role of the High Commission

The High Commission represents the New Zealand Ministry of Foreign Affairs in the UK — managing New Zealand's political, economic and trade relations with the United Kingdom and Ireland. For New Zealanders in the UK, the important functions of the High Commission are consular and information services.

You will deal with the staff there if:

- You need a New Zealand legal document — an affidavit, affirmation, statutory declaration etc. — witnessed or certified. There's a small fee involved. For details see www.nzembassy.com/uk.
- You are involved in an accident, are hospitalised, arrested or detained and need guidance (although they can't pull out a diplomatic badge to bust you out of jail or send in a helicopter if you fall down Ben Nevis). Always deal with the local authorities first.
- You lose a bag or wallet containing your New Zealand passport or driver's licence or similar. There's a slight possibility it could end up making its way to the High Commission.
- You are making arrangements following the death of a New

Zealander in the UK or Ireland. The New Zealand High Commission's consular staff can provide guidance if you need it.
- You are getting married in the UK and you want to have it witnessed so you can have a New Zealand marriage certificate.

If you lose your passport you'll deal with the Department of Internal Affairs Identity Services Office in New Zealand House (see below).

> **The New Zealand High Commission — contact details**
> Phone 020 7930 8422
> email email@newzealandhc.org.uk
> website www.nzembassy.com/uk
>
> The website should always be your first point of call for enquiries. And if you're planning to visit the New Zealand High Commission or the passports office, always check opening hours for the relevant service on the website.

Registering with the High Commission

New Zealand diplomatic posts overseas are increasingly encouraging New Zealanders to register with them while they are in the country, in case of emergencies — such as your mum calling up all worried because you haven't emailed in a week and there's been a terrorist attack in Outer Mongolia. You give them basic contact details and your passport number. In the UK you can do this online at www.nzembassy.com/uk. Don't forget to update your details if they change.

Information office

The New Zealand High Commission has an information office which can help with general enquiries from New Zealanders in the UK. Information office opening hours are limited.

However, before you contact the office:
- Check if your question can be answered on its thorough website www.nzembassy.com/uk. It has all sorts of information and links.
- If you have queries relating to the UK or Ireland, you should contact the appropriate organisation in that country.

- If you need to contact the New Zealand government or a department or agency, you might find what you are looking for on the government website www.govt.nz. There are also tourism, immigration and trade representatives in New Zealand House (contact details below) who you can contact directly.
  Information office contacts:
  phone 0207 316 8989, email email@newzealandhc.org.uk.
  Written enquiries can be addressed to: The Information Officer, New Zealand High Commission, New Zealand House, 80 Haymarket, London SW1Y 4TQ. It's best to telephone or email the office before visiting in person.

Library

The New Zealand High Commission has a small library of New Zealand general interest books and some magazines — opening hours are limited (see www.nzembassy.com/uk). You can also buy magazines at Kiwifruits The New Zealand Shop *(see 'Getting your Kiwi fix')*. The High Commission once had a much larger library but the collection was gifted to Edinburgh University. New Zealand books can be sought on interloan from Edinburgh University Library, 21 George Street, Edinburgh EH8 9LD, phone 0131 650 1000, website www.edinburgh.ac.uk.

Honorary consuls

There are also honorary consuls in Northern Ireland and Scotland, although it's best to contact the High Commission in London for most queries. In 2004 the honorary consuls were:

BELFAST
New Zealand Honorary Consul Jill McIvor, Ballance House, 118a Lisburn Road, Glenavy, Co Antrim, BT29 4NY, phone 028 9264 8098, email ballancenz@aol.com.

EDINBURGH
New Zealand Honorary Consul Iain Scott, 5 Rutland Square, Edinburgh EH1 2AS, phone 0131 222 8109, email iwscott@blueyonder.co.uk.
For details of embassies and consulates elsewhere in Europe, see below.

New Zealand government in the UK and Europe

Other New Zealand government agencies in New Zealand House

Defence

It's unlikely you'll need to personally call out the New Zealand Defence Force while you're in the UK, but they have a post in New Zealand House; phone 020 7930 8400, email nzdeflon@dircon.co.uk.

Department of Internal Affairs Identity Services Office

You're most likely to deal with the Identity Services Office if your passport is lost or stolen. You can apply for a replacement passport through the office.

LOST OR STOLEN PASSPORTS

If your passport has been lost or stolen, you should immediately report it to your local police and get a police report.

The standard replacement service takes ten days, or there's an urgent three-day service. In 2004 the standard service cost £45 for an adult, and double that for the urgent service. You will need to fill in the PAS/OS 'Application for a New Zealand Passport' form, which you can download from www.nzembassy.com/uk, or get by emailing passports@dia.govt.nz, from New Zealand House, or by calling 020 7930 8422.

If you have a UK work permit or similar you'll need to apply to the Home Office to get it stamped into your new passport.

Contact: The Home Office Immigration Department, 40 Wellesley Road, Croydon, CR9 2AR; phone 0870 606 7766, www.homeoffice.gov.uk.

New Zealand Immigration Service

You'll deal with the Immigration Service if you want to take a British partner to New Zealand to live, and need a Spouse Visa for him/her.

Call centre 09069 100 100, email info@immigration.govt.nz, website www.immigration.govt.nz.

Tourism New Zealand

Tourism New Zealand has an office in New Zealand House; phone 020 7930 1662, call centre 09069 101010, website www.purenz.com.

New Zealand Trade and Enterprise

May be able to help if you are trying to bring a New Zealand product into the UK; phone 020 7973 0380, email london@nzte.govt.nz, website www.nzte.govt.nz.

Voting in New Zealand elections

A voting booth is set up in New Zealand House in London for every New Zealand general election. Because of the time difference it's not actually open on election day, but for three weeks beforehand. If you can't get there you can apply to Elections New Zealand to cast a postal or email vote. You can enrol online. You must have at least visited New Zealand in the past three years to vote.

Details: Elections New Zealand, Electoral Enrolment Centre,
PO Box 190, Wellington 6015, New Zealand
phone +64 4 801 0700
email enrol@elections.org.nz (for enrolment enquiries) or
vote@elections.org.nz (for voting enquiries)
website www.elections.org.nz.

Keep an eye on www.embassy.com/nz in the lead-up to an election for further instructions.

> ### Voting in UK elections
> Once you have lived in the UK for a year, you can enrol to vote. Some New Zealanders have found it handy to be on the UK electoral roll for identification and credit check purposes. Commonwealth citizens aged over 18 are eligible to vote in the UK.
>
> You can download a voter registration form from the Electoral Commission website, www.electoralcommission.gov.uk.

New Zealand diplomatic posts in Europe

If you get into strife while travelling, you can seek help from New Zealand's Ministry of Foreign Affairs posts and overseas representatives. The embassies and consulates in Europe are listed below.

New Zealand government in the UK and Europe

For representatives in other countries, look on the website www.mfat.govt.nz before you travel.

You can email the embassies in advance to tell them basic contact details and travel plans just in case — especially useful if you're entering a volatile area. It's a good idea to note their contact details before you travel. They can't always sort your life out for you, but they can help you to help yourself.

They can assist with:

- Issuing a manual passport if yours is lost or stolen. (The replacement passport will be valid for only 12 months. Outside New Zealand, only the New Zealand High Commission in London or Sydney can issue full-validity, machine-readable passports.)
- Helping you contact relatives or friends back home to arrange a money transfer, if you get into financial difficulties.
- Providing you with a list of English-speaking lawyers in the case of detention or arrest, and helping you contact family and friends.

They cannot:

- Pay your hotel, travel or other bills, bail or medical expenses.
- Help you with arrangements that could be handled by local organisations — banks, lawyers, travel agents, undertakers.
- Give you legal advice or get you out of prison.
- Get you better conditions in prison or hospital than a local would receive.
- Give you a loan, other than in a real emergency and only after consultation with family and friends in New Zealand.
- Trace missing persons or investigate a crime.
- Operate a personal mail service for you.

Many of the embassies and high commissions listed take responsibility for more than one country. For information, check out the Ministry of Foreign Affairs website, www.mfat.govt.nz, and the website for New Zealand embassies, www.nzembassy.com. Details are correct for 2004.

For more information, contact: Consular Division, Ministry of Foreign Affairs and Trade, Stafford House, 38–42 The Terrace, Wellington, phone +64 4 494 8500, email cons@mfat.govt.nz.

AUSTRIA
Vienna: New Zealand Consulate-General, K1 Neusiedlerstrasse 23B, A — 2041 Fischamend, Austria
phone +43 2 2327 6632; email p.sunley@aon.at.

BELGIUM
Brussels: New Zealand Embassy, Square de Meeus, 1, 1000 Brussels; phone +32 2 512 1040; email nzemb.brussels@skynet.be; website www.nzembassy.com/belgium.
Antwerp: New Zealand Consulate, Braderijstraat 15 (cnr Grote Markt), 2000 Antwerpen 1; phone +32 3 233 1608; email primepacific@acom.be.

CROATIA
Zagreb: New Zealand Consulate, Hrvatska Matica Iseljenika, Trg Stjepana Radica 3, Zagreb 1000; phone +385 1 6151 382 or +385 1 6115 116; email nzealandconsulate@matis.hr.

CYPRUS
Nicosia: New Zealand Consulate, Kondalaki 6, 1090 Lefkosia, Nicosia; phone +357 22 818 884; email tony.c@actionprgroup.com.

FINLAND
Helsinki: New Zealand Consulate, phone +358 2 470 1818; email paddais@paddais.net.

FRANCE
Paris: New Zealand Embassy, 7ter, rue Leonard de Vinci, 75116 Paris; phone +33 1 4501 4343; email nzembassy.paris@wanadoo.fr; website www.nzembassy.com.

GERMANY
Berlin: New Zealand Embassy, Atrium Friedrichstrassem, Friedrichstrasse 60, 10117 Berlin; phone +49 30 206210;
email nzembassy.berlin@t-online.de; website www.nzembassy.com.
Hamburg: New Zealand Consulate-General, Zurich Haus, Domstrasse 19, 20095 Hamburg; phone +49 40 442 5550;
email hamburg@nzte.govt.nz.

New Zealand government in the UK and Europe

GREECE

Athens: New Zealand Consulate-General, 268 Kifissias Avenue, 15232 Halandri, Athens; phone +30 210 6874 700; email costas.cotsilinis@gr.pwc.com.

HUNGARY

Budapest: New Zealand Consulate, Teréz krt 38, 1066 Budapest phone +36 1 42 82 208; email nzconsul@freestart.hu.

IRELAND

(The New Zealand High Commission in London is responsible for Ireland.)
Dublin: New Zealand Consulate-General, 37 Leeson Park, Dublin 6, Republic of Ireland; phone +353 1 660 4233; email nzconsul@indigo.ie.

ITALY

Rome: New Zealand Embassy, Via Zara 28, Rome 00198 phone +39 06 441 7171; email nzemb.rom@flashnet.it; website www.nzembassy.com.
Milan: New Zealand Consulate-General, Via Guido d'Arezzo 6, 20145 Milan; phone +39 02 4801 2544; email charles.haddrell@nzte.govt.nz.

MALTA

Valleta: New Zealand Consulate, Villa Hampstead, Oliver Agius Street, Attard, Valletta, BZNO3; phone +351 21 435 025; email jill.camilleri@mail.com.

THE NETHERLANDS

The Hague: New Zealand Embassy, Carnegielaan 10, 2517 KH The Hague; phone +31 70 346 9324; email nzemb@xs4all.nl; website www.nzembassy.com/netherlands.

NORWAY

Oslo: New Zealand Consulate-General, Billingstadsletta 19B, Asker, Olso; phone +47 6677 5330.

POLAND

Warsaw: New Zealand Consulate, Ul. Grecka 3, 03 971 Warsaw; phone +4822 672 8069; email office@nzconsul.pl; website www.nzconsul.pl.

RUSSIA

Moscow: New Zealand Embassy, 44 Ulitsa Povarskaya (formerly Vorovskovo), Moscow 121069; phone +7 095 956 3579 or 956 3580; email nzembmos@online.ru; www.nzembassy.msk.ru.

SLOVENIA

Ljubljana: New Zealand Consulate, Lek d.d, Verovskova 57, S1 1526 Ljubljana; phone +386 1 580 3055; email janja.bratos@lek.si.

SPAIN

Madrid: New Zealand Embassy, 3rd floor, Plaza de La Lealtad 2, 28014 Madrid; phone +34 91 523 0226; email nzembmadrid@santandersupernet.com; website www.nzembassy.com.

Barcelona: New Zealand Consulate, 4th floor, Travesera de Gracia 64, 08006 Barcelona; phone +34 93 209 0399.

SWEDEN

Stockholm: New Zealand Consulate-General, Norrlandsgatan 15, 103 95 Stockholm; phone +46 8 506 3200; email michael.frie@twobirds.com.

SWITZERLAND

Geneva: New Zealand Consulate-General, 2 Chemin des Fins, Grand Saconnex, Geneva 19; phone +41 22 929 0350; email mission.nz@itu.ch.

TURKEY

Ankara: New Zealand Embassy, Level 4, Iran Caddesi 13, Kavaklidere 06700, Ankara; phone +90 312 467 9054/6/8; email newzealand@superonline.com.

Istanbul: New Zealand Honorary Consulate-General, Inonu Caddesi No 92/3 80090 Taksim, Istanbul; phone +90 212 244 0272; email nzhonconist@hatem-law.com.tr.

14. Tracing your family history

about four-fifths of New Zealanders are of European origin, predominantly from the British Isles, according to Statistics New Zealand. So there's a good chance you're one of them.

Getting started

Get as much information from your immediate family as possible before embarking on family tree research. If you have names, dates and places for the British people you're descended from you can search for public records in the UK to fill in the gaps, using documents such as census material and birth, marriage and death certificates.

For example, if you know your great-grandfather came from a certain town in the UK and you know roughly when he was born, you can search for his birth certificate (in the local parish archives or by mail through the General Register Office), on which his parents' names will be listed. You can then trace them back, and so on.

More information

The British High Commission in Wellington has an exhaustive list of public record offices and other useful contacts on its website www.britain.org.nz.

You can also get advice and help (sometimes for a fee) from:

- Society of Genealogists, phone 020 7251 8799, website www.sog.org.uk.
- The Institute of Heraldic and Genealogical Studies, phone 012 2776 8664, website www.ihgs.ac.uk.
- Federation of Family History Societies, website www.ffhs.org.uk.
- The Scots Ancestry Research Society, phone 013 1552 2028, website www.scotsanc.co.uk.
- The Honourable Society of Cymmrodorion (Wales), phone 020 7631 0502, website www.cymmrodorion1751.org.uk.
- Ulster Historical Foundation (Northern Ireland), phone 028 9033 2288, website www.ancestryireland.co.uk.

15.
Travel on the Continent and beyond

at some time during your stay in the UK a British person will ask you why the hell you're living here when you could be in the paradise that is New Zealand. Say it's because of the British climate and the fabulous customer service. The real answer is, of course, the Continent.

Europe covers an area about the size of Australia, but it's far more than the sum of its land mass. It will assail your senses. From the sweet smell of tulips in spring in the Netherlands to the stink of urine in the streets of Paris in summer. From the haunting tune of the fado singer in a Lisbon bar to the cacophony of traffic in Rome. From the unaccountable magic of the simplest and freshest food in Tuscany to an expensive stale sandwich on a budget airline. From the silky turquoise waters of the Croatian coast to the bedbug-ridden room in a dodgy hostel. From beautiful classical architecture to the Soviet-era slums of Russia.

It can be expensive and hard work, but it is always interesting and rewarding. The advice below is by no means an exhaustive guide to European travel. It's more of an added-value list of travel tips, to complement what's in your Europe guidebook and help you make the most of your time and money.

The Big OE Companion

Planning

The beauty of living in the UK is that you don't have to do Europe in one go. A day trip here, a weekend there, a month here, a summer there. There are certain places you shouldn't miss, but don't get too obsessed with following a tick sheet of places to go. People will tell you, 'You haven't been to Europe unless you've been to (insert place name here),' but you might find your nirvana somewhere else. You won't know unless you follow your own nose.

Timing

Most places in Europe are worth seeing at any time of year, but it's best to avoid the biggest tourist magnets in the height of summer (late June to late August), when the air can be stifling, accommodation scarce and expensive, and public transport packed. Europeans tend to take their holidays en masse in July and August, so you'll be fighting them for rooms, views and restaurant tables.

The big festivals of Europe

January	La Tamborada, San Sebastian, Spain Northern Lights, Scandinavia
February	Snow Carnival, Avoriaz, France Carnevale, Venice
March	St Patrick's Day, best celebrated in Ireland, naturally
April	Feria de Abril (April fair), Seville, Spain Queen's Day, Amsterdam, the Netherlands
May	Cannes Film Festival, France
June	Midsummer celebrations, Finland, Sweden, Norway Rock festival, Roskilde, Denmark
July	Il Palio (a horse race), Siena, Italy (also in August) Wife Carrying World Championships, Sonkajarvi, Finland

Travel on the Continent and beyond

In the shoulder seasons — April, May, September and October — the kids are at school, the students are at university and the grown-ups are at work, yet the skies are often clear, if inclement, and the travelling cheaper.

And certainly don't discount travelling in winter, when the queues are far smaller and the air just feels clearer. And there's a romance that is missing at other times of year — Christmas markets in Vienna, ice-skating in Moscow, deserted streets in Venice, a cosy restaurant in Paris, skiing in the French alps, frozen forests in Finland — or you can just hole up in a German beerhall and drink yourself warm.

If you're flying out of the UK on a bank holiday be prepared for massive queues at the airports and expect flight delays.

Guidebooks

The most popular guidebooks for independent travel in Europe are *Rough Guides* and the ubiquitous *Lonely Planet*. They're well tried and tested,

July *(cont.)*	Bastille Day, France
	Fiesta de San Fermin (The Running of the Bulls), Pamplona, Spain
	Berlin Love Parade, Germany
	Galway Arts Festival, Ireland
August	Il Palio (a horse race), Siena, Italy
	La Tomatina tomato fight, Valencia, Spain
September	Oktoberfest, Munich, Germany (until early October)
	Festes de la Merce, Barcelona
October	Oktoberfest continues
November	Christmas markets (most notably in Vienna and in German cities and towns)
December	Christmas markets continue.

For UK festivals, see 'Enjoying the UK'.

which has many advantages in saving you time and money and keeping you safe, but it follows that if hordes of people are reading them then hordes of people are going to be staying at the hostels and other accommodation they recommend. Buy one by all means, and use it as a baseline, but don't be scared to check out a town or hostel that's not listed. You might find the next big thing — and it might be far less crowded. A good lesser-known alternative is *Time Out* city guides.

(It's an interesting exercise to flick through the *Lonely Planet* and *Rough Guides* New Zealand editions. You'll find that they recommend towns you wouldn't send your grandmother to on a garden tour, for fear she'd get bored.)

A handy pocket-sized option for Europe is the *Inside-Out* city guides. These can be picked up from WH Smith (often in the airport on your way to your plane) and contain two or three easy fold-out maps on the left and annotated information on where to go, what to see, where to eat and shop, etc. Ideal for that long weekend to Venice, Malta or Amsterdam, and a great advantage over lugging your heavy *Lonely Planet* or *Rough Guide* with you, if you've already sorted accommodation. And it's up to you whether or not you use the dinky travel compass that accompanies it (not its most useful feature!).

— Kushla McIndoe

Travel insurance

You're taking an enormous risk if you don't have travel insurance. The market for insurance in the UK is extremely competitive. You'll probably want some kind of annual multi-trip insurance, which covers you for multiple trips to Europe, each trip up to a maximum number of days. Standard annual multi-trip insurance should cost you about £50. As with any kind of insurance, read the fine print. There can be all sorts of exceptions and catches — for instance, if your gear gets stolen from a car at night or if there are current travel warnings about your destination from the British government you might not be covered. Make sure you're covered if you're going to be skiing or doing other adventure sports, check the excess (you can buy a lower excess) and make sure it covers expensive items such as a camera and jewellery.

Travel insurance firms court New Zealanders through the antipodean publications, and they regularly advertise in the Tube. Shop around, and don't buy it with your holiday — that's usually the most expensive way.

A couple of tried and tested firms are:

- Kiwi-owned Downunder Insurance,
  phone 0800 393 908 (+44 207 402 9211 from overseas),
  email info@duinsure.com, website www.duinsure.com.
- Travelplan Direct, phone 08707 747 377,
  website www.travelplan-direct.co.uk.

Note the emergency contact phone numbers, and keep them with your travel insurance documents.

For more advice, go to the Association of British Insurers website www.abi.org.uk or the Consumer Association website www.which.net.

Travel warnings

Keep an eye on the New Zealand Ministry of Foreign Affairs and Trade website www.mfat.govt.nz for travel warnings. Cross-check with its British counterpart, the Foreign and Commonwealth Office, www.fco.gov.uk.

Visas

New Zealanders can get into most countries in Europe without a visa. The exceptions are some former Communist bloc countries. Visa policies change, so it pays to check with that country's embassy in the UK before you book a ticket.

Leave a record

Before you leave, photocopy the identity page of your passport, the page with your UK visa, and your airline tickets, and write down on a piece of paper your passport details, visa details, bank and credit card emergency phone numbers, travel insurance details, traveller's cheque numbers, phone numbers of some friends and family members, airline ticket details, itinerary, etc. Photocopy it twice. Leave one copy with someone in London and carry two with you, one in your day bag, the other in your main bag.

Flight/hotel packages

For short trips, booking a flight and hotel together can be a hassle-free way to travel in Europe, and you can get some great deals, especially in the shoulder season. The big newspapers often sponsor good specials or you can try these websites: www.lastminute.com, www.expedia.com, www.statravel.co.uk, www.cheaptickets.co.uk and www.ebookers.co.uk, or a travel agent. Before you book, test the deal by checking the costs of booking your flight and accommodation separately, over the internet. And always check the location of the accommodation.

Money

Euro

The dominant euro has been blamed for pulling up prices in formerly cheap countries but it does make the logistics of travelling easier. No longer do you have to hurriedly change currencies between countries, and end up with a pile of useless (if interesting) coins at the end of your trip, and no longer do you have to stand at a stall doing complicated equations to figure out how much something costs. However, don't get blasé and assume every country you arrive in uses the euro — even within the EU several countries are still holding out. Check first.

Most other European currencies are fully convertible, which means you can change them readily across the Continent. The exception is coins — even if a coin is worth a lot of money in its country of origin, or you have £20 worth of them, you probably won't be able to get them changed — buy yourself a treat before you cross the border. You lose money in commission and other charges every time you convert, so it's cheaper in the long run to change bigger amounts. The cheapest place to change money is usually a bank. The most expensive is usually a hotel.

Credit cards

Don't let your credit card out of your sight when a transaction is being processed — it's easy for a dodgy shop assistant to swipe your card twice and forge your signature. And check your credit card bills regularly.

ATMs

In the age of the ATM it's no longer necessary to change all your trip money in the UK before you leave for Europe — you can usually get a stash of local currency at a money machine when you arrive. However, some airports and other ports don't have them, so it's a good idea to keep some readily changeable sterling or euro notes with you. (The UK post office will change currency for no commission.) Some of the more primitive countries only have ATMs in main cities or don't have them at all. Check first. You will be charged for each ATM transaction — and withdrawing money by credit card can be costly.

Tipping

Tipping is more commonplace in Europe than in the UK. At a restaurant or bar, check the receipt to see if there is a service charge. If there is, don't tip. If not, you can round up the bill or add about ten percent.

Communications

Internet

You'll find internet points everywhere in Europe. Often they're free at tourist offices and public libraries. It's especially comforting if you're travelling alone to be able to converse — even virtually — with people you've known for more than a few hours. But it's very easy to get addicted to checking emails, to the extent that you might find yourself organising your day around your emailing time — a recipe for homesickness. If this is you, set yourself internet-free days to force yourself to go out and smell the roses without thinking of home.

Phones

It can be very tempting to use your UK mobile phone in Europe, since it's so convenient. But be aware of how much you're paying for it. In some countries it can cost you a pound to send a text message, and receiving calls while you're in Europe can drain your money faster than a Moroccan scam artist. It is usually far cheaper to have an international calling account or card *(see 'Communications and media')*, or to buy a public phonecard in the country you're visiting.

Cycle touring

Cycle touring through Europe is a great healthy, environmentally friendly, demanding and rewarding way to travel. You meet like-minded people along the way and tour together for a couple of days. You get an authentic tourist experience and see things you wouldn't see if you were in a vehicle or train. We were invited for dinner with locals and came close to the wildlife. Getting lost, changing plans and learning to adapt and overcome the obstacles is all part of the fun.

I travelled without maps or guidebooks. Had a plan from looking at a children's picture atlas to travel east across Belgium and the southern tip of the Netherlands into Germany until I hit the Rhine. Judging east by the sun's position in the sky was a challenge on overcast days. Once hitting the Rhine I planned to travel south through Germany, France and Switzerland, following its banks. I discovered great cycle paths and no traffic. Once in Schaffhausen, Switerzland I left the Rhine with no real idea of how I would make it to the Danube River. My plan had been to rely on asking locals, which cycle touring, as I found, necessitates you to do.

However, before I had the chance to do this, luck would have it that I came across a small village hotel and decided I needed a beer pretty badly after covering 147 km that day. I ordered the local beer, Furstenburg Pilsener, and took the only table alfresco. When I say I travelled without any guide I'm lying a little. I did carry one guidebook, Michael Jackson's *Pocket Beer Book*. While enjoying the beer I looked up its entry and discovered that 'the Furstenburgs are aristocrats of note who have been brewing beer for 500 years'. The family had a collection of German masterpieces in the Furstenburg Museum at the palace of Donaueschingen in the Black Forest. 'In the palace grounds the Danube emerges from its underground source,' the guide said. Breakthrough! I just needed to get to Donaueschingen and from there I could then follow the Danube. I cycled until my departure date loomed, then caught the nearest train to the airport.

The Netherlands has to be the best first-time tour. Their cycle paths are more like cycle highways, with directions, dual lanes, and cars giving way. My best ride would have to be in Italy, once away from the big cities cruising through the hill-top towns.

Tips for cycle-touring

- Weight is vital — the lighter the better. Decide what you want to take then halve it.
- Eat salty food to replace salts lost through perspiration.
- The European continent is well serviced by cycle shops and it is a lot cheaper to buy supplies there than in England.
- Always carry water (cemeteries always have taps).
- Carry tools and spare parts — long-nose pliers, bike multitool, small adjustable spanner, screwdriver (multihead attachments), spare spokes, tire puncture repair kit.
- Check that the trains you plan to take will carry bikes.
- Use a dish cloth as a towel as it holds heaps of water and wrings out easily and dries quickly.
- Don't take cooking equipment as this is unnecessary weight and part of the experience is tasting the local cuisine. Don't ride past a supermarket, always have food on you, as you never know when you may have to stop or have a problem. Supermarkets are relatively cheap.
- Carry a roll-up grass mat as there are a lot of little biting insects in the grass.
- Make sure you have an ergonomically designed saddle.
- Carry a citronella candle and take insect repellant.
- Take a torch and spare batteries, a sink plug, compass, a good guidebook.
- Make sure your bike has had a service and is in tip-top condition.
- Flowing soap can double as your clothes wash and hair wash.

— Philip Lash

The Big OE Companion

Transport tips

Trains

- By far the best way to get from London to Paris is by train. Jump on the Eurostar at Waterloo (www.eurostar.com) and voilà, you're in the middle of Paris three hours later. From there you can catch a train to anywhere in France and a dozen European cities. No big trek out to an airport in a London extremity or trek in at the other end, no long waits in airport lounges.
- Trains are by far the most comfortable and romantic way of travelling within Europe. Rail passes can significantly reduce your costs in Europe, especially if you're under 26. For all but a few country passes, you must book before you leave the UK. You'll have to pay a supplement of a few pounds for express trains and if seat reservations are compulsory. It's frustrating to be forced to book a seat on a deserted train, but there you go. For information, go to www.eurail.com.

Buses

- Buses tend to be far cheaper than trains, although they take a lot longer. You can go for national buses (usually very cheap), international buses — Eurolines is the big player (www.eurolines.com) — and hop-on-hop-off bus routes targeted mainly at young travellers, such as Busabout, phone 020 7950 1661, email info@busabout.com, website www.busabout.com.

Driving

- Having a car has advantages and drawbacks. You can set your own pace, save money by sleeping rough and camping, and get to out-of-the-way places. But you are a bit tied down, logistics can be tricky, the driving can be stressful and you might find yourself more at the mercy of dodgy border guards than if you were on foot.
- If you're taking a car to Europe from the UK you'll need the Vehicle Registration Document, your driver's licence and, in some countries, an International Driving Permit from the Automobile Association.

- Third-party insurance is compulsory. For more information, contact the RAC, phone 08705 722 722, website www.rac.co.uk, or the AA, phone 0870 600 0371, website www.theaa.co.uk.
- You usually get cheaper rental cars through internet brokers who deal with the big companies than by going direct to the companies or booking through travel agents. Do a web search of UK sites (you can do this through www.google.co.uk) for something like 'cheap car hire'. Shop around for the best deals. The company behind easyJet also has a cheap rental business, www.easycar.com.
- Renault Eurodrive (www.eurodrive.co.nz) is a variant on the car rental option — it's a short-term car lease, handy if you're travelling for a month or more. It needs to be organised through New Zealand (you can do this from the UK via the internet) and you get a Renault Scenic/Clio at various pick-up points in Europe for approximately £500 for one month or £800 for two months.
- In many countries you'll get by with a New Zealand driver's licence, but others might insist on an International Driving Permit. If you don't have one, you can apply by mail to the New Zealand Automobile Association. You'll need to send them a photocopy of your New Zealand driver's licence, a passport photo, give them your date of birth and town/city of birth, a permanent New Zealand address, and an overseas address for the permit to be posted to, and a fee (about NZ$20, but check first with the AA). Apply online or post to International Driving Permits, NZAA, PO Box 5, Auckland. AA contacts: phone +64 9 966 8979, email internationalmotoring@nzaa.co.nz, website www.nzaa.co.nz.

Budget airlines

Travellers have a lot to thank budget airlines for. They've opened up many parts of Europe to air travel and have forced some conventional airlines, most notably British Airways, to cut prices. They can be a ridiculously cheap way to travel. In some cases it can be cheaper to fly from Europe City A to London and back out to Europe City B than to take a train or ferry between the cities. Budget airlines are especially useful for one-way trips, as they don't hike up one-way prices as conventional airlines do. And keep an eye out for 'free' flight specials (but note 'free' means you still pay fees and taxes).

Navigating London's terrestrial airports

Allow plenty of time for journeys between London and Stansted or Luton, in particular. Trains can be delayed, and if a bus is full you'll have to wait for the next one, which could make you late for check-in. If you're a sound sleeper and you're catching an early flight, it can be less hassle — and cheaper — to travel to the airport the evening before and bed down for the night. If there are a few people to split the cost, check the cost of a minicab *(see 'Transport and orientation')*. Buses are the only cheap 24-hour option. *For Heathrow transport, see 'Your first week'.*

Gatwick   Phone 0870 000 2468, website www.baa.com.
Train:
- Gatwick has a relatively fast and cheap regular train connection with London Victoria (via Clapham Junction); phone 0870 830 6000, website www.southcentraltrains.co.uk.
- The Gatwick Express is a non-stop service between the airport and Victoria, which takes around 30 minutes; phone 0845 850 1530, website www.gatwickexpress.co.uk.
- The Thameslink service goes to several stations, including London Bridge and King's Cross on its way to and from the airport; phone 0845 330 6333, website www.thameslink.co.uk.

Coach:
- The cheap National Express 025 service goes to and from London Victoria; phone 08705 757 747, website www.nationalexpress.com.

London City   Phone 020 7646 0000, website www.londoncityairport.com.

London City airport is only 16 km from the West End and 10 km from the City. A cheap 10-minute airport shuttle links up with Canning Town, Canary Wharf and Liverpool Street stations; phone 020 7646 0088.

Luton   Phone 01582 405 100, website www.london-luton.co.uk.
Train:
- A handy regular Thameslink service links Luton Airport Parkway

station with the city. There's a free bus between the airport and the train station 1.8 km away. Stops include West Hampstead, London Bridge, Blackfriars, Farringdon and Kentish Town, but the most regular stop is King's Cross. Phone 0845 330 6333, website www.thameslink.co.uk.

Coach:
- The Greenline 757 goes between the airport and central London and the West End. Stops include Brent Cross, Finchley Road, Baker Street, Marble Arch and Victoria. Phone 0870 608 7261, email enquire@greenline.co.uk, website www.greenline.co.uk.

Stansted Phone 08700 000 303, website www.baa.com.

Train:
- The Stansted Express is a fast train between the airport and Liverpool Street Station and Tottenham Hale. It's fairly expensive — around £14 one-way. Trains depart every 15 or 30 minutes and the average journey time is 45 minutes. Phone 0845 8500 1500, website www.stanstedexpress.co.uk.
- The regular train service from Liverpool Street is cheaper but takes far longer, stopping at about a dozen stations on the way; phone National Rail enquiries 0845 8500 150, website www.nationalrail.co.uk.

Coach and bus:
- The A6 coach service connects Stansted with London Victoria, via Golders Green, Finchley Road Underground Station, St John's Wood, Baker Street, Marble Arch and Hyde Park Corner.
- The A9 travels between Stansted and Stratford in east London.
- The A7 goes between the airport and Victoria Street, via Marble Arch and Liverpool Street Station. Contact National Express, phone 0870 5747 777, website www.nationalexpress.com.

Shuttle:
- The Terravision Express Shuttle is a non-stop service between Stansted Airport and London Victoria; phone 012 7966 2931.

The Big OE Companion

THE PITFALLS

- Budget airlines have a different grasp of geography to the rest of us, and they're not always upfront about it. For instance, you'll find on the Ryanair website that it lists two of its Swedish airports as Stockholm (NYO) and Stockholm (VST). On further investigation you'll find that neither flies into Stockholm. One lands in a town called Nykoping, 100 km south of Stockholm, and the other in a city called Vasteras, 85 km west of Stockholm. Always check how easy it will be to get transport into the city.
- Similarly, the budget airlines use cheaper London airports that are miles out of the city. By the time you've paid for transfers you may as well have flown a national carrier. And if you're only going away for a weekend, the extra time it takes to get to and from obscure airports can really cut into your holiday.
- If you're making a return trip, make sure you check the price conventional airlines are offering — you may be surprised.
- The advertised prices are usually one-way, exclusive of taxes, which can double the cost of the ticket.

Case study — how a £9 flight can break your budget

Cost of a one-way flight from Amsterdam to London Stansted with Netherlands budget airline Basiq Air, booked five weeks in advance (31 July 2003)	£9.00
Airport tax, insurance and administration fee	£27.15
Other fees	£5.00
Food and drink for the flight	£8.00
Taxi home from Stansted at 2am after flight is delayed five hours because of airline error	£87.00
TOTAL	**£136.15**
Cost of return British Airways flight from Amsterdam to Heathrow, booked in advance, taxes included	£84.00

- You don't usually get a seat assigned to you, so you'll have to fight through a scrum upon boarding.
- The flight times are often inconvenient. A 7 am departure from Stansted might look like a cheap option, but you'll have to check in by 5.30 am, so you'll either have to get a bus there (which takes at least 90 minutes) or an expensive taxi. Similarly, if you arrive at an obscure European airport late at night, you might have no choice but to take a taxi.
- You don't get free food and drink on board.
- Check terms and conditions — most budget airlines won't be held responsible for cancellations or delays to your flight even if it's their error.

There are four airports servicing London, but to say that they are London airports requires a good stretch of the imagination. Three of them are known as London Gatwick, London Luton and London Stansted. This is a bit like saying Auckland Hamilton, Auckland Tauranga and Auckland Whangarei. Often the airfare from these airports sounds too good to be true, but once you factor in the cost and inconvenience of completing your journey into London from there, then sometimes it's not so great. If you catch a black cab to London, then be prepared to have the equivalent of Liberia's foreign loan debt in your pocket. There are many who believe that London City Airport doesn't actually exist. This is not surprising, as you would be challenged to find anyone who has ever been to it. The only real evidence that it is there at all is that it features in the opening credits of *EastEnders* in the aerial map of London.

— Andrew Knight

Bus tours

Independent travellers get a bit sniffy about people who go on organised tours, particularly the 20-countries-in-15-days organised bus tours, but if you're tempted, don't let that put you off. It's rare to meet bus tour veterans who didn't enjoy the trip, even if they get a bit sheepish about having it on their travel CV. Indeed, you could well spend your three weeks in too much of a booze- and orgy-fuelled haze to even notice where you're going, and there are guaranteed to be people who will get on your tits. However, it's a good way to meet your future flatmates/

girlfriend/boyfriend/drinking buddies — especially if you're new to the UK — it's a hassle-free way to travel, and it can give you a taste for places you'd like to explore further.

SOME BUS TOUR COMPANIES
(You'll find dozens of others in the antipodean publications and websites in the UK.)

- The Backpacker Company, phone 020 8896 6070, email info@backpacker.co.uk, website www.backpacker.co.uk.
- Contiki, phone 0208 290 6777, email travel@contiki.co.uk, website www.contiki.com.
- Kumuka, phone 0800 068 8855, email enquiries@kumuka.com, website www.kumuka.com.
- On The Go, phone 020 7371 1113, email info@onthegotours.com, website www.onthegotours.com.
- PP Travel, phone 020 7792 4444, email info@pptravel.com, website www.pptravel.com.
- Topdeck, phone 020 8879 6789, email res@topdecktravel.co.uk, website www.topdecktravel.co.uk.

Kiwi pilgrimages

Van Tour

It's a great antipodean tradition to buy a beat-up Kombi van at the beginning of summer, decorate it in All Blacks colours, put a mattress in the back, assemble a few of your most laid-back mates and hit the three-month Van Tour trail through some of the best festivals and beaches of Europe, getting horrendously drunk at every campsite along the way. Van Tour has a dubious reputation as a travelling party, and some little villages might close their shutters in fear when they see a painted van shuddering down the road. You won't learn too much about the local way of life, but you'll have some fun.

GETTING A VAN
It's essential to get a decent van. It doesn't have to be a Kombi van — in fact the fleet is looking a bit worse for wear these days, and parts can be hard to come by. You might be able to buy a van that made it back from

Travel on the Continent and beyond

last year's Van Tour (which is pretty good testament to its hardiness) or you might be able to get a cheap second-hand workman's van which you can build a bed into. Start your search by asking around, and looking in *Loot* newspaper (www.loot.com), *Autotrader* (www.autotrader.co.uk) the classifieds in *TNT Magazine* (www.tntmag.co.uk) and *New Zealand News UK* (www.nznewsuk.co.uk), and on www.thegumtree.com. There's also a van market in Market Road N7, London, off Caledonian Road. Plan on spending about £1000-2000. It might pay to get a mechanic to check it out before you buy. And if you have a mechanic mate, offer to subsidise his/her trip if he or she comes along.

The best time to buy a van is straight after summer, when dozens of antipodeans are sitting in their vans on Caledonian Road, desperate to get rid of them. The best time to sell is in the months leading up to summer, when demand is highest. If you buy at the beginning of summer, when prices are at their peak, and sell when they dive at the end of summer, you could lose a bit of money. Thus, if you are going to buy a van, you will be better off buying it in advance and holding onto it for a while.

You could also fly into Europe and rent a van.

For hire car advice and the rules on driving a car from the UK to the Continent, see 'Transport tips' earlier in this chapter. For advice on buying a vehicle, see 'Transport and orientation'.

INSURANCE
Downunder Insurance (phone 0800 393 908, email info@duinsure.com, website www.duinsure.com) has a Van Tour insurance policy.

THE ROUTE
The route goes roughly from London through France to Pamplona in Spain for the very messy Running of the Bulls festival in July — the unofficial starting point. From there the vans go all over Europe and Eastern Europe, usually in search of beaches and/or cheap beer, and most of the surviving vans end up at Oktoberfest in Munich in September/October.

Running of the Bulls in Pamplona
In recent years the New Zealand and Australian embassies in Madrid have pooled resources in a (usually futile) campaign to dissuade their

young citizens from going to the Running of the Bulls. They also issue a travel advisory, which usually goes something like this: Listen to the police and don't cross police barriers, don't block the route, don't overcrowd balconies, don't run if you're not fit, and don't attempt to run the whole course, don't carry anything, don't impede other runners, don't challenge, touch, distract or run towards the bulls, if you fall, protect your head with your hands and lie still until the bulls have passed, when inside the bullring get behind the barriers quickly, and leave wounded runners to the health workers. For more information, check www.nzembassy.com.

There are less touristy Running of the Bulls-type festivals elsewhere in Spain, and in some places in France.

Anzac Day in Europe

GALLIPOLI

Just when the numbers of New Zealanders and Australians going to Gallipoli for Anzac Day services was getting out of hand, along came September 11 (2001), followed a couple of years later by Al Qaeda bombs in Istanbul. The terrorist threat immediately cut the numbers making the April 25 pilgrimage and consequently made it a far more sombre and meaningful experience.

If you plan to go, maintain an appropriate sense of decorum and keep in mind that it's not a party — save that for your onward travel around Turkey. Be prepared to do a lot of uphill walking (consider it your personal tribute to the diggers). In recent years camping equipment and large backpacks have been banned and security has been beefed up. Take a sleeping bag and warm clothes, because it'll be very cold before dawn. Keep an eye out for travel advice from the New Zealand government, on www.nzembassy.com/uk and www.mfat.govt.nz.

There are a few options for organising your travel. You can get a package deal including airfares; find your own way to Turkey and meet up with a tour there; or do the whole thing yourself (few people do this because the tour companies book most of the accommodation in the vicinity). For deals, keep an eye out for advertisements in the antipodean media.

While you're there, spring is a good time to tour Turkey — it's inexpensive, not too hot and less crowded than in summer.

Gallipoli on Anzac Day
It was amazing looking out on Anzac Cove as the sun rose, and the Kiwi service in the afternoon was very moving. There wasn't a dry eye. I was pleased to see it wasn't a big booze-fest — everyone was quite subdued.
— Rachael O'Brien

The Maori Battalion was a highlight — their songs and haka were amazing. We felt very emotional and proud of New Zealand.
— Peta Norris

FRANCE AND BELGIUM

Gallipoli is the obvious focus for Anzac Day commemorations, but it's also a very important day in parts of France and Belgium where the Anzacs fought. The biggest event is held in the French town of Le Quesnoy, which Kiwi troops liberated in World War I. There are also services in Paris, Dublin, Berlin, and Messines and Ieper (Ypres) in Belgium. For information, contact the appropriate New Zealand embassy *(for contact details, see 'New Zealand government in the UK and Europe')*, or look on www.nzembassy.com.

If you want more information on New Zealand's role in the battles of France and Belgium, get a copy of historian Ian McGibbon's book *New Zealand Battlefields and Memorials of the Western Front* (Oxford University Press, 2001). It's part touring guide, part history book.

For Anzac Day events in the UK, see 'Enjoying the UK'.

Accommodation tips

If you haven't booked accommodation, try to arrive at your destination early in the day before everything fills up, and so you've got time to look.

Camping

As you'd expect, camping is the cheapest way to sleep in Europe. Best done with a car — otherwise you'll have to cart around a lot of gear, and you might have difficulty getting to campsites, which tend to be on the outskirts of cities.

Hostels

Some hostels are great, others terrible, but spend long enough in them and you'll grow to dread them all. In summer and at other busy times always book ahead. Internet booking is handy for advance bookings (try www.hostelworld.com, www.hostels.net and www.hihostels.com), but you should call the hostel direct if you want to book accommodation less than a week out. Confirm hostel bookings a day or two in advance.

Private rooms

In many places in Europe, and especially Eastern Europe, you'll find hordes of persistent little old ladies outside train stations offering private rooms. Sometimes you'll stumble on a gem complete with home cooking, other times you'll find yourself in a Soviet-era apartment in the middle of nowhere with a crazed, lonely old woman who wants you to marry her inbred son/daughter. Get a handle on where it is and how much, and ask to inspect it before you commit yourself. Some tourist offices and travel agents also arrange private rooms, which will probably cost more but will be more reliable.

Bed and breakfast

B&Bs are underrated in Europe. They can be almost as cheap as a hostel, friendlier and far more comfortable. And you get to meet the locals. Check the location before you book.

Luggage tips

- Unless you're planning to go camping in Europe, and need all the paraphernalia that goes with it, you won't need your 90-litre backpack with zip-on daypack. A backpack of 60 litres or smaller is ideal for most trips, even long ones — big enough to fit a few changes of clothes and shoes and your other bits and pieces, but small enough to carry for long distances. Expandable packs are good because you can adjust them to suit the length of your trip. Make sure your pack has a well-fitting harness. The best place to buy packs in London is on High Street Kensington, where there are about a dozen good outdoors stores. There is a branch of New Zealand outdoors store Kathmandu in London, at 1 Berners Street

(just off Oxford Street), W1; phone 020 7436 7499, website www.kathmandu.co.nz.
- Avoid carrying big, unwieldy suitcases, but it can be handy to own a small suitcase on wheels, preferably small enough to classify as carry-on luggage on planes. You can get them cheaply, and they can be very handy for weekend city breaks, when you know you won't have to lug your bag far. But be aware that wheels are often useless on cobblestones.
- Don't pack until the seams are bursting. Leave some room in case you want to buy anything on your travels.
- Attach strong name and address tags to your luggage, inside and outside, and get padlocks to fit every opening. If you leave bags anywhere that looks even a little bit dodgy, don't leave anything valuable in them.

Take only cabin baggage for weekends on the Continent if you are flying. It saves hours waiting in the likes of London Heathrow for baggage handlers to come off their coffee breaks and actually do some work.

— Adrian McCloy

Packing tips

- Pack light, especially in summer. You're unlikely to regret having to leave a few CDs at home, or having to wash your clothes more often, but you will regret it if you take too much. Depending on your size and strength, aim for a maximum of 10–15 kg for most trips, long or short.
- Bedding. Unless you're camping, you probably won't need a sleeping bag. They're banned in many hostels in Europe because of the health risk, and the hostel will provide a blanket instead. If you take a sleeping bag, buy a compression sack from a camping store, which compacts it to about half its size. Hostels also provide pillows, but you'll need a pillowcase. Most also insist that you have a sleeping sheet — a couple of single sheets sewn into a sleeping sack.
- Buy a tube of clothes-washing detergent and a small twisted elastic washing line, both available from camping stores. Don't even think of putting some washing powder in a plastic bag. Ever thought about how dodgy that looks at Customs?

- A sarong doubles as a sheet, towel, skirt, picnic rug, rope and curtain.
- Get a medium-sized travel towel from a camping store. They take up far less room and dry far more quickly than normal towels.
- If you're going to be staying in hostels, pack your belongings in cloth bags rather than plastic bags. You'll make far less noise, which will endear you to your dorm-mates a lot more than if you arrive at midnight and rustle around for an hour.
- Get an eye mask and good earplugs. You might feel like a schmuck, but a good sleep takes precedence over image when you're travelling.
- Take one absorbing book. Many hostels have a book swap facility, so you'll never be short of one.
- If you have a big Europe-wide guidebook, it can be more convenient to (carefully) rip out the chapters you need for each trip, rather than lugging the whole thing around when you only need ten pages of it at any one time. If you can't bear to do that, photocopy it.
- Pack a blank journal. No matter how illiterate you think you are, it can be great to look back on, and a healthy vent for your fury and angst if something goes wrong.
- Buy film in bulk before you leave the UK, especially if you're heading to touristy places. Always carry spare camera batteries with you.
- Buy sunscreen before you leave the UK. In countries like Italy and Spain, where the locals don't tend to use it, they hike the price up for tourists.
- If you have a digital camera, have at least one spare memory card on hand and carry spare camera batteries.
- A small torch can be handy if you're hostelling or camping.
- Don't bother taking an alarm clock or calculator if you have a mobile phone. It doubles as both.
- Consider getting a mini disc player or iPod and a set of tiny speakers. You'll be the most popular person around at impromptu parties — and you get to choose the music.
- Get a multi-way power adaptor if you're taking CD players, mini discs, mobile phones, etc.
- Get a roll-up compartmentalised toiletries bag that you can hang up.
- To save room, buy a set of travel-sized bottles for your toiletries.

Travel on the Continent and beyond

- Keep medicines in their original packaging. If you've been prescribed restricted drugs bring a letter from your doctor or similar.
- You might feel like a boy scout or girl guide, but it's not a silly idea to pack a small compass, especially if you're geographically challenged. Most maps have compass points on them, so you could avoid walking 2 km in the wrong direction down a street in Paris.

> I had a carabiner [rock climbing tool] attached to my bag and whenever I sat down at a cafe or anywhere else I clipped it around the leg of the table or chair. It makes it very hard for thieves to grab and run with your bag (as a chap on the back of a scooter found out). Plus, if you're travelling on a really crowded train, like in Greece, keep your bags at your feet. It's a lot harder for pickpockets to get to bags on the floor. Also if going to a humid country buy packs of silica gel to keep in your pack. It takes the moisture out and helps dry your gear if you get it wet.
> — Brendon O'Hagan

In case of emergency

If you are the victim of a crime, contact the local police first. If they're not much help, you can contact your nearest New Zealand consulate or embassy *(for a list, see 'New Zealand government in the UK and Europe')*. If you've been robbed, get a report from the police — you'll need it to make a travel insurance claim.

If you're unlucky enough to be caught in a disaster or terrorist attack, turn to the local authorities first. Inform your nearest New Zealand consulate or embassy of your situation — even if you're okay — and try to contact family and friends to reassure them as soon as possible. The media will get word of events to them first, and things can look far scarier to a worried mum watching a television screen half a world away than they do on the ground. (Even if you're hundreds of miles away from the event, your family will probably worry, so it's not a bad idea to give them a call.)

If your passport is lost or stolen, report it to the local police, then to your nearest New Zealand embassy or consulate.

The Big OE Companion

It's so great living on the doorstep of Europe, with most places a cheap flight away. I'm not getting free flights from Ryanair or easyJet for saying this, but get your arse out of London. Take a long weekend and see some awesome cultures and great places. Yes, we are lucky tigers; New Zealand does have it all. But when I was growing up I never thought that I would be able to fly to Belgium for bugger all, eat their chocolates, drink their beer, then be back behind my desk first thing Monday morning.

— Al Pitcher

A highly subjective list of where to go and how long for

A weekend (preferably a long one)
Barcelona
Munich
Prague
Stockholm
Madrid
Bruges
Amsterdam
Reykjavik
Berlin
Venice

A fortnight
Moscow to St Petersburg
Croatia
Greek Islands
Northern Scandinavia
Ireland
A villa in Italy or Spain
Mainland Greece
Portugal's coast

As little time as possible
Athens
Gibraltar
Airports, anywhere
Sorrento
Any Moroccan bus station
Albanian seaside resorts
Pisa
British home-away-from-home seaside resorts

A week
Paris
Champagne or Bordeaux
Rome
The Alps (skiing or walking)
Vienna and Salzburg
Norway's fjords
Cinque Terre in northern Italy
Sailing the Med
French Riviera
New York (no, it's not Europe, but it's not far)

A month or more
Italy — top to bottom
Turkey
The Middle East
Morocco
Eastern Europe
The trans-Siberian railway
Doing a language course
Chilling out in a cute European village
Cycling in Europe

16.
What next?

Not ready to leave?

There are a few ways to extend your stay in the UK, depending on your visa. It's not as difficult for Working Holidaymakers as it once was since switching into Work Permit employment was officially sanctioned in 2003. You can even download the forms from the internet.

> **Immigration and Nationality Directorate**
> Home Office Immigration and Nationality Directorate
> Enquiry bureau phone: 0870 606 7766
> Email: indpublicenquiries@ind.homeoffice.gsi.gov.uk
> Website: www.ind.homeoffice.gov.uk.
>
> **Work Permits (UK)**
> Phone: 011 4259 4074
> Email: wpcustomers@ind.homeoffice.gsi.gov.uk
> Website: www.workingintheuk.gov.uk
> Address: Work Permits (UK), Home Office, Level 5, Moorfoot, Sheffield S1 4PQ

Work Permits

After a year on a Working Holiday Visa, or once you graduate with your degree if you're a student in the UK, you can apply for a Work Permit. You'll need to convince an employer to sponsor you, and convince the immigration people that you're the best person for the job. Some employers will do it all for you, others might be happy to sign the forms if you organise it all and pay for it.

You can do it yourself through the Home Office's Work Permits (UK) or employ the services of a work permit company — advertised in antipodean publications and websites. Get application forms and information from Work Permits (UK) (downloadable from their website).

Getting British citizenship

You can apply for a certificate of naturalisation if you have lived legally in the UK for five years, you're aged 18 or over, you're 'not of unsound mind', you speak English, and you 'stay closely connected with the United Kingdom'. Also, the last year you have spent in the UK must have been free from a time limit — that is, you must already have indefinite leave to remain (see Ancestry Visas below) or an equivalent. Thus, if you have a visa with an expiry date on it you're not eligible.

The wife or husband of a British citizen can apply for naturalisation after having lived in the United Kingdom legally for three years. As in the standard naturalisation process, you must be aged 18 or over, not of unsound mind, and 'must be of good character'.

To meet residence requirements, you must not have been absent from the UK for more than 450 days over the five-year period, or for more than 270 days over the three-year period. In each case, you must not have been absent for more than 90 days in the last year of the period. Get application forms from the Home Office Immigration and Nationality Directorate (downloadable from their website, above).

Ancestry Visas

After four years of continuous work on a UK ancestry visa, you are eligible to apply to live in the UK permanently as long as you continue to meet the immigration rules. You'll have to apply for further leave to remain or indefinite leave to remain. Get application forms from the Immigration and Nationality Directorate.

Leaving?

Sorting out your finances

BANKING AND CREDIT CARDS

It is best to shut down your bank accounts and credit cards when you leave, unless you are pretty sure you'll be returning, or you'll have outstanding transactions. You will have to advise your bank in writing of your intention to close the account, and you may be asked to cut and hand in your credit cards. You can ask the bank to transfer the balance to your New Zealand account, for a fee of about £15–20 (read on for more international money transfer options). You can also do this by writing a letter to the bank once you are back in New Zealand. Make sure you cancel all automatic payments and ensure all credit and debit card payments have been processed.

DEBTS AND CONTRACTS
Pay off any debts and shut down any contracts for services you no longer need. Don't just take off thinking they won't be able to find you in New Zealand — your credit rating is at stake.

TAX
You'd be a mug not to do a final tax return, because you can be due for a nice rebate if you haven't worked for the entire tax year (April 6 to April 5). Make sure your employer gives you a P45 tax form that signals the end of your employment and records your salary and tax details.

You'll need to get a P85 Leaving the United Kingdom form, which you can download from www.inlandrevenue.gov.uk, or phone the order line, 0845 7 646 646.

It's dead easy to fill out the form and send it in yourself (with your P45) — you don't even have to do any calculations. Make sure Inland Revenue has your contact details in New Zealand. You can get them to pay a rebate into a bank account or by cheque. If it hasn't come through within a couple of months, ring them to follow up.

If you have a limited company, don't forget to close it down.

If your tax situation is difficult or you can't be bothered doing it yourself, you can enlist the help of a tax company. Some are listed in *'Money matters'*, earlier in the book, or check the antipodean publications *(listed in 'Getting your Kiwi fix')* for advertisements.

For information about National Insurance rebates, see 'Money matters'.

Mobile phones

If you have a contract you might want to consider changing it to a prepaid account — you can keep your number — about a month before you leave. Then you can pay the last bill in good time, and load up your account to cover you for your remaining time in the UK, your trip home and even for a week or so when you get there. *See 'Communications and media' for more advice on mobile phones, and using them internationally.*

Other logistics

- Get references from your landlord and employer.
- Get travel insurance for the trip home *(see 'Travel on the Continent and beyond')*.
- Make sure your name is taken off any lease and utility bills in your flat.
- Leave some time to say goodbye to the UK and go to the tourist places you've always been meaning to get to.

Going home?

Eventually the British winters will probably get you, if your visa doesn't get you first. If you go back to New Zealand be prepared to see it in a far different light than before. You'll get a renewed appreciation for the lifestyle, or you'll wonder where all the people are and pine for a bit of variety, or a bit of both. But you don't have to go straight home if you don't feel ready. There's a whole world out there.

The Myers/Inkson study *(see 'The OErs')* concluded that the travellers they interviewed returned home mainly for family-related reasons. Others felt they had been away too long or needed a break. A few were forced to return when their visas expired. Few cited career reasons. Most resumed a similar kind of work to that they'd been doing when they left, although others capitalised on overseas work experience by venturing into new jobs or starting their own businesses. Others went back to tertiary study, several indicating that this was a result of a reappraisal of their lives during their time overseas.

Significant numbers said they'd had difficulties readjusting to life in New Zealand. Some said their jobs simply did not match up in terms of interest or responsibility. 'Those who had made their way in the big wide world may find the constraints of being over-controlled in an Auckland accounts department just a tad restrictive,' Myers and Inkson commented.

How to know you've been in London too long

These lists have been doing the email and website rounds for years. Here are some of the best offerings.

- You consider eye contact an act of overt aggression.
- You call an 8' x 10' plot of patchy grass a garden.
- You think Hyde Park is nature.
- You pay £3 without blinking for a beer that cost the bar 28p.
- Your idea of personal space is no one actually physically standing on you.
- You can't remember the last time you got up to 30 mph in your car.
- You say 'all right' back and finish every sentence with 'yeah?'
- £1 doesn't seem like too much to pay for a Crunchie.
- You've just realised you have lost your sunnies. In Greece. Two years ago.
- Your sunburn cream is the stuff you brought from home.
- You call soccer football . . .
- . . . and you have a team . . .
- . . . and it's not Manchester United.
- You believe that Monday, Tuesday, Wednesday, Thursday, Friday and Saturday are all good nights for drinking. Sunday during the day is also entirely reasonable.
- You have given up explaining why you are half an hour late to work as no one notices or cares.
- You don't even bother looking out of the window to check the weather. You know it is overcast.
- You dissolve in laughter at hearing your mother's accent on the phone.
- A Tube jumper isn't so much a tragedy as an inconvenience.

Shipping your belongings to New Zealand

You may have turned up with just your Macpac, but it's inevitable you'll end up with at least four times that. Since shipping your stuff home can take a while to organise, and it can take months to get there, plan a few months ahead.

STEP 1

Audit your belongings and get rid of anything you don't need, especially if it's cheap but heavy (and therefore inordinately expensive to take home). You can sell valuable stuff through the antipodean publications and websites *(see 'Getting your Kiwi fix')*, or *Loot* newspaper, www.loot.com. Don't be too ruthless, though — there's not much point in getting rid of £400 worth of stuff to save yourself £50 in shipping costs. Consider how expensive these things would be to buy in New Zealand.

STEP 2

Weigh your gear. Separate out what you'll take on the plane — you'll have a 20-kg allowance if you travel home via Asia and 32 kg if you go via the United States, plus cabin baggage. If there's anything you'll need desperately when you get home — such as a suit for job interviews or worker's tools — take it with you. Whether you freight by air or sea, quoted time frames are notoriously unreliable. It's not unusual for your things to arrive months after they were expected. And don't discount the possibility of using the plain old postal system to send home smaller bits and pieces. Surface mail can be pretty cheap. See www.royalmail.com.

STEP 3

Shop around for quotes. And then shop around some more. You can start your search with the antipodean publications and websites. This is big business and the companies court the antipodean market.

Starting points: some companies targeting the New Zealand market:

 1st Contact Shipping, phone 0800 039 3099,
website www.1stcontact.co.uk.
 Anglo Pacific International, phone 020 8965 1234,
email info@anglopacific.co.uk, website www.anglopacific.co.uk.
 Excess Baggage Company, phone 0800 783 1085,
email sales@excess-baggage.com, website www.excess-baggage.com.

What next?

- Seven Seas Baggage, phone 0800 216698,
  email info@sevenseas.co.uk, website www.sevenseas.co.uk.

TIPS FOR CHOOSING A COMPANY

- Read the small print — check for extra charges, such as money you'll have to pay to collect your goods in New Zealand, Customs charges and storage costs.
- Check time frames. Shipping can take up to three months, and air freight up to four weeks.
- Companies will offer pick-up or delivery options — the most expensive is door to door, UK to New Zealand, but you can save money by delivering your goods to the company in the UK and/or by picking them up yourself from the port in New Zealand. If you opt for the latter option, there will be extra charges to get your belongings released by Customs in New Zealand, so check first.
- Compare prices for sending by sea and air. If you don't have much stuff it might be worth paying a little extra for air freight, which is much quicker than sea freight.
- Check where they deliver — any company will do Auckland, but some also go to Wellington, Lyttelton and Dunedin.
- Check if the company uses a volumetric weight calculation for large but light belongings, such as surfboards. This means they'll take into account both its weight and its size, and you could get stung.
- It's best to go with a reputable company. You don't want the company to disappear, leaving your gear anywhere between the UK and New Zealand.
- You can check that they're affiliated to:
  — The International Furniture Movers Association (Federation Internationale des Demenageurs Internationaux or FIDI), phone +32 2 426 5160 (Belgium), email fidi@fidi.com, website www.fidi.com, or
  — The British Association of Removers, phone 020 8861 3331, email info@bar.co.uk, website www.removers.org.uk.
- Opt for insurance. The company should be able to offer you a reasonable deal — about three to five percent of the value of your belongings. As with any insurance policy, check the small print and for exceptions and exclusions. Find out how to make a claim — it's

best if you can deal with a company in New Zealand if anything goes wrong.

STEP 4
Packing tips:
- If the shipping company doesn't supply its own boxes and/or tea chests and packing materials, you should be able to get boxes free from your local supermarket or other shops. Don't pack your gear in fruit boxes. New Zealand MAF staff might get suspicious that they contain traces of fruit and insects.
- Pack carefully, using heaps of padding material, and put everything in plastic bags to avoid water damage. Your boxes might get chucked around a bit — and ships attract water.
- Secure your belongings as best you can. The company might offer security bags at extra cost, but you can take your own precautions, such as buying security mesh from a camping store for your backpacks. There's nothing much you can do to protect your gear while it's en route, but if your security measures have obviously been tampered with, you might have a stronger claim for insurance.
- Weigh your stuff as you go. Make sure it's under the weight restrictions — going overweight can attract disproportionate charges.
- Clean any camping equipment, shoes, sports equipment, garden equipment, horse-riding equipment and the like, to avoid it attracting MAF's interest in New Zealand.
- If for some crazy reason you're taking a vacuum cleaner, throw out the dust bag.
- You can't send plants or drugs or anything explosive, flammable, poisonous, alcoholic or pressurised, and it's best not to send food or anything else perishable, or liquids. Also, your insurance probably won't cover cash, bonds or jewellery.
- Send your photographs separately from your negatives, so you don't lose the lot if something goes wrong.

STEP 5
Do the paperwork. Be pedantic and precise to avoid problems at the other end. Keep a detailed list of everything in your boxes and bags, to declare to Customs when you pick up your gear in New Zealand. If your

What next?

> **New Zealand Customs Service in Europe**
>
> The nearest New Zealand Customs Service office to the UK is at the New Zealand Embassy in Brussels, Belgium. If you are returning to New Zealand with items or sending belongings home and can't find answers to your questions on the New Zealand Customs website:
>
> www.customs.govt.nz,
>
> you can email the Brussels office: nzcusbru@compuserve.com.

stuff will arrive in New Zealand before you do, you can nominate someone to pick it up on your behalf.

STEP 6

Wave your stuff goodbye and cross your fingers that you'll see it again. (There is a small element of risk, but it's rare for things to go missing.) Make sure the company gives you copies of all documents, including insurance policies and phone numbers of the company to contact in New Zealand to arrange collection.

STEP 7

Once home, chase your gear up. This may involve lots of phone calls. Before you get your gear you'll have to fill out a MAF Quarantine Declaration. MAF might decide to check your shipment. They will charge up to NZ$45 to clear your goods, and if they decide to check them, you could face a bill of up to NZ$100. You'll also have to fill out a New Zealand Customs form stating that your consignment is personal baggage. If you've been away for less than 21 consecutive months, you're liable for duty and GST on anything purchased or acquired overseas, except clothing and apparel.

> I checked three companies to begin with (for air freight prices) and they were much the same — up to £20 a kilo. It was only when I expanded that to ten companies that I found some that charged £5 a kilo. Some of the most popular companies with Kiwis and Aussies are also the most

expensive ones. A good place to find the good companies is on the Gumtree [www.thegumtree.com], I found. If you work for a big company and you can get away with it, send small things home through your company mail — bit by bit. By the time they get suspicious, you'll be long gone.

— Anonymous

Sending money home

There are a few ways to send money home, and costs vary to a ridiculous degree so shop around. Check currency exchange rates on www.xe.com/ucc.

Ways to send money home:

- Through a bank transfer. This can be a convenient and safe option. You can get a same-day transfer, but it's cheaper to get one that'll take a few days.
- You can send a sterling cheque home to someone trustworthy to deposit into your account. The bank in New Zealand will charge to convert it into dollars.
- Through a money-wiring service, often operated out of a travel agency, or online — such as Western Union, www.westernunion.com, or MoneyGram, www.moneygram.com. This is usually the most expensive and most complicated way. You nominate a Western Union or MoneyGram office in New Zealand to send it to, and nominate a person to pick it up, and they will have to show a passport to collect it.
- Through an internet-based company. This might sound risky, but it's the 21st-century way to do things — and significantly cheaper than any other option. You set up an account with the company, then wire the money from your UK bank account to your New Zealand bank account via their website. To protect yourself, only transfer small amounts to start with. Tried and tested ones are www.easyexchange.co.uk, www.paypal.com/uk and *TNT Magazine*'s transfer service, www.tntex.com.

Booking a flight

By the time you come to book a trip home, you're probably an expert on getting good deals. You'll know to shop around for a flight, and get quotes from travel and airline websites as well as travel agents. One-way

What next?

flights with the major airlines can be inordinately expensive. Check the fares for return flights too. On some airlines a return flight can be cheaper than a one-way flight.

Delay tactics

There's an advantage to New Zealand being almost the polar opposite of the UK — almost any part of the world is 'on the way home'. It's a good idea to take a break between leaving the UK and going home, to give you a chance for a breather.

> **Taking the long way home**
> - Do an African truck safari. You can go overland all the way from London to Cape Town, from Cairo to Cape Town, or just jet in to Kenya or South Africa. It's not always cheap to get to New Zealand from South Africa, but there are very few times in your life when Africa is on the way home.
> - Fly to New York, rent or buy a car and a tent and drive at leisure to Los Angeles, where you can pick up a flight to New Zealand.
> - Chuck on a backpack and head home through Asia or South America.
> - Spend a week chilling out on a tropical beach in Asia.
> - Choose your favourite spot in Europe and spend a week there. You might not get to have another holiday in Europe for a while.
> - Spend three months on a language course somewhere exotic.

Reverse culture shock

There seem to be two types of returning New Zealanders — those who appreciate it far more than they did before they left, and those who find it claustrophobic and spookily familiar and spend the next decade reminiscing about some great weekend at an All Blacks game in Cardiff.

A 'To do' list on your return

- Take a deep breath and smell the clean air (unless you're from Rotorua, in which case you'll probably be able to smell the sulphur for the first time in your life).

Things to expect
- People's accents will sound cartoonish. You'll chuckle when the New Zealand airport intercom voice says, 'Wulcum to Niew Zillind. Please keep all your buggage with you ut all toimes.'
- You'll get teased for 'speaking like a Pom', even though you've spent the last few years being teased about your Kiwi accent.
- Your parents will look old.
- You'll get sunburnt in the shade at 6 pm on an overcast day.
- New Zealand will seem small and friendly and oh so quaint . . .
- . . . and deserted.
- Your relationships with your friends will have changed and you'll have to re-establish them.
- You'll be regularly tempted to drop the UK into your conversation. (Try to resist.)
- You might find your priorities have changed. No longer are you saving all your money for travel.
- New Zealand will seem so far away from the world.
- Everything will seem expensive — probably because you're used to seeing smaller numbers on price tags.
- You'll be surprised at getting friendly customer service.

Dealing with culture shock
- Go away to one of your favourite places and remember the things that make New Zealand great.
- Don't get stuck into a job immediately, but if you can't shake the feeling of being unsettled, you'll find that once you get a job and find somewhere to live, life will start to recover.
- If you find yourself bored and wistful about the UK, try living in a different place in New Zealand.
- If things get really bad, buy a one-way flight to Heathrow.

What next?

- Tell Inland Revenue you're back. If you've been a non-resident for tax purposes you'll have to switch status back, and if you have a student loan you'll have to change your repayment plan.
  Phone 0800 377 774 (general enquiries)
  0800 377 778 (student loans)
  website www.ird.govt.nz.
- If you have a British driver's licence, exchange it for a New Zealand one (you have a year to do this).
- Get your mobile phone unlocked, if necessary, and get a new connection.

Moving on?
Other Working Holiday Visas

If you don't yet fancy returning to New Zealand and you're under 30, you can apply for a Working Holiday Visa to more than a dozen other countries.

After interviewing 50 New Zealanders who'd gone on OE, academics Barbara Myers and Kerr Inkson *(see 'The OErs')* concluded that the Anglo-centrism of the OE might limit its value. They wrote:

> The overall focus on London is apparently caused by the colonial history of New Zealand, OE traditions, the British working visa system, the cultural and language similarity of the two countries, and the natural tendency of travellers not to change too many parameters of their lives all at once.
>
> However, the result may be that OE travellers do not learn to be citizens of the world but instead act as little Englanders, though, of course, Britain (and particularly London) is a much more cosmopolitan community than it once was.
>
> A riskier and more eclectic choice of destinations — for example, countries with contrasting cultures where English is not the main language — might provide better preparation for New Zealand's future global workforce. New Zealand does, after all, have visa arrangements for working holidays in at least 14 other nations.

All the visas listed below last for a year, forbid you from bringing dependents, and require you to be aged 18 to 30. In most cases the age restrictions apply at the time of application, but you can turn 31 while you're there. An exception is Ireland, for which you'll need to be 30 or younger for the entire year of your visa.

Each country has a quota and the counter usually starts at the beginning of the year, so for popular visas it's best to get in early. Some countries insist you apply while you're in New Zealand, and will want to see proof that you have enough money for a ticket home and to support yourself on arrival, and that you have comprehensive travel and medical insurance. New Working Holiday Visa deals are being signed every year, so check www.mfat.govt.uk for an updated list.

CANADA
One of the most popular programmes. Operates on a strict first-come-first-served basis, starting in mid-January. There are extra hurdles to cross if you want to work in childcare or health, or as a schoolteacher. You can apply from outside New Zealand.

> Contact: Canadian High Commission in Wellington, 61 Molesworth Street, PO Box 12049, Wellington
> phone +64 4 473 9577
> email nzwhp-pvt@dfait-maeci.gc.ca or wlgtn@dfait-maeci.gc.ca
> website www.dfait-maeci.gc.ca/newzealand.

CHILE
Requires you to be living in New Zealand at the time of your application. You can't work for the same employer for more than three months or take a permanent job.

> Contact: Embassy of the Republic of Chile, 19 Bolton Street,
> PO Box 3861, Wellington
> phone + 64 4 471 6270
> email echile@embchile.co.nz.

DENMARK
You can only work for six months of the 12-month visa, and you can't work for the same employer for more than three months. You can apply in New Zealand through Denmark's Singapore embassy, or from the UK.

What next?

In New Zealand, contact: Royal Danish Embassy, 101 Thomson
Road, #13-01/2 United Square, Singapore 307591
phone +65 6355 5010
email embassy@denmark.com.sg.
In the UK, contact: The Passport and Visa Office, Royal Danish
Embassy, 55 Sloane Street, London SW1X 9SR
phone 020 7333 0200
email lonamb@um.dk, website www.denmark.org.uk.

FRANCE

You can apply from outside New Zealand, but you must do it through the French embassy in Wellington.

Contact: Embassy of France, 34-42 Manners Street,
PO Box 11343, Wellington
phone +64 4 802 1590
email consul.france@actrix.gen.nz, website www.france.net.nz.

GERMANY

You must apply while you're in New Zealand, and you can only work for 90 days.

Contact: Embassy of the Federal Republic of Germany, 90-92
Hobson Street, Thorndon, PO Box 1687, Wellington
phone +64 4 473 6063
email GermanEmbassyWellington@xtra.co.nz
website www.deutschebotschaftwellington.co.nz.

IRELAND

Applications open in October each year for visas for the following year. You must be resident in New Zealand when you apply. You must not be due to turn 31 during the year of the visa. You are supposed to take only 'casual or temporary' work.

Contact: Consulate-General of Ireland, 6th floor, 18 Shortland
Street, Auckland 1001, PO Box 279, Auckland
phone +64 9 977 2252
email consul@ireland.co.nz, website www.ireland.co.nz.

ITALY

You must be 'ordinarily resident in New Zealand'. You can work for only six months of the year, and spend no more than three months with one employer.

Contact: Embassy of Italy, 34–38 Grant Road, Thorndon,
PO Box 463, Wellington
phone +64 4 474 0951
email visaoffice@ambwell.co.nz, website www.italy-embassy.org.nz.

JAPAN

You must be living in New Zealand when you apply. The initial visa is for six months, which can be extended by another six months while in Japan.

Contact: Embassy of Japan, Majestic Centre, 100 Willis Street,
PO Box 6340, Wellington
phone +64 4 473 1540
email japan.emb@eoj.org.nz, website www.nz.emb-japan.go.jp.

THE REPUBLIC OF KOREA

You cannot work as an entertainer or hostess or in a professional job.

Contact: Embassy of the Republic of Korea, Level 11, ASB Bank Tower, 2 Hunter Street, PO Box 11143, Wellington
phone +64 4 473 9073/4
email korembec@world-net.co.nz.

MALAYSIA

You must have been living in New Zealand for at least six months prior to your application. Visa lasts for six months.

Contact: High Commission for Malaysia, 10 Washington Avenue,
Brooklyn, PO Box 9422, Wellington
phone +64 4 385 2439 or 4 801 0943
email mwwelton@xtra.co.nz, website www.imi.gov.my.

THE NETHERLANDS

You must 'ordinarily reside in New Zealand', although you can apply at any Netherlands embassy worldwide.

Contact: Royal Netherlands Embassy, 10th Floor, Investment House (PSIS Building), cnr Ballance and Featherston Streets, PO Box 840, Wellington
phone +64 4 471 6390
email wel@minbuza.nl, website www.netherlandsembassy.co.nz.

SINGAPORE
Contact: Singapore High Commission, 17 Kabul Street, Khandallah, PO Box 13140, Johnsonville, Wellington
phone +64 4 470 0850
email shcwlg@xtra.co.nz.

SWEDEN
You must be 'ordinarily resident in New Zealand at the time of application'.
Contact: Embassy of Sweden, 5 Turrana Street, Yarralumla, Canberra, ACT 2600, Australia
phone +61 2 6270 2700
email sweden@austarmetro.com.au
websites www.embassyofsweden.org.au
and www.migrationsverket.se.

URUGUAY
You can't work longer than three months in the same job, or study longer than three months.
Contact: Uruguayan Consulate-General in Sydney, Level 24, Westpac Plaza Building, 60 Margaret Street, Sydney 2000, Australia
phone +61 2 9251 5544
email curuguay@bigpond.net.au.

Living in Amsterdam
There are no soaring mountains, the weather is identical to London's, and there's an excellent reason as to why you seldom see Dutch restaurants outside of Holland. But despite all this, the Netherlands is a terrific alternative for the jaded Kiwi in the UK, particularly if mention of the Underground causes your eye to twitch uncontrollably. You'll soon be gliding up and down the grachten (canals) on your fiets (bike), stopping

occasionally to pick up tulpen (tulips) and wiet (cannabis). Language isn't a problem as the Dutch are delighted to show off their mastery of English and will be correcting your grammar in no time. Finally, it's a mere 45 minutes from London, should you get wistful for your local greasy spoon. Goede reis en veel geluk (happy travels and good luck)!

— Ian Haigh

Other overseas working options

- Put your name into the annual US Green Card lottery. For information, contact the United States Embassy in Wellington, phone +64 4 462 6000, website www.usembassy.org.nz.
- Work at a summer camp in the US. Some websites: www.iep.co.nz, www.campcounselors.com, www.campamerica.co.nz.
- Teach English in Japan. The best scheme to apply for is the official government one, called Jet. You must have a bachelor's degree and apply from within New Zealand. Contact: Japan Information and Cultural Centre, Wellington, phone +64 4 472 7807, website www.mofa.go.jp.
  Two big private schemes are GEOS Corporation (ww.geoscareer.com) and Nova (www.teachinjapan.com).
- Do a Teaching English as a Foreign Language (TEFL) course almost anywhere in the world, and then work overseas teaching English. Check that the course is validated by a reputable body or university.
- Volunteer as a staff member for an international expedition with the charity Raleigh International. Phone 020 7371 8585, email staff@raleigh.org.uk, website www.raleigh.org.uk.

Returning to New Zealand is great. As long as you don't get too many postcards or emails from exotic destinations. I'm loving being back. Rediscovering all those old haunts — cafés you'd forgotten about, little shops you don't remember until you walk past them again — and just how great is Borders on Queen Street? The Japanese restaurant we used to go to all the time, that café on K'Rd, the Comedy Club, checking out what's changed and what's exactly the same as when you left. It's all new and exciting again. Even the views and the scenery you used to take for granted are something special.

— Kate Ellis

What next?

Quiz — what next?
Your ideal beach is:
A: A wide open space you can play cricket on.
B: A one-metre-square stake of sand and a striped changing shed.
C: Regent's Park in your underwear in your lunch hour. (You mean beaches are supposed to have sand and water?)
D: Turquoise seas and tepid water.

Your idea of a good night out:
A: A barbecue at the beach and a skinny dip.
B: Straight to your local after work to down a pint every 15 minutes until the bell rings.
C: Catching the first tube home tomorrow.
D: Dinner at 11 pm, followed by a drink in the taverna.

Your ideal holiday:
A: Chuck your togs and three mates into the Holden and away you go.
B: A beach in Majorca populated by your entire neighbourhood.
C: Holed up watching football on the telly.
D: Somewhere new and exotic.

You usually see sunset from:
A: A deserted beach.
B: Sunset? Isn't that when *EastEnders* is on?
C: Your office window at 4 pm.
D: Alfresco in a café in the old town over a cerveza, birra or bière.

Your policy on public transport delays:
A: Dunno. I drive.
B: Hey, so lines buckle in summer, ice over in winter, attract leaves in autumn and get washed out in spring. You can't expect a train to get through one centimetre of snow!
C: Gives me time to read the *Evening Standard*.
D: You're thrown if your train is one second late.

The Big OE Companion

Britain is:
A: Dingy, depressing, dreary, dark, dismal, dire, dingy, depressing, dull, damp, dank, disheartening . . .
B: The mother country.
C: Something that happens on the other side of the M25, so they say.
D: Only three hours from Paris by train.

When you think New Zealand, you think:
A: Paradise. The best place to bring up kids. Why did I ever leave? Sniff.
B: Britain in the 1950s. How quaint.
C: Tumbleweed in Queen Street.
D: A place you'll get back to some time. Maybe. For a holiday.

The *Lord of the Rings* movies are:
A: A sweeping, gorgeous advertisement for New Zealand.
B: A tribute to Britain, directed by a fellow colonial. Isn't that naice?
C: Something I'll get around to seeing when I get time.
D: If it doesn't have subtitles it's not worth seeing.

Best food while stumbling home from a night out:
A: Fish and chips and a paua fritter, don't spare the tomato sauce.
B: A curry or kebab.
C: Breakfast at the greasy spoon.
D: Pizza in the piazza.

Your closest friends:
A: Own a weatherboard house on a quarter-acre section and are engaged, married and/or having kids.
B: Our Trace from over the yard.
C: Are all here in London. I don't know exactly where they live, we just meet in the West End.
D: Oh, Pierre, Natalia and Yoris are doing fine, thanks.

What next?

On royalty:

A: An outdated, archaic institution. Although between you and me that Prince William/Zara Phillips (delete where appropriate) is a bit of all right.

B: That reminds me, I haven't polished the souvenir Coronation plate today.

C: Holding up traffic on the Mall. Again!

D: Oh, we sail past them all the time in the Med.

Your ideal pet:

A: A dog. The bigger the better.

B: Cats. The more the better.

C: One that doesn't need to be fed every week.

D: Fits in my Gucci bag.

Results

Mostly As: Jump on the first Air New Zealand flight to Auckland and put the whole trip down to experience.

Mostly Bs: You've definitely been in Britain too long. There's no hope. You may as well apply to stay.

Mostly Cs: You've been swallowed up by London and have lost touch with the world beyond the M25. A year in rural France is the only hope.

Mostly Ds: Your New Zealand passport is an embarrassment. Find a European one to marry.

Acknowledgements

Thanks to the following people for their contributions, help and support: Winston Aldworth, Angel Ash, Kelly Blanchard, Rebecca Cameron, Chris Drum, Kate Ellis, Barbara and Chris Else, Ian Haigh, Kylie Harris, Lyndon Hogg, Michelle James, Phillip Lash, Adrian 'Gus' McCloy, Kushla McIndoe, Nadia Millar, Peta Norris, Rachael O'Brien, Brendon O'Hagan, Al Pitcher, Adam Ray, Geoff Slater, Natasha Speight, Mike Stead, Alicia Stenhouse, Nicola Topping, Wesley Tuszynski, Ben Watson, Anna Williams, Reuben Woods; Rachel Broadmore, Rob Hole, Angela Phillips and their colleagues at the New Zealand High Commission in London; and Bryan Nicolson, Stacey Buckland and their colleagues at the British High Commission in Wellington. Special thanks to Christine Sheehy for her enthusiasm and advice and to Andrew Knight for his inspirational contributions.

And special thanks to token Australian Brad McEvoy, my greatest overseas experience.